313.6 Kit
The kite runner

$105.00
on1126338849

CRITICAL
INSIGHTS

The Kite Runner

CRITICAL INSIGHTS

The Kite Runner

Editor
Nicolas Tredell

SALEM PRESS
A Division of EBSCO Information Services, Inc.
Ipswich, Massachusetts

GREY HOUSE PUBLISHING

Publisher's Cataloging-In-Publication Data
(Prepared by The Donohue Group, Inc.)

Names: Tredell, Nicolas, editor.
Title: The kite runner / editor, Nicolas Tredell.
Other Titles: Critical insights.
Description: [First edition]. | Ipswich, Massachusetts : Salem Press, a division
        of EBSCO Information Services, Inc. ; Amenia, NY : Grey
        House Publishing, [2020] | Includes bibliographical references
        and index.
Identifiers: ISBN 9781642653779 (hardcover)
Subjects: LCSH: Hosseini, Khaled. Kite runner. | Hosseini, Khaled--Criticism
        and interpretation. | Male friendship in literature. | Guilt in literature. |
        Redemption in literature. | Afghanistan--In literature.
Classification: LCC PS3608.O832 K583 2020 | DDC 813./6--dc23

First Printing

Contents _____

Resources _____

About This Volume

Nicolas Tredell

This Critical Insights volume provides a rich variety of fresh and searching perspectives on Khaled Hosseini's *The Kite Runner*, a bestselling, popular, and widely studied novel that has, as yet, received relatively little sustained critical attention. The essays assembled here explore a range of important aspects of Hosseini's first novel: its style, structure, and narrative technique; its treatment of physical and psychological trauma, particularly in the forms of rape and war; its representations of Afghanistan and America; its historical contexts; its critical reception; its relation to other texts that examine similar areas; and its movie, stage, and graphic novel adaptations. This volume offers new ways of reading, enjoying, appreciating, interpreting, discussing, and thinking and writing about *The Kite Runner* that will enrich and advance the critical discourse on and around Hosseini's first and later novels.

In the first essay in this volume Calum Kerr, a world expert on *The Kite Runner*, offers a vivid and vigorous account of his discovery of the novel, his increasing fascination with it as a reader, writer, critic and teacher, his growing admiration for its achievement, and his detailed critical and contextual explorations of its many facets. As he says, there are many ways in which to approach and discover it: "it is an historical novel, but also a post-colonial one. It is a coming of age story, and also a love story. It opens itself up to almost every critical perspective you care to apply, but is also an engaging and absorbing read." This combination of high readability and an openness to a wide range of interpretative approaches is crucial to a full understanding of the novel's dynamics.

A brief biography of Khaled Hosseini by Angela Tredell follows Kerr's essay, and we then move into the "Critical Contexts" section of this volume.

Critical Contexts

The "Critical Contexts" section opens with an essay by Calum Kerr on the historical context of *The Kite Runner*. Kerr points out that Afghanistan's geographical position "has made it a crucial territory for those seeking expansion, and as such it has been overrun and occupied on several occasions, by a variety of different colonisers." This has produced "a country with a range of cultural identities, and a great deal of internal tension, much of which can be seen played out over the course of *The Kite Runner*'s narrative." Kerr affirms that "[a]n understanding of some of this history is therefore crucial to a deeper understanding of the book." He navigates us through this "tangled narrative of external interference and internal tensions," from the pre-Independence period in which Afghanistan was a pawn in "The Great Game," as it was dubbed, between the British and the Russian Empire, through the period of Afghan independence from 1919 to 1978, the Soviet occupation and mujahideen resistance from 1978–92, the rise of the Taliban from 1992–2001, and their overthrow and its aftermath. Although "The Great Game" may have concluded around 1919 with Afghan self-rule, Kerr cites Rudyard Kipling's remark, in his novel *Kim*, that it will never be over until "everyone is dead," and suggests it may have continued in some form throughout the twentieth and into the twenty-first century, with the United States replacing Britain as the major world power to oppose Russia. Given the importance of America in the novel, Kerr also surveys the relevant history of the United States from the early 1980s to 9/11 and beyond. He relates the history of both Afghanistan and the United States closely to the characters and events in *Kite*.

The second "Critical Contexts" essay surveys the critical response to *The Kite Runner* to date. It discusses key examples of early reviews by David Kipen, Edward Hower, Amelia Hill, and Sarah A. Smith; goes on to consider later and more reflective critiques by Ronny Noor, Meghan O'Rourke, and Fatemeh Keshavarz; discusses the thoughtful and insightful monographs by Judi Slayden Hayes and Rebecca Stuhr; examines Harold Bloom's introduction to his critical anthology on *Kite*; and explores later essays by Timothy Aubry, David Jefferess, Barbara Bleiman, Rachel Blumenthal, and Dominic Davies. Mainstream literary discourse, whether in newspaper review columns or academic journals, has been slow to get to grips with *Kite*, either in itself or as one of the three substantial novels Hosseini has now produced, which poses the question of how far the criteria by which it has been assessed and sometimes found wanting are useful and appropriate in the twenty-first century.

In the third "Critical Contexts" essay, Calum Kerr examines the novel through the lens of narratological theory. Though *Kite* can seem a simple story, it in fact offers, Kerr suggests "a very complex interweaving of narratives which revolve around two key events, namely the attack on Hassan in the alley, and the rescuing of Sohrab from the Taliban." He draws on Paul Cobley's narrative system consisting of three components, story, plot, and narrative, and suggests that *Kite* has one story and one plot but numerous narratives that arise from the "ripples" that spread out from those two key events and overlap. In analyzing these narratives, Kerr draws on Christopher Booker's *The Seven Basic Plots*. While acknowledging that Booker's outlines of these plots are "perhaps simplistic" and "undermined by the later examinations in his own book, as he explores the fact that combination and divergence are key to differentiation." Kerr nonetheless contends that "these schema form a classic exercise in narratology, and provides us with useful templates for recognising different narrative arcs." The "seven basic plots" are as follows: "Overcoming the Monster"; "Rags to Riches"; "The Quest"; "Voyage and Return"; "Comedy"; "Tragedy"; "Rebirth." Kerr demonstrates how each of these, applied to *Kite*, offer insights into how the novel works, and why it has such an appeal.

The fourth "Critical Contexts" essay offers a comparative analysis of *The Kite Runner* and Mohja Kahf's *The Girl in the Tangerine Scarf* (2007). Both are highly readable and entertaining novels; both can be seen as *Bildungsromane* and coming-of-age novels; both confront and recreate trauma; both evoke the complexities and conflicts of certain kinds of immigrant experience in the United States; both engage with Islam as a major religious faith; and both have a sense of a lost homeland to which they cannot permanently return. But *Kite* has a male protagonist, *Scarf* a female one; *Kite* is a third-person, *Scarf* a first-person narrative; *Kite*'s engagement with Islam is intermittent, *Scarf*'s intense; *Kite*'s lost homeland is Afghanistan, *Scarf*'s is Syria; *Kite* is chastened, *Scarf* exuberant. Reading them alongside each other brings out the remarkable qualities of both and their vital contribution to twenty-first century fiction.

Critical Readings

In the first essay in the "Critical Readings" section, Georgiana Banita focuses on *Kite*'s "representation of sexual violence during armed conflict" to "show that Hosseini acts from a position of humanitarian sympathy with the victims and faith in the ability of fiction to do its part in investigating the complex causes and victimology of this vile crime." By "exposing sexual violence in this way," Banita contends, *Kite* "illuminates the role of sexuality and gender in the shaping of modern conflict while also highlighting the ability of literature effectively to expose and denounce human rights atrocities carried out beyond the gaze of international observers." Banita points out that *Kite* "is a rare example of a novel that depicts sexual violence perpetrated against boys" but "it nonetheless rests on male/female gender hierarchies" in that the violence against Hassan and, later, Sohrab aims to feminize them. These hierarchies marginalize women. As Banita puts it, "[f]emale characters stand out through their prolonged absence from the main narrative strand of the novel." While she acknowledges the partial truth of the charge that *Kite*'s representation of sexual violence could serve to justify American military intervention in Afghanistan, she nonetheless affirms that "portraying sexual attacks against Hazara children in a book aimed at a mass audience is a fundamental step in recognizing the illegitimacy of wartime rape. By naming and shaming a rapist, Hosseini makes clear that sexual violence is an affront to social order and human rights that deserves global scrutiny as an issue of principle."

Lucky Issar also highlights the marginalization of women in *Kite* and links it with the repression of a range of forms of perceived deviancy. "Only men—Pashtuns, masculine, seemingly heterosexual—inhabit social space fully in *The Kite Runner*. Everything else such as transgressive women, effeminate men, non-normative bodies or sexualities that can disrupt the dominance of Pashtun men in society are either discarded or severely subdued." He links this with "the Hindu 'cultural' practice of untouchability" and examines "how ideas of caste 'purity' and caste's interface with sexuality unfold in an Afghan society whose history in terms of both its religion and culture intersects with Indian culture." Issar argues that homophobia and repressed homosexuality are crucial but under-articulated elements of the narrative. Baba is a "hypermasculine" figure who detests what he sees as "feminine" elements in Amir. But Baba's own heterosexuality is insecure—for example, since he is a highly eligible widower in a society that would expect him to remarry, why does he never do so? Amir, despite his own "feminine" traits, internalizes these heteronormative attitudes, which surface most strongly in his own rejection of Hassan after the rape. Here Issar offers an intriguing speculation: Amir might be the real rape victim. Not a wholly reliable narrator, Amir may have constructed an idealized, fairy-tale version of his friend and half-brother, "generous, sacrificial, and ever-smiling," and turned him into the victim in a screen memory or cover story that serves to evade the full force of his own trauma.

Alla Ivanchikova contends that the "distance of almost two decades" from the first publication of *Kite* "gives us a vantage point from which to view [its] literary success, its shortcomings, and its lasting legacy." She highlights "three issues that anyone who reads, studies, or teaches *The Kite Runner* should be aware of." First, that *Kite* "became a runaway bestseller" because "it fed into the political climate in which the U.S.'s political establishment sought support for the invasion of Afghanistan and the reading publics were hungry for stories that explained not only the tragedy of Afghanistan, but also the tragedy of 9/11." *Kite* is significant "as the first post-9/11 bestseller that reframed how Americans were to relate not only to Afghanistan, but also to the Muslim world in the twenty-first century." Second, *Kite* "should not be taken as a window upon Afghanistan and its culture," even though it "often fills precisely this role." Third, *Kite* should now be seen in light of Hosseini's two later novels, *Suns* and *Mountains*, "both of which reframe and revise *The Kite Runner's* approach to narrating Afghanistan's tragic history" and "become increasingly complex, reflecting both Hosseini's enduring struggle to explain the tragedy of Afghanistan to his readers in the West and exemplifying the disappointments regarding humanitarian wars that characterize the second decade of the 9/11 wars era." Ivanchikova contends that "[b]y positioning the first novel within this larger arc" created by his two subsequent novels, "we are able to see both *The Kite Runner's* success and limitations in a different light."

Calum Kerr's essay focuses "on one of the clearest themes" in *Kite*: "the relationships between fathers and sons." The novel presents "many different fathers—biological, adoptive, chosen— and many different sons— legitimate, illegitimate, lost and found— and the relationships between them are shown in many different ways, and they change as the text— and narrative time—progresses." Kerr traces the complexities of these relationships, looking in turn at Baba and Amir, Ali and Hassan, Rahim Khan and Amir, General Taheri and Amir, Amir and Hassan, and Amir and Sohrab. These relationships can assume a range of wider significances of an historical and mythological kind. For example, when the narrative moves to the United States, we can see Baba as "the representative of the old, pre-coup Afghanistan," and Amir as "more a part of a Western liberal democracy." In this perspective, Baba's very active role in Amir's wedding can look like "a last flicker from that old Afghanistan" and his death soon afterwards seems "the passing of a torch from Baba's liberal, secular Afghanistan, to Amir's diasporic, Afghan America." On a mythological level, we could regard Rahim Khan, in Chapter 17 of *Kite*, as "performing the key function of the mentor figure within the hero's journey as described in Joseph Campbell's *The Hero with a Thousand Faces*: he is ushering Amir across the threshold of adventure," if rather late in the narrative; but as Kerr points out, "most of Amir's life up until that point has been a rejection of calls to adventures."

The next essay approaches *Kite* from "the perspective of cognitive literary theory, which assumes a continuity between the ways human sensory and cognitive processes operate in everyday life and the ways they operate in the reading of imaginative literature." In this perspective, perception "involves both sensation, as experienced in the interactions between the external world and the senses of sight, hearing, smell, taste and touch, and cognition, knowing and understanding things, often through inferences from, and verbal and conceptual constructions of, sensations." We can see "imaginative literature" as "a simulation, a kind of virtual reality experience, which [readers] do not confuse with actuality but which they inhabit and respond to as if it were real." "A key reason for the success of *Kite*," the essay argues, "is its evocation of both sensation and cognition, which the reader experiences imaginatively on the body and in the mind." The essay "analyses *Kite*'s evocation of seeing, hearing, smelling and touching" and of "the sensations and cognitions of pain, particularly of the kind of physical and psychological distress caused by respiratory difficulty, a recurrent motif in the narrative." It relates these to a range of key incidents in the novel, such as Hassan's rape, Amir and Baba's escape from Afghanistan to Pakistan in the nearly suffocating interior of a fuel tanker, and Amir's close encounter with the Taliban, and it explores the ethical and metaphorical implications of the idea and physical reality of being able "to breathe more freely."

The sixth essay in the "Critical Readings" section challenges the late Harold Bloom's magisterial judgment that *Kite* was full of clichés. It acknowledges that the novel "eschews stylistic exhibitionism" but contends that its style shows both "felicity and originality." The essay first examines and defends the few specific examples Bloom adduced to support his case, putting them back into their contexts and showing how they work for a reader who engages sympathetically, imaginatively, and intelligently with the text. It goes on to explore more widely the "three main ways" in which *Kite* reanimates its "alleged clichés": "by drawing attention to them, effectively saying 'I know these are clichés,' but affirming their appropriateness and thus prompting us to look at them afresh—

in effect, defamiliarizing them; by putting them into different contexts that reawaken and extend their possibilities of meaning; and by developing them in ways that give new emphases to their original phrasing and meaning." The essay moves on to discuss clichés of situation, those "stock situations" that recur in narrative fiction and in drama," and then suggests that we can define the genre of *Kite* as "neither tragedy nor comedy" but as occupying "the kind of territory explored most famously in those late Shakespeare plays we now call "romances"—*Cymbeline, Pericles, The Winter's Tale* and *The Tempest*— in which characters create through their own folly seemingly intractable situations that are eventually resolved in a partly magical and improbable way."

The next three essays in the "Critical Readings" section examine, in turn, three important adaptations of *Kite* into different media: film, theatre, and graphic fiction. Robert C. Evans surveys the review responses to the 2007 movie which, he points out, "was much less well received" than the novel and indeed "even helped generate some second thoughts" about it: "some reviewers suggested that the film highlighted flaws already evident in the general structure, individual characterizations, and specific plot developments" of *Kite*. As Evans's examples show, reviewers recurrently applied terms such as "melodrama," "sentimental[ity]," "tearjerkery," and "coincidence" (and various variations on these) to both novel and film, often perjoratively. Evans finds, however that "[a]lthough positive responses were less numerous than negative and mixed reactions, the film did receive some very enthusiastic praise," including a rave review from the leading American film critic of that time, Roger Ebert. Evans garners many interesting and insightful observations on both the original novel and the movie, assessing a range of aspects of the latter. These included its script by David Benioff, its direction by Marc Forster and its acting, especially the performances of Homayoun Ershadi as (highly praised), Ahmad Khan Mahmoodzada and Ali Danish Bakhtyari as, respectively, Amir, Hassan and Sohrab as boys (generally commended), and Khalid Abdalla as the adult Amir (usually judged disappointing). The reviews also considered such aspects of the film as its visual qualities, especially in the special-effects kite flying scenes; its representations of Aghanistan and America; its deployment of Dari (Farsi) rather than English at times; its use of Western China as a location to stand in for Kabul; its handling of Hassan's rape; and its generic elements.

The essay on the stage version of *Kite* examines the adaptation that Matthew Spangler, an experienced adaptor of prose fiction, made in close cooperation with Hosseini. It explores the differences between the novel and the published script of the play, the ways in which the adaptation aims at fidelity to the original but must necessarily make changes. It addresses the difficult issue of its representations of violence, especially the rape of Hassan. It broadens the discussion to encompass not only violence but also physical action on stage more generally and the theatrical value of this. It lends an ear to its rich aural tapestry of musical effects from both Eastern and Western sources. Finally, it samples the review reception of the play's several different productions. There is no doubt that Spangler's stage adaptation of *Kite* is now both an important adjunct to the novel and a potent theatrical event in its own right.

The penultimate essay looks at the adaptation of *Kite* into the form of the graphic novel, a very important twenty-first-century mode that is often a vital means through which classic and contemporary literature is now disseminated to a wide audience. With powerful artwork by Fabio Celoni (ink) and Mirka Andolfo (color) and a script sensitive but not slavish to the original, the graphic novel of *Kite* makes a strong impression. The essay explores three main aspects of it: the interaction between its narrative voice and its visual images; the impact and import of the capitalized and often onomatopoeic words that are one of the most distinctive features of graphic novels and of comic books more generally, such as "THUMP" (110), "CRASH" (116) and "BAM" (116); and those very significant moments in a graphic novel when panels appear that have strong visual images but no words at all. Like Spangler's stage adaptation of *Kite*, the graphic novel version is an important adjunct to the original and a strong visual-verbal work.

The final essay in this volume explores how *Kite* has been reconfigured both by Hosseini's own retrospective remarks on his first novel and by the appearance and critical reception of his two subsequent novels, *A Thousand Splendid Suns* and *And the Mountains Echoed*. It draws on interviews in which he looks back on *Kite* affectionately but not uncritically and on a range of thoughtful reviews that show an increasing appreciation of Hosseini's positive qualities as a writer of fiction, even if they cannot always quite bring themselves to throw off the residue of the critical disdain with which he was initially greeted. The searching essays in this volume will contribute further to that reconfiguration of *Kite* and of its author's whole *oeuvre* and will help to move Hosseini studies into a new phase at this vertiginous moment of the twenty-first century.

Discovering *The Kite Runner*_____

Calum Kerr

Part One: Writing the *York Notes* on *The Kite Runner*

In 2008, when I was working part time at a university teaching a range of English Literature and Creative Writing subjects, an opportunity arose to write a full academic textbook on twentieth-century literature. Although my application was not accepted, it led to another offer—writing the *York Notes* study guide for *The Kite Runner*, by Khaled Hosseini, which I agreed to do.

I had heard of *The Kite Runner*, which had been published with some fanfare back in 2003, and had also been aware of the press coverage when the film was released in 2007. When I started to read *The Kite Runner* for the first time, little did I know that it would be the first of at least seventeen complete read-throughs.

The first read-through of a book you are going to write about should be the same as the first read-through of any book. You let it take you on its journey, you ride the highs and lows, and you let it sweep you along its emotional trail to its ending. This had been true for my first reading of *The Kite Runner*, which I found to be a hugely affecting read, with every twist in the tale of Amir and his family catching and carrying me. Although I knew I was going to have to read it more times, now with a more critical eye, I first sat down to research the book to see what academic material might have been written about it that could inform my understanding and my writing of the *York Notes*.

There was next to nothing. Scouring through the academic journals that would normally contain articles about the book, I found several reviews. Some had a few useful insights, but in the main they were the standard fare of reviews—recounting of some of the plot, some of the details, an assessment of quality, and a statement of the reviewer's opinion. They didn't, however, add very much to what I had already been able to discern from my own reading of the book. Beyond that, I couldn't find anything more in-depth. Searches of the various libraries—academic and public—that I had access to, yielded nothing more.

Realizing that I was on my own was, at first, somewhat daunting. When you write a study guide about *Henry V*, or *Waiting for Godot*, or even *Fight Club*, there is already a wealth of material to steer you. Here, I could chart my own course. I could delve into the book, see what I found, and express it to the world. I could be Columbus!

Writing a synopsis would be the first step, one that I thought would be a fairly straightforward task. As I started, however, I found myself more and more having to refer back to the book. For what had been absorbed as a fairly simple read, the summation of it was proving fairly complex. This was where *The Kite Runner* started to change from a book I had enjoyed to a book I was starting to respect and admire. In trying to boil the book down to its essential elements, and express them in a way that a student could easily understand, I had to do a lot of explaining to make the incorporation of past events, and the foreshadowing of future events, fit into my simplified narrative.

Continuing the writing of the synopsis also revealed to me the webs of different relationships in *The Kite Runner*, and I started to make notes on things I would have to discuss later in the writing of the *Notes*. It occurred to me, and it's something that I've passed on to students ever since, that if you really want to understand all the ins and outs of a novel, write a full synopsis of the book in just 2–3000 words.

Once I had completed the full synopsis, I wrote another, this time a breakdown of the text in more detail, covering handfuls of chapters at a time. By the time I finished this section, I was starting to dream parts of *The Kite Runner*. I could quote whole portions, and no longer needed to flick through to find a particular quote, as the page numbers were becoming emblazoned in my memory.

I also wrote three "'extended commentaries'" on key sections of the book: Amir and his relationship with his father—including the winning of the kite competition; the crucial scene in the alley; and Amir's arrival back in Afghanistan.

The next part was to find all the interesting things in the book, and write about them. The process of examining the narrative—three times—in such detail had brought me to that point. I knew what I wanted to say and was eager to say it.

I had moved from someone who simply enjoyed the book to someone who was deeply immersed in it almost to the point of worship. Now I wanted to share all the little things—and big things—I'd noticed and encourage others to enjoy and get excited about them.

I started with what I felt was the most obvious—the relationships between fathers and sons, which I have expanded upon in this collection—and moved on to concepts of race and religion, storytelling, redemption, and the ways in which personal and global history weave together throughout the novel.

After thematic considerations, the next section I tackled was the narrative structure of the book. This is one of my particular areas of interest. As a writer of fiction, I find that the theoretical areas of structuralism, and narratology especially, are of more use to me than post-structuralist theories, at least during the process of creation. I unpicked some of the ways in which the book was structured and explored them in as much space as I was allowed. Although I was restricted by length and format, I was realizing that *The Kite Runner* was a book about which so much could be discussed around the way it worked and delivered its ideas beyond just the plot and the characters.

With that done, it was on with the theory, writing sections utilizing post-structuralist concepts to examine the text, into post-colonial, Marxist, and psychoanalytical viewpoints. This allowed me to finally stretch out into some of the ideas that had been occurring to me as I was painstakingly picking over the narrative. As Afghanistan was a pawn in the fight for territory between Russia and Great Britain in the nineteenth and early twentieth centuries, known colloquially as "The Great Game" (Wahab and Youngerman, 83–84), and this was such a key underpinning for the narrative, post-colonial theory was particularly useful. It allowed me to explore the ideas of members of a previously marginalized group finally finding their own voice but also the influence of the West on Hosseini's voice and perspective.

A Marxist viewpoint allowed me to look at the power relations in the book and discuss the role of religion in supporting that power. A psychoanalytic approach let me delve a little more deeply into the relationships between fathers and sons but also the absent and present mothers in the text. These sections were my favorite to write, as I was aware that I was planting footsteps, albeit shallow ones, into the virgin landscape of serious academic writing about this text.

Other areas of the *York Notes* led me to explore the history of Afghanistan—which I have written much more extensively on in a later chapter, but which is tortuous and bloody, and sadly fascinating—as well as Hosseini's own autobiography and the literary landscape of which the book was a part.

If it had been any other study writing job, my task would have come to an end at that point. However, a special feature of the *York Notes* books—a host of marginalia—meant that my work was far from over.

These notes appear in boxes at the sides of the page and take many forms: links to other books, links to films or other media, questions for the reader, contextual notes, and so on. In total, I wrote over 180 of these tiny snippets, and they took me away from the book itself and into the larger world of which it is a part. I had to watch the film to see where it supplied me with new information or perspectives that could deepen a student's understanding. I read other books emerging from post-Taliban Afghanistan and the wider Afghan diaspora, and in a repeat of the way I first delved into *The Kite Runner*, I read Hosseini's second novel, *A Thousand Splendid Suns*, in a single sitting.

I was also taken into the world of literary terms and definitions, writerly effects and techniques, and historical minutiae. In total, writing these little extras took me almost as long as writing the main text itself. But in the end, it was worth it. The finished *Notes* was, and is, something of which I am immensely proud: not just because it is a good job of work that does what it is supposed to; but also because it allowed me to do that one thing I had been steering my

English Literature students away from for years when they were writing their essays. For once I had been given not just the leeway but the injunction to "write everything you know about the book." It was quite a liberating experience.

Part Two: After the *York Notes*

After the *York Notes* was finally published in July of 2009, I thought that that might be the end of my interaction with *The Kite Runner*.

However, the following year a student raised her hand to ask, "Are you the same Calum Kerr who wrote the *York Notes* on *The Kite Runner*?"

I admitted that I was, and the student excitedly added, "I need to thank you. You got me through my A level!"

I responded that I hoped that she had read the actual book and thought about it for herself, too. She had, so she said, and then it transpired that half of the class had actually used copies of my notes when studying the book for their exams. The half that hadn't, it seemed, had been taking their exams with a different Board where *The Kite Runner* wasn't a set text.

The class took a turn then, from being about Contemporary Literary Theory to *The Kite Runner*. I saw that the ideas I had had in writing about the book, and the excitement I had felt in sharing them, had been communicated effectively. I also saw that, unlike some other texts they had been forced to read for their A levels, there was a genuine affection for the book which, despite my repeated rereadings, I could still identify with.

Those in the class who hadn't read it wanted to know more about the book, and as the other students started to unpick the story and the themes and meanings within it, I heard how some of my own ideas had been assimilated by them, and also new thoughts and concepts that I may have considered but not had the space, or the brief, to explore.

So, when, a month later, I was contacted by the Head of English at a Sixth Form college to come and teach a session to her A level students about the book, I jumped at the chance. Realizing that this would be different from just having a conversation about the book, and that students would have to write essays and answer exam questions about the book, I returned to my, somewhat battered, copy of *The Kite Runner* about two years after I had finished writing the *York Notes* on the book, I wasn't prepared for how fresh it still felt. As I reread it the story unfolded for me again as it had the first time, and I was once more impressed with how strongly drawn the characters were, and how well—if occasionally heavy-handedly—the themes were explored.

The session in the college went very well, and as I talked about the book I realized how much I had retained about it, how my exploration of it in writing the *York Notes* had given me real insights into it, and also how much I still enjoyed the book, the story, the characters, and its messages. I even enjoyed talking about the problems with the text that some of the students raised—the obvious uses of imagery, the representation of women, the westernization of the viewpoint. We were even able to get into a discussion on the problems of this kind of story being told in English and the cultural biases that emerge from language. It was a very enjoyable session.

The college invited me back for the following year, and in the meantime, I was invited to two more to do the same session. All told, in the three years after the release of the *York Notes*, I delivered five sessions to A level students about the book, and always found them to be rich and rewarding.

One of these was one of my favorite sessions of all time, but that was due more to the location than the content. The Head of English from a school near to where I grew up invited me to come and talk to his A level students about the book. This teacher had taught me when I was in Secondary School and had had a great influence on my decision to become a writer and an academic. Being able to stand up in front of his class, with him looking on, while I taught his students about a book about which I had unwittingly become an expert, will always be one of the highlights of my career.

After that, my career moved on, and so did I. I was no longer being asked to teach the sessions, and that was okay. I more or less forgot about *The Kite Runner.*

Part Two (a): Writing the *York Notes* on *The Kite Runner* (again)

In early 2012, however, I was approached to write a new version of the *York Notes*.

This was an expansion of the previous version, now with a specific focus on the needs of AS and A2 students (the two levels that now made up the A level). It required a full synopsis of each chapter, which sent me diving back into the novel looking for new details. It also expanded the sections on characters and themes, as well as introducing a new section engaging with the Critical Debates. Thankfully, in the time since I had written the first Notes, there had actually been some critical debates, so now I was able to engage with the work produced in the world of academia discussing the issues I had already seen in the text.

However, what sticks out most in my memory from the writing of the new version of the *York Notes*, was a section towards the end, which required me to produce sample A level essays, of differing quality, all in answer to the same question. For the first time in writing these books, I was daunted. I never took English A level. I never had to write an A level essay, nor answer a question in an A level exam. I studied sciences instead, until a change at university brought me back to Literature. This was the first time I had to write an A level essay—and samples that met A*, A, B, C, D and Fail marking criteria.

I have since used this experience in my teaching, as a way to encourage students to engage with their essay writing as well as their study of texts. Writing the same essay, but at varying degrees of quality, depth, and engagement, really shows you how to understand an aspect of a text. Those notes were published in July 2012, and I thought (again) that was the end of it.

Part Two (b): After the *York Notes* (continued)

In late 2018, teaching Creative Writing at the University of Portsmouth, *The Kite Runner* could not have been further from my mind. And then, in mid-2019 I was approached to write essays for this collection. "Would I like to contribute something about *The Kite*

Runner?" A small part of the back of my brain woke up and shouted, "Yes!"

It turned out I still had things to say about the book, even ten years later, and I relished the chance to delve even deeper into some of the more intriguing parts of the book.

Within this collection you will read three other essays by me. My first choice, perhaps surprisingly, was to explore the historical context. When I was writing the *Notes*, it became obvious that this was absolutely central to the novel, and in writing the study guide it was something of which I was only able to scratch the surface. In the essay, I got to unpick all the aspects of history that impacted on *The Kite Runner*—The "Great Game" between England and Russia, the coups, the invasions, the Soviets, the rise of the Taliban, and not to forget the impact of "Reaganomics." It was a much bigger undertaking than I expected, as what had already seemed like a very confused and confusing history turned out to be even more complicated than I'd expected. But then that's why it's so crucial to the book. Without the confusion and the complexity, a story like *The Kite Runner* couldn't be told, and probably wouldn't need to be told, so an understanding of the historical context is crucial.

The second essay engaged with the narrative structure of the book. Even in my first reading I found myself excited and surprised by the complex nature of the structure. At first glance it seems straightforward, with a mostly chronological structure, but there are two key moments—the attack in the alley near the beginning, and the adult Amir's fight with Assef near the end—around which the rest of the narrative revolves in two concentric circles. The narrative before the first leads us to it, then afterwards keeps looking back towards it. We then enter the middle section, which becomes a *Bildungsroman* all of its own, before we move into the second circle, which leads us to the fight and the release of Sohrab, and afterwards causes us to look back to it until we reach the conclusion. It also starts with a scene *in medias res* [in the middle of things], which is not what it seems, and twists in ways that mimic the surprises of real life more than those of a traditional narrative.

The third essay I elected to undertake was the one on Fathers and Sons. This had seemed to me to be the crucial focus of the book, so having a chance to explore it was exciting. After all, the roles of Baba and Amir, as well as Ali and Hassan, are obvious. The relationship between Hassan and Sohrab and then Amir and Sohrab complicates things. Beyond this, there are the father roles played by both Rahim Khan and General Taheri, each providing different models of fatherhood and, thereby, producing different results in the "sons." The centrality of this in the book does throw into sharp relief the side-lined roles of women in the text—dead, absent, left behind–that would also make for a fascinating exploration, but it was in the classically literary area of father and sons—Hamlet, anyone? —that I was happy to spend my time.

Part Three: *The Kite Runner* Discovered

There is one final story to tell about my interaction with *The Kite Runner* and the journey that the book has taken me on. Back in September 2019, the new university term had just started, and as well as teaching, I was working on my essays for this collection. Telling my students about the work I was doing served a useful purpose in showing them that I was also working hard on researching and writing, and they weren't alone in their struggles. I also mentioned that it had come about because of my work on the *York Notes*.

When we returned after the Christmas break, a first-year student came up to me. "I have to tell you something," she said, "about *The Kite Runner.* I couldn't believe it when you said you'd written the *York Notes* for it. I studied the book for my A Level, and I bought your notes. They were so helpful. I love *The Kite Runner*. It's so good!"

After I made all the right responses of thanks and shared appreciation, she told me that while she was home for Christmas she bumped into her former English teacher, who had shared her love for the book.

"You know *The Kite Runner*"? the student asked.

"What, this?" the teacher responded, and pulled her copy of Hosseini's book from her bag. . . along with the *York Notes*.

The student then showed the teacher my name on the inside of the *York Notes*, explaining that I was now one of her tutors.

After the student told me this story, we walked slowly from the classroom, and talked for 30 minutes more about *The Kite Runner*, and once again I found myself connecting with the book in a new way, seeing fresh things about it as we discussed it.

The Kite Runner has many ways to approach it and many ways to discover it. In many ways it is an historical novel, but also a post-colonial one. It is a coming-of-age story, and also a love story. It opens itself up to almost every critical perspective you care to apply but is also an engaging and absorbing read. And I can honestly say that it is a book which, no matter how I try, won't leave me alone.

Work Cited

Wahab, Shaista, and Barry Youngerman. *A Brief History of Afghanistan.* 2007; Checkmark Books, 2010.

Biography of Khaled Hosseini_____

Angela Tredell

Khaled Hosseini was born in Kabul, Afghanistan, on March 4, 1965, into an upper-middle-class family. His father, Nasser, was a diplomat in the Ministry of Foreign Affairs in Kabul and his mother, Maimoona, was a Farsi language teacher at a high school for girls. He was the eldest of five children: his parents had three more sons and one daughter. In 1970, his father was posted to the Embassy of Afghanistan in Tehran in Iran, and the family lived there for the next three years. The family returned to Kabul in 1973, and in July that year Hosseini's youngest brother was born.

In 1976 Hosseini's father was posted to Paris, France, and again the family moved with him. This was meant to be only a temporary absence from Afghanistan, so most of their possessions were left in their Kabul house. In 1978, however, the communists mounted a violent coup in Afghanistan, known as the Saur Revolution, and Russian troops invaded the country in 1980, beginning the Soviet-Afghan War. It became evident that it was not safe for the Hosseini family to return home. One of his father's colleagues who went back to Kabul was killed there. "That sent a very clear message" (Young 2007). So, the family sought political asylum in America. As Hosseini said, "My father felt we had greater opportunities in the US" (Young 2007).

They arrived in San José, California, in a very precarious financial position. As Hosseini recalled, "They just had the clothes on [their] backs" (Young 2007) and his parents, as immigrants, could no longer find middle-class professional jobs: his father became a driving instructor and his mother a waitress. Hosseini was determined to become a doctor in the future to ensure financial security.

Hosseini knew Farsi and French but spoke no English on his arrival in the United States. He found this meant he was marginalized at first when he started attending Independence High School in San

José. However, he graduated in 1984 and moved on to Santa Clara University. He graduated from there in 1988 with a bachelor's degree in Biology. In 1989, he entered the University of California, San Diego School of Medicine, and he earned his M.D. in 1993.

In October 3 the same year, he married Roya, a lawyer born of Afghan parents in Bethesda, Maryland. They would go on to have two children: a son, Haris, born on December 22, 2000, and a daughter, Farah, born on January 6, 2003. Hosseini completed his residency in internal medicine at Los Angeles Cedars-Sinai Medical Center, and in 1996 he became a practicing doctor as a Medical Internist at Kaiser Hospital, Mountain View, California.

In 1999, Hosseini discovered from a news report that the Taliban had banned kite flying in Afghanistan. This prompted him to write a 25-page short story about two boys who fly kites in Kabul. Hosseini had grown up as a storyteller (influenced by the Persian storytelling tradition) and had been a writer from the time he scripted plays as a child that "he cajoled his younger brothers and cousins into performing" (Jones 2007). He submitted his short story to *Esquire* and *The New Yorker*, but both publications rejected it.

In March 2001, Hosseini rediscovered the manuscript of the short story in his garage and, responding to positive feedback, he decided to expand it into a novel, writing in the early morning before going to work as a primary-care doctor. He was two-thirds of the way through *The Kite Runner* when the terrorist attacks took place in America on September 11, 2001. His first impulse was to abandon the book as he felt "Why would any American readers feel any empathy now for this tortured country or its people"? (Jones 2007). He recalls saying to his wife Roya "I don't want to finish this novel. The Afghans are the bad guys now." Roya persuaded him to finish the book, using her legal skills to present a convincing case "that his book 'could maybe show a different face of Afghanistan.'" (Jones 2007) In June 2002, Hosseini sent the manuscript to the literary agent Elaine Koster in New York City, who took him on as a client.

On May 29, 2003, *The Kite Runner* was released in hardback by Riverhead Books, with an initial printing of 50,000 copies. While it was in production, Hosseini had made his first visit to Kabul since he had left as a teenager. The sight of the burqa-clad women begging in the streets, often accompanied by several ragged children, was the inspiration for his second novel, *A Thousand Splendid Suns* (2007).

Hosseini continued to practice medicine for some time after *The Kite Runner* was published. "[E]ven while patients of his were coming in just to have their copies signed, he continued to work at the clinic for a year and a half" (Hoby, 2013). In 2013, however, when *And the Mountains Echoed* was published, he was quoted as saying that he did not "miss medicine one bit." (Hoby, 2013). Hosseini has often been asked about how he felt about his two rather different professions of medicine and writing. In 2007, Tamara Jones had written: "Medicine was like an arranged marriage he grew fond of; writing was the grand romance between high school sweethearts" and later in her article she quotes him as saying that "writing was always kind of a diversion from medicine."

In 2004, he stopped practicing medicine and started writing *A Thousand Splendid Suns*. The paperback edition of *The Kite Runner* was released, and it was then that it really took off. It became popular with Book Groups and received the endorsement of no less a figure than the First Lady of the United States, Mrs. Laura Bush, who called it "really great." In September of that year *The Kite Runner* started appearing on bestseller lists where it remained for over 240 weeks, four of them in the number one position. It achieved several accolades including winning the South African Exclusive Books Boeke Prize. In March 2005, it was number one in the New York *Times* Best Seller list.

In 2006, Hosseini became a Goodwill Envoy for the United Nations. In 2007, Matthew Spangler, a teacher at San José State University, adapted *The Kite Runner* for the stage, in close consultation with Hosseini. His adaptation was performed at the University by the Arizona Theatre Company. On May 22, *A Thousand Splendid Suns* was published in hardback by Riverhead Books and by Simon Schuster as an audio CD. The original title was "Dreaming in Titanic City," referring to a neighborhood of Kabul that for a while was known as Titanic City. The revised title comes from a line in the poem "Kabul" by Saib Tabrizi, a seventeenth-century Iranian poet, in the translation by Josephine Davis. Columbia Pictures bought the film rights to this book and confirmed their intention to make a movie out of it.

During this year Hosseini also pursued his work for refugees and went on a trip to Afghanistan under the auspices of UNHCR (United Nations High Commissioner for Refugees). On this trip several village elders told him stories of young poor children dying in the harsh Afghan winters. This made him start to think about the novel that became *And the Mountains Echoed*.

The adaptation of *The Kite Runner* into other media continued when it was made into a film with a screenplay by David Benioff. On September 16 Hosseini was present at a screening of the film at the White House for President George W. Bush and Mrs. Laura Bush. Also at the screening were Vice President Dick Cheney; Secretary of Defense Robert Gates; Chairman of the Joint Chiefs of Staff General Peter Pace; National Security Advisor Stephen Hadley; Ambassador Said T. Jawad of Afghanistan; former Ambassador to Afghanistan now US Ambassador to the United Nations Zalmay Khalilzad; former US Ambassador to Afghanistan Ronald E. Neumann; and President of the American University in Afghanistan Tom Stauffer. The fifteen-year-old who had arrived in America in 1980 as an impoverished immigrant knowing no English was now fêted at the pinnacle of American political life.

The film of *The Kite Runner* was scheduled to premiere on November 2, 2007, but the release date was put back six weeks to evacuate the Afghan child stars from the country after they had received death threats. The film was eventually released on December 14. In 2007 and 2008 it was nominated for several awards. On October 4, 2007, an illustrated edition of *The Kite Runner* had been published in hardback.

In 2008, inspired by his UNHCR trip, Hosseini established The Khaled Hosseini Foundation in Afghanistan. This is a non-profit organization providing funding for "relief and shelter to families, economic opportunity for women, and healthcare and education for children in Afghanistan" (Foundation). In an interview in 2013 he said, "There's a sense of guilt about your own undeserved good fortune and that was part of the impetus of starting my own foundation." (Goodreads 2013).

In 2008 *A Thousand Splendid Suns* won two literary awards: Richard & Judy Best Read of the Year (United Kingdom); and Book Sense Book of the Year Adult Fiction Winner. In the previous year it had been awarded the California Book Award Silver Medal for fiction awarded by the Commonwealth Club, California. In 2009 Steven Zaillian finished writing the first draft of the screenplay of *A Thousand Splendid Suns* and Scott Rudin was signed on as producer.

Hosseini went on a further UNHCR trip to Afghanistan in 2009. His meeting with two young sisters in a remote village outside Kabul provided material for *And the Mountains Echoed* in the relationship between Abdullah and Pari.

On March 21, 2009, the world premiere of the theatrical adaptation by Matthew Spangler of *The Kite Runner* was performed by the Arizona Theatre Company at San José Repertory Theatre. This run lasted until April 19. There were two more runs of the play in 2009; September 10–October 3 performed by the Arizona Theatre Company at the Temple of Music and Art in Tucson; and October 8–25, performed by the Arizona Theatre Company at the Herberger Theater Center in Phoenix. On October 29, 2009, an illustrated edition of *A Thousand Splendid Suns* was published.

The year 2010 saw more performances of the play of *The Kite Runner*: August 31–September 25 at the Actors Theatre of Louisville; and October 15–November 11 at Cleveland Playhouse. In 2011 the Graphic Novel edition of *The Kite Runner* was published. The illustrations were by Fabio Celoni (ink) and Mirka Andolfo (color) and the script was by Tommaso Valsecchi. In 2012, the play of *The Kite Runner* had a run at the New Repertory Theatre of Watertown, Massachusetts, from September 9–30.

The year 2013 was another landmark year for Hosseini. By this year over seven million copies of *The Kite Runner* had been sold in the United States. The play of *The Kite Runner* was performed in Canada at the Theatre Calgary, Alberta, from January 29–February 24, in a co-production with the Citadel Theatre, Edmonton. The

European premiere of the play took place at the Nottingham Playhouse, England, on April 26 and ran until May 18. Riverhead Books celebrated the tenth anniversary of the publication of *The Kite Runner* by releasing a special anniversary edition with a gold-rimmed cover and a Foreword by Hosseini.

In an interview carried out by Goodreads on June 4, 2013, Hosseini made a range of interesting statements about why and how he writes—for example, "I write because I can't help it" and "I've never known the ending of any of my books." To the charge that he was a didactic novelist who wanted to educate his readers, he replied "I have never set out with the intention that I'm going to bridge the gap between people in the West and the region where I'm from or educate anybody."

On May 21, 2013, *And the Mountains Echoed* was published by Riverhead Books. The title of this book was inspired by the line "And all the hills echoed" from William Blake's poem "Nurse's Song: Innocence." Hosseini carried out a five-week promotional tour of 41 cities across America. In October it was confirmed that there were plans to translate *And the Mountains Echoed* into 40 languages including Icelandic and Malay. The novel was also the winner of the Goodreads Choice Award for Best Fiction. In May Columbia Pictures had confirmed the tentative release date of 2015 for the film of *A Thousand Splendid Suns*. However, this film does not yet seem to have appeared.

On December 21, 2016, the play of *The Kite Runner* came to Wyndham's Theatre, London, and ran until March 11, 2017. Since then there have been further tours of the play including one around the United Kingdom in 2017–18. A revised adaptation by Matthew Spangler started touring in the United Kingdom early in 2020. Although the spread of the Covid-19 virus halted this tour, it is hoped to revive it in 2021.

The year 2017 saw the first theatrical adaptation of *A Thousand Splendid Suns*, which premiered on February 1 at the American Conservatory Theater in San Francisco, California, (co-produced by American Conservatory Theater and Theatre Calgary). A theatrical production of *A Thousand Splendid Suns*, adapted by Ursula Rani

Sarma, had a brief run at Birmingham Repertory Theatre May 2–18, 2019.

Hosseini's most recent book, *Sea Prayer*, started out in 2017 when *The Guardian* newspaper asked him to write the narrative for "an illustrated story animated in a virtual reality film" to commemorate the death of a three-year-old Syrian refugee, Alan Kurdi, on September 2, 2015, when he had been drowned crossing the Mediterranean Sea in a small inflatable boat fleeing the Syrian Civil War. The text was originally written as part of a speech that Hosseini gave at a charity fundraising event for refugees in 2017. On September 1, 2017, *Sea Prayer* was released "as a virtual reality experience in collaboration with UNHCR, the *Guardian* and Google" "to mark the second anniversary" of Kurdi's death. The film was accompanied by music from the Kronos Quartet. In September 2018, to mark the third anniversary of Kurdi's death, *Sea Prayer* was published in print and e-book form by Riverhead Books with watercolor illustrations by Dan Williams. It was stated that "[a]uthor proceeds from the sale of *Sea Prayer* will go to the UNHCR, the UN Refugee Agency, and The Khaled Hosseini Foundation."

Hosseini is now a prominent figure in highlighting the plight of refugees through a variety of channels such as The Khaled Hosseini Foundation in Afghanistan and his speeches at fundraising and awareness-raising events. His life has been a variation on the traditional "Rags to Riches" story. In his case it has been a story of "Riches to Rags to Riches," from his privileged early years as the son of an Afghan diplomat to his late teens and twenties as an impoverished immigrant to America to his success as a best-selling novelist. His current influential status has enabled him to become an advocate for the many unfortunate refugees still requiring assistance.

Perhaps like Amir, in *The Kite Runner*, this also serves the function of assuaging guilt. In Hosseini's case it is the "survivor's guilt" of having escaped the suffering and death experienced by many of his friends and family who remained in Afghanistan; one of his cousins he grew up with flying kites "died in a fuel truck trying to escape Afghanistan" and his cousin's father was "shot."

He acknowledged that "I've this sense of being spared somehow and granted this incredible luck. It would be wasteful not to do something" (Young 2007). He continues to encourage affirmation and aspiration in spite of his strong awareness of human suffering. As he said in his Foreword to the 2007 illustrated edition of *The Kite Runner*: "May your kites soar far and high."

Works Cited

Hosseini, Khaled. Foreword, Illustrated edition of *The Kite Runner*, Riverhead, 4 Oct. 2007.

_____. "Interview with Khaled Hosseini." Interview by GR. Goodreads. 4 June 2013, www.goodreads.com/interviews/show/869. Khaled_Hosseini.

_____. "If I Could Go Back Now, I'd Take *The Kite Runner* Apart." Interview by Hermione Hoby. *The Guardian*, 1 June 2013, theguardian.com/books/2013/jun/01/khaled-hosseini-kite-runner-interview.

_____. "An Old, Familiar Face: Writer Khaled Hosseini, Lifting the Veil on Afghanistan." Interview by Tamara Jones. *The Washington Post*, 28 May 2007, washingtonpost.com. [Paywall].

_____. "Despair in Kabul." Interview by Lucie Young. *Telegraph*, 19 May 2007, www.telegraph.co.uk/culture/3665261/Despair-in-Kabul.html.

Khaled Hosseini Foundation in Afghanistan website. www.khaledhosseinifoundation.org/.

CRITICAL
CONTEXTS

From The Great Game to 9/11: The Historical Context of *The Kite Runner*_____

Calum Kerr

The Kite Runner, a book that covers Amir's life in both Afghanistan and the United States, was published in 2003, at an historical moment that saw the two countries linked by the terrorist attacks of September 11, 2001. However, what the book highlights, is that the history of Afghanistan is a complex one in which it has often been a pawn in the political and global machinations of other countries. This would seem largely to be the result of its geographical location, lying as it does between Pakistan, India, and China to the East, and Iran to the West. To the north lie the countries that were formerly part of the Soviet Union and before that the Russian Empire. This unique positioning has made it a crucial territory for those seeking expansion, and as such it has been overrun and occupied on several occasions, by a variety of different colonizers. The outcome is a country with a range of cultural identities, and a great deal of internal tension, much of which can be seen played out over the course of *The Kite Runner*'s narrative. An understanding of some of this history is, therefore, crucial to a deeper understanding of the book.

Pre-Independence Afghanistan and "The Great Game"

Over the centuries, Afghanistan's geographical location has made it a target for invasion many times. Often this has not been because the country is a goal in itself but has been used as a stepping stone for further invasion into other territories. These have included the Macedonian empire of Alexander the Great and the Mongol expansion of Genghis Khan. However, taking and holding Afghanistan has always been a problem, leading to the country gaining the nickname "graveyard of empires."

In his 2017 article in the *Diplomat*, Akhilesh Pillalamarri discusses this epithet and attributes three causes:

First, because Afghanistan is located on the main land route between Iran, Central Asia, and India, it has been invaded many times and settled by a plethora of tribes, many mutually hostile to each other and outsiders. Second, because of the frequency of invasion and the prevalence of tribalism in the area, its lawlessness led to a situation where almost every village or house was built like a fortress, or qalat. Third, the physical terrain of Afghanistan makes conquest and rule extremely difficult, exacerbating its tribal tendencies. (Pillalamarri)

These issues mean that control of Afghanistan has passed from conqueror to conqueror but rarely to be held for any length of time. In more contemporary times, and in an example that seems to have the first major bearing on *The Kite Runner*, it thus became the focus of what became known as "The Great Game" (Wahab and Youngerman, 83–84).

This somewhat cheerily titled period of history encompasses a period of conflict between the British and Russian empires stretching from the early parts of the 1800s to around the time of the First World War, and includes at least two Anglo-Afghan wars and two Anglo-Sikh wars. The term itself was popularized by Rudyard Kipling in his novel, *Kim*. The exact start and end dates of this period, as so often with history, are contested, with different specific events being seen as the markers. However, what characterized the period was an expanding British Empire which, having secured India and other parts of the subcontinent, was looking to move West towards Turkey. The British then came into competition with the Russian Empire, which was expanding southwards and seeking to find seaports in the Persian Gulf.

Just as Russian and British historians differ on the dates that mark the beginning of The Great Game, they also disagree on the end-date, though it is possible, as Kipling said in *Kim*, that it will never be over until "everyone is dead" (418). However, one ending would seem to be the Third Anglo-Afghan War, known in Afghanistan as the War of Independence, which ran from May 6 to August 8, 1919. The conclusion of this war saw Afghanistan achieve self-rule, winning back control of its affairs from Britain, and seeing the British government finally recognize it as an independent country.

1919–1978: Independence and Growth

King Amanullah Khan emerged as the leader of Afghanistan in the era of independence, but his attempts to modernize the country were seen as too radical in some quarters. These included: a relaxation on the dress code for women, creation of schools for both boys and girls, and a general incorporation of equal rights and individual freedoms. Disagreements over these modernizations led to a civil war that ran from November 1928 to October 1929 and saw Amanullah Khan's deposition and an exchange of power. When the war finally ended, Muhammad Nadir Khan became ruler of the country. He reversed many of the liberal edicts of his predecessor, taking a more hard-line approach in a move to pacify religious forces.

Muhammad Nadir Khan's death is also of note. He was assassinated in 1933 by a man named Abdul Khaliq who, like Ali and Hassan in *The Kite Runner*, was an ethnic Hazara. An understanding of this historical moment draws a clear line for readers of *The Kite Runner* to understand the different sides in the internecine conflicts between the various ethnic groups in the country. In *The Kite Runner*, this is the year in which Baba is born, and so there is a connection here between these larger ethnic tensions and the relationships between Baba and Ali and later between Amir and Hassan.

Following the assassination, Nadir Khan's son became Shah. Mohammed Zahir Khan ruled from his father's death in 1933, until he was overthrown in a coup in 1973, by Mohammed Daoud Khan, who was both Nadir Khan's cousin, and his former Prime Minister. Daoud Khan established a republic, abolishing the monarchy, and instead of King, became the country's first President. It is of note, and a harbinger of what was to come, that this coup was achieved with the backing of the Soviet Union. This also shows that Kipling may have been right and that this was another move in The Great Game.

During Zahir Khan's rule, there was progress in Afghanistan, with a series of modernizing measures, albeit less revolutionary than

---

those proposed by Amanullah Khan. During his reign, there were improvements to infrastructure and communications, the founding of the first modern university, and greater attempts to create links with other nations (Barfield 200–10), He also oversaw the creation of a new constitution that allowed for a parliament, free elections, universal suffrage, and an extension to both civil and women's rights. However, many of his proposals were blocked by continuing political fighting between the various factions in the country. After the coup, Zahir Khan lived in exile until after the US invasion of Afghanistan and the defeat of the Taliban. He then returned to Afghanistan in 2002, where he was given the title 'Father of the Nation,' and lived in Kabul until his death in 2007. His return was largely welcomed by the Afghan people, and his rule seen as an extended period of peace. It was in this period that Amir was born. Although the exact year of his birth is not given in *The Kite Runner*, it is this period that provides the backdrop for the earlier, more stable, scenes in his life, before the coups of 1978 and 1979, and the Soviet invasion. Amir comments directly on the idea of this being the end of the peace and declares that their "way of life had ended" (32).

As we reach this period, the history of Afghanistan starts to intersect directly with Amir's story. Amir is born and lives his early life during the last peaceful years of Zahir Khan's reign. In Chapter 5 we have a report of the 1973 coup. The kite-fighting tournament, and Hassan's subsequent assault in the alley, then takes place in 1975. This is directly between Daoud Khan's coup and his establishment of the republic, and the later coups that led to the Soviet invasion of the country—moments from which we see later in the book. The time of the tournament was a period of relative stability in the country, but also one in which tensions were gathering that would lead the country to chaos. Daoud Khan's rule was characterized by a more controlling and repressive state (Wahab and Youngerman 138). This was a useful period for Hosseini to set the story, as it allowed him to mirror events in Afghanistan with the events in Amir's life.

In Chapter 5, where the first coup is reported, we are also introduced to Assef, the bully who will prove so influential in Amir's life, both as a childhood tormentor, Hassan's attacker, and later as a member of the Taliban. This serves, in the form of a character, to presage the new Afghanistan that is emerging, one in which the Hazara will be badly treated, and "bullying" will become institutionalized. Amir tells us that this was when Afghanistan changed forever, but it is clear that he is referring to both his internal and external reality.

1978–1992: Soviet Occupation and the Mujahideen Proxies

By 1978, there were a range of different political and cultural tensions pulling at Afghanistan. Daoud Khan's rule had mobilized many to oppose him as he was seen as dictatorial. Previously solid ties to the Soviet Union were weakening, and what were seen as disturbing alliances with the United States were emerging. Daoud did little to garner support from his parliament or the military, leaving him in a precarious situation. Then, in April 1978, Mir Akbar Khyber, a leader of Daoud Khan's main opposition, the People's Democratic Party of Afghanistan (PDPA), was murdered. Khan was blamed for this, although there was also a belief that the CIA may have been involved. Whatever the truth, it seems that fear for their safety led to the PDPA, aided by the military, undertaking a coup against Daoud Khan and removing him from power. An announcement was broadcast via radio that "a military council had taken power and would rule in accord with Islam to benefit the people of Afghanistan" (Wahab and Youngerman 140).

Although the PDPA were then nominally in charge until 1992, this, as with most things in Afghanistan, was not straightforward. Though there is little evidence that the Soviet Union was directly involved in the 1978 coup, or that they were even aware that it was coming, they became heavily involved in the subsequent government, and became the de facto rulers of the country after invading Afghanistan in 1979.

This links us directly to Baba and Amir's flight from their country, in 1981, as detailed in Chapter 10 and the scene in which we see Baba confront the Russian soldier as he inspects their truck (99–102). The invasion, and the new government, saw a kind of radical socialism imposed on the country. Several of the Islamic activities in the country were made illegal, and many of the rich middle classes found themselves stripped of their wealth. This is precisely what led Baba to flee to America. At a time when Afghans were fleeing to whichever countries would take them—mainly Pakistan and Iran—Hosseini's use of America is key in the text as the symbolic opposite of the Soviet Union, but it was also the place where Hosseini himself was taken at a similar age to Amir, feeding into the autobiographical nature of the novel.

The Soviets attempted to solidify their control of the country during the 1980s; however, it was not a trouble-free occupation. Many of the Afghan people, not wanting to lose their identity or their right to practice Islam, fought back. In particular, the Soviets' fight was against the mujahideen: militia groups of guerrilla fighters, who made use of their knowledge of Afghanistan's geography to wage war on the occupiers. These mujahideen were supplied via Pakistan and Saudi Arabia and supported by the United States with money and weapons. As such, this war was in many ways a heated version of the Cold War, played out via the people of Afghanistan. Once again, in a further development of The Great Game, the country was a pawn in larger political machinations.

Much support also came from individual donors and religious charities across the Muslim world, and historians have connected the anti-Islamic practices of the PDPA and Soviet Union, and this support, to the subsequent rise of the Taliban. In addition to money, some Muslim countries and groups wanted to send their own fighters to aid the efforts against the USSR in Afghanistan. Rich backers provided money for camps to train these fighters, and this included a wealthy Saudi called Osama bin Laden. He helped to train fighters from several countries, and as a result of this founded al-Qaeda towards the end of the war, in 1988 (Wahab and Youngerman 212–16).

The war lasted until 1989, with damage done to many of the larger cities and the country's infrastructure. It ended when international pressure finally caused the Soviet Union to withdraw its troops. This withdrawal was aided by the rise of Mikhail Gorbachev to General Secretary of the Communist Party in the USSR. His desire to modernize his country and reverse the economic declines presided over by his predecessors made a withdrawal from the Afghan conflict an attractive prospect. However, even after the withdrawal, the USSR continued to provide some support to the Afghan government until the collapse of the Soviet Union in 1992. Some historians have linked the withdrawal from Afghanistan with the collapse of the USSR, claiming that the forced retreat undermined the powerful image of the Red Army around the world and demonstrated a weakness at the heart of the Soviet Union.

1992–2001 The Rise of the Taliban

With the fall of the USSR, so, too, came the end of the Afghan government they had supported. A new government was formed, thanks to the Peshawar Accords, which saw an agreement formed between some, but not all, of the groups of mujahideen who had fought against the Soviets. However, several groups did not sign up to the Accords, and the new Islamic State of Afghanistan never had much of a chance to realize itself. Fighting between disparate groups of mujahideen attempting to seize control of the government broke out almost immediately, and a civil war commenced that lasted until 1996.

One group that formed was composed of religious students who believed that the problems in Afghanistan were being caused by a failure to follow the strict teachings of Islam that they had learned in their religious schools or *madrassas*. This group was known as the Taliban, after the Pashto word for student: *talib* [the plural is *Taliban*] (Wahab and Youngerman 211). It was composed of native Afghans as well as some Islamic students from neighboring countries, plus returning refugees from Pakistan. Upon its formation it declared its intention to bring peace to Afghanistan by imposing strict Islamic law. After some fighting with the poorly established Islamic State of Afghanistan, the Taliban overran Kabul in September 1996 and set themselves up as the de facto government of what was now to be called the Islamic Emirate of Afghanistan.

The Taliban then spread until they were ruling much of the country, albeit with some resistance. They imposed strict adherence to Islamic law that was characterized by increasingly tight restrictions and increasingly harsh punishments as their reign continued. They remained in power until they were overthrown by US forces in the wake of the attacks on the United States on September 11, 2001. During these five years, the Taliban were responsible for a huge number of deaths of Afghan civilians, the destruction of homes and farms, ethnic cleansing, and the destruction of cultural monuments. All this was part of a push to make the Pashtun the dominant—if not the only—tribal group in the country. Most of their actions were condemned by the international community, although there was little concrete response, other than attempts to provide aid, until the US invasion. It is notable that it was one of their smaller actions, the banning of kite-flying in 1999, which led Hosseini to write *The Kite Runner*.

The rule of the Taliban obviously has a large impact on the second half of the narrative in *The Kite Runner*, and more of this will be discussed below; however, it is worth noting at this point that the massacre that occurred in Mazar-i Sharif, in which Hassan is killed, was a real event that took place in August 1998 (Marsden 87). During the preceding years, the city had become a notable rival to the Taliban's regime, ruled over by a former Afghan Army commander, General Abdul Rashid Dostum. The city did not adhere to Islamic law and was, for all intents and purposes, a secular state existing by itself within the larger country. It was relatively peaceful and prosperous and provided a haven for persecuted groups. During the attack in 1998, it is reported that the Taliban drove along the streets of the city, shooting anyone they could find, and particularly seeking out Hazara. By the end of two days, they had killed between 6–8000 people, and then they refused to allow the bodies to be buried according to Islamic tradition. This event is seen as one of the worst single atrocities of the Taliban regime. Mazar-i Sharif was also one of the first cities to be relieved by what was known as the Northern Alliance, or the United Islamic Front for the Salvation of Afghanistan—the Taliban's main challenger during their reign, composed largely of deposed officials from the former Islamic State of Afghanistan—following the US Invasion of 2001.

Amir's return to Afghanistan in *The Kite Runner*, and his rescue of Sohrab, comes in the late summer of 2001, just before the terrorist attacks on America. In retrospect, it is easy to imagine that the US forces were the cause of the downfall of the Taliban, but in reality their grip on power was already weakening, with efforts being made to unite the various factions in the country, to introduce some form of democracy, and with disaffected Taliban members joining the United Front. It is in this time of slight decline, and perhaps a growing desperation to hold onto their power, that Amir arrives. As such, the Taliban he meets are, as depicted, slightly more febrile and committed, as those who may have been more moderate would already have defected. That Assef is portrayed as one of these hard-line Taliban—seduced by power and reluctant to let it go—gives us a clear indication of the state of the nation at the time.

1980–2003 The United States from the 1980s to September 11 and Beyond

While the history of Afghanistan forms the majority of the backdrop of *The Kite Runner*, the framing device, and the central section, take place in America, so it is also useful to look at US history for this period, both in terms of its appearance in the book and its influence on Amir's character.

The main contact with American culture in the book starts in the 1980s. The decades preceding this time had been tumultuous in America, with World War II, the Korean War, the Civil Rights movement, Vietnam protests, and the countercultural movement. This last seems particularly relevant as Baba and Amir settle in the San Francisco area, and later Amir moves to the city itself. San Francisco, of course, was seen as the center of the countercultural movement, associated with hippies, free love, and very liberal political attitudes. This ties in with Amir's description of his father as he considers the man following his death: "[. . .] an unusual Afghan father, a liberal who had lived by his own rules, a maverick who had disregarded or embraced societal customs as he had seen fit" (157).

President Jimmy Carter is mentioned in the book, as a leader Baba disliked, and it is fitting with Baba's somewhat mercurial nature that, even though a liberal himself, he is reported as having a great liking for President Ronald Reagan. Reagan, a former Hollywood actor and Governor of California, became President of the United States in 1981, and served two terms, stepping down in 1989. His period in office was characterized by strong conservative economic values, which became known as Reaganomics, but are policies largely still followed by Republicans today: low taxation, smaller government, less regulation, and low inflation. The result of these policies was seen by many to benefit the rich and disproportionately penalize the poor. This is even commented upon by Amir, who expresses surprise at his father's admiration of Reagan considering that his policies were so hard on them when they first arrived in America.

Reagan's time in office also saw increased communication with the USSR, largely due to the election of a moderate leader in the form of Mikhail Gorbachev. Talks over the two countries' nuclear arsenals saw a reduction in their size, and many historians link Reagan's call in 1987 to tear down the Berlin Wall with its eventual fall in 1989, and then the eventual collapse of the Soviet Union nearly three years later, and three years after Reagan left office. Such a link is often seen as tenuous, though Reagan's call has become celebrated, in parts of the American media at least, as the rallying cry that led to the end of the USSR. The date of 1989 is key, as we saw above, as it was a point in time at which the Soviet Union faced internal strife and weakening power and was also the point at which they withdrew from Afghanistan.

One effect of the fall of the USSR was to place the United States as the world's sole remaining superpower—the rise of China as a challenger was still to come, as was Russia's slow resurgence. This made the United States both a popular country for other nations seeking trade or protection and a target of envy and hatred. As a representative of "The West," America's power made it the eventual target of Islamic extremists.

In 1990–91, under Reagan's successor, President Bill Clinton, the United States became engaged in what became known as the "Gulf War" wherein more than thirty countries, led by America, responded with force to Iraq's invasion of neighboring Kuwait. This was not the first time that the United States had intervened in countries in the region and around the world but was perhaps the most significant in modern times in solidifying some extreme groups in their opposition to the country. This conflict is now seen as a precursor to the 2003 Iraq War that occurred following the terrorist attacks in 2001, as part of the so-called "War on Terror," and that encompassed much fighting in Afghanistan. Many commentators, however, see both conflicts as being more to do with oil, and alliances with other Middle Eastern regimes, than with the aggressions of Iraq's leader during the wars, Saddam Hussein. As such, and as seems to be the case underlying much of the history relevant here, we can see the Great Game continuing, though under American control now rather than British.

On September 11, 2001, the United States was given a stark notification that its involvement in the Middle East had been significant, when members of Osama bin Laden's al-Qaeda hijacked four planes within the United States and flew them toward various targets. The Twin Towers in New York and the Pentagon were both struck, while the hijackers on the fourth plane—originally bound for Washington—were overpowered and the plane crashed in Pennsylvania. These attacks sparked a retaliation from the United States that led to invasions of both Afghanistan and later Iraq, commencing initially on October 7, 2001, with attacks on Taliban and al-Qaeda camps. This led to the overthrow of the Taliban and the instatement of the Afghan Interim Administration and later the current Islamic Republic of Afghanistan. Its leader, Hamid Karzai, had been involved with the mujahideen during the Soviet occupation and temporarily in the governments following the Soviet withdrawal—including the first years of Taliban rule. After the Taliban reportedly killed his father, he worked, in exile, with the Northern Alliance and campaigned for a free democratic Afghanistan. The war in Afghanistan continued until 2014.

The Writing and Publication of *The Kite Runner*

It is clear from the only brief mention of the events of September 11, 2001, and the book's publication in mid-2003 (given the usual 12–18 month lead time for publication) that this event happened late in the creation of the manuscript and was not the key factor in Hosseini's inspiration. He has cited that it was the banning of kite flying in Afghanistan in 1999 that served as his inspiration. As a native Afghan, Hosseini would have been influenced by much of the history above. Like Amir, he left the country as a boy, to emigrate to America, in the early years of the Soviet Occupation. However, he did not return to Afghanistan until 2003, after the fall of the Taliban, so autobiographical parallels can only be drawn so far. It was certainly fortuitous for Hosseini that he decided to write his book when he did. With the American attacks fresh in everyone's mind, and the war in Afghanistan in its early stages, there was a receptive audience for a book that could give some insight into Afghanistan both before and during the Taliban regime.

Conclusion

The history of Afghanistan forms a tangled narrative of external interference and internal tensions. This has led to centuries of instability marked with only short periods of relative stability and growth that have often been quickly overturned by the next destabilizing event. This is not just something that predates the events in *The Kite Runner*, but with the "War Against Terror" that followed the 9/11 attacks, Afghanistan was once again caught up in international tensions, and sectarian violence. Although that war in Afghanistan officially ended in 2014, the country is still working towards stability, and at the time of writing, there are still many deaths occurring there every year, plus the Taliban are once more jockeying for a position of power. What *The Kite Runner* highlights is a long procession of troubles that have affected the Afghan people, and while as a fictional narrative it has a positive ending, the reality for the inhabitants of that country is likely to remain uncertain for a long time to come.

Works Cited

Barfield, Thomas. *Afghanistan: A Cultural and Political History*. Princeton UP, 2010.

Hosseini, Khaled. *The Kite Runner.* 2003. Bloomsbury, 2004.

Kipling, Rudyard. *Kim.* 1901. The Floating Press, 2009

Marsden, Peter. *Afghanistan: Aid, Armies & Empires*. 2009. I.B. Taurus & Co., 2009.

Pillalamarri, Akhilesh. "Why Is Afghanistan the 'Graveyard of Empires'"? *The Diplomat*, 30 June 2017, thediplomat.com/2017/06/why-is-afghanistan-the-graveyard-of-empires/.

Wahab, Shaista, and Barry Youngerman. *A Brief History of Afghanistan*. 2007; Checkmark Books, 2010.

Catching *The Kite Runner*: A Survey of Critical Responses_____

Nicolas Tredell

Looking back from the vantage point of 2020, it may seem that Khaled Hosseini's *The Kite Runner*, first published in 2003, was inevitably destined for the bestselling success it has since achieved; but this was not necessarily anticipated at the outset. It received the range of favorable reviews that any reasonably competent debut novel, and especially one with an unusual setting, might be expected to muster, but the praise was sometimes modest and hardly ever unqualified, raising doubts about *Kite*'s stature, style, and structure that later critics would pursue in various ways. We shall sample those reviews first and then move on to key examples of later criticism in articles, an interview, books, and essays.

Fair to Middling: Review Responses 2003–04

We find the mixture of negative and positive observations characteristic of some early responses to *Kite* in David Kipen's review in the *San Francisco Chronicle* (June 8, 2003). His patronizing, bet-hedging assessment of Hosseini's first novel combined deprecating comment with faint praise: he called *Kite* a "middlebrow but proficient, timely novel from an undeniably talented new San Francisco writer." Later in the same review, he demoted the novel from "middlebrow" to "popular" status, describing it as "informative, sentimental but nevertheless touching popular fiction." [M–1] It is as if Kipen, a cultural journalist, broadcaster, and editor, were anxious to signal to his readers that he knew the difference between high-quality literary fiction and "middlebrow" and "popular fiction" and that *Kite* fits into, or hovers between, those two latter categories, so that any praise he offers must fall within the limits those categories imply. Such doubts about the status of the novel will continue into later criticism.

Kipen's more specific objection to *Kite* was that the first-person narrator-protagonist, and sometimes other characters such as Rahim Khan, were "given to overly explicit musings." "Hosseini," Kipen contended, "shows a much more natural talent when he stops telegraphing his themes and lets images do the work for him" (M–1). Here, Kipen was deploying a distinction, which goes back to the novelist Henry James, between "telling" and "showing" in fiction, with the latter seen as superior. This distinction, however, belongs to an earlier critical era, like the categories of "middlebrow" and "popular." *The Kite Runner*, and its widespread success, effectively challenges such distinctions.

In the *New York Times* (Aug. 3, 2003), the novelist, short-story writer, and essayist Edward Hower was more generous and less constrained by outdated critical assumptions than Kipen. He called *The Kite Runner* "powerful," "vivid" and "engaging," though he did find that, when Amir meets Assef again on his return visit to Kabul to rescue Hassan's son Sohrab, the narrative "descends into some plot twists better suited to a folk tale than a modern novel." This implicitly raises the question, which later critics would pursue, of the genre(s) to which *Kite* should be assigned. Hower affirmed, however, that "in the end we're won over by Amir's compassion and his determination to atone for his youthful cowardice."

The short storywriter and critic Aamer Hussein, in the UK newspaper *The Independent* (Sept. 20, 2003), found *Kite* "a first novel of unusual generosity, honesty and compassion" and compared Hosseini to the Korean American novelist Chang-rae Lee in his "ability to reach the core of experiences of love and loss." Hussein did feel, however, that "Hosseini's apparent wish to memorialise occasionally leads him into didacticism" and that the "pace" and sometimes "the prose" of the novel were "uneven."

In *The Observer* (Sept. 7, 2003), Amelia Hill identified Hosseini as "the first Afghan novelist to fictionalise his culture for a Western readership" in "an epic tale," a "shattering" novel that gave "a sharp, unforgettable taste of the trauma and tumult experienced by Afghanis as their country buckled." She found Amir's narrative "simultaneously devastating and inspiring" and his "world [. . .] a patchwork of the beautiful and horrific."

Sarah A. Smith, in *The Guardian* (Oct. 4, 2003), was more critical. While she warmed to the simple and powerful evocation of "old Kabul and the Afghan community in exile" and praised the novel's "richly detailed characterisation," she found most of the incidents in the last part of the book, which supposedly effect Amir's partial redemption, "nothing but schlock [cheap, inferior goods]" and concluded that a novel that "starts as a fiercely moral but subtly told story" declines into "an unconvincing melodrama, more concerned with packing in the action than with fictional integrity."

In *World Literature Today* (2004), Ronny Noor judged *Kite* a "lucidly written and often touching novel" that "gives a vivid picture of not only the Russian atrocities but also those of the Northern Alliance and the Taliban" (148). But while it worked well as "a novel of sin and redemption," it offered, in Noor's view, "a selective, simplistic, even simple-minded picture" of the civil conflict in Afghanistan (148), failing to mention possible covert US involvement in the rise of the Taliban and placing too much trust in Hamid Karzai, the President installed by the allied forces. Noor concluded with the rhetorical question: "There is no Hollywood-style solution to such grave problems of a nation steeped in the Middle Ages, is there?" (148). Here Noor addressed, more explicitly and controversially than most earlier reviewers, the issues at the interface of literature and politics that *Kite* raises and that some later critics will pursue, such as Fatemeh Keshavarz in the next section of this survey. The year after Noor's review, however, it was clear that *Kite*, whatever its literary quality and/or political import, was becoming a phenomenon that exceeded critical control, as Meghan O'Rourke points out below.

A Must-Read or a Mislead? Responses 2005–07

By 2005, only two years after its publication, *Kite* had soared from a relatively modest launch-pad to stellar heights. It raised the question posed in the title of Meghan O'Rourke's article on Hosseini's novel in *Slate* (July 25, 2005): "Do I Really Have to Read It?"

Literary editor and poet O'Rourke summarized some of the signs of its success at that point: 1.25 million paperback copies sold; the spread of its reputation spreading through the Internet; top of the *New York Times* bestseller list in Spring 2005; the choice of many municipalities for their "Community Reads"; the accolade of the First Lady, Laura Bush, wife of the incumbent 43rd president of the United States, who praised it as "really great" (qtd. O'Rourke). But O'Rourke identified a "mystery": "Why have Americans, who traditionally avoid foreign literature like the plague, made *The Kite Runner* into a cultural touchstone?"

O'Rourke offered two answers. One was that Hosseini's novel provided much-needed information about Afghanistan at the time of the military presence of the United States in the country. The other and more enduring reason was "the appealingly familiar story at the heart of the novel: a struggle of personal recovery and unconditional love, couched in redemptive language immediately legible to Americans." But she discerned in *Kite* two conflicting elements, which she characterized as "the journalistic travel guide approach and the language of redemption." *Kite*, O'Rourke argued, made simultaneous attempts "to deliver a large-scale informative portrait and to stage a small-scale redemptive drama, but its therapeutic allegory of recovery can only undermine its realist ambitions." O'Rourke did not regard the novel as "merely exoticizing Afghanistan as a monolithically foreign place" or as "succumbing to the Orientalist fallacy." She felt, however, that *Kite* strived so hard to appeal to the emotions of American readers that it had little energy left to address differences between Afghans and Americans. This is an aspect of a more general criticism O'Rourke made: that *Kite* lacked any extensive "exploration of the subtleties of assumptions that do divide people."

Two years later, however, the Iranian American poet, scholar, and critic Fatemeh Keshavarz did see *Kite* as "succumbing to the Orientalist fallacy"—or rather, contributing to the "New Orientalist" fallacy. In 2007, Keshavarz published *Jasmine and Stars: Reading More Than* Lolita *in Tehran*, a mixture of memoir and analysis, and the article "Banishing the Ghosts of Iran" in the *Chronicle of Higher*

Education. In both book and article, as the allusion in the subtitle of the former suggests, her chief target was Azar Nafisi's *Reading* Lolita *in Tehran* (2003) and in the article she saw Nafisi's book, along with Åsne Seierstad's novel *The Bookseller of Kabul* (2003) and *Kite*, as examples of what she called the "New Orientalism" (B6; Bloom 70). The old Orientalism, which Edward W. Said identified, analyzed and criticized in his seminal book *Orientalism* (1978), was the kind of construction of the East in eighteenth-, nineteenth- and twentieth-century Western discourses and images that represented the "Orient" as an "Other" that was exotic but also backward, inert and inferior, and fallen from former greatness, a place of attraction and adventure but also of threat, peril, barbarism, and savagery. In Keshavarz's view, Nafisi, Seierstad, and Hosseini in *Kite* do the same, in a twenty-first-century, post 9/11 key: "they all reduce the cavernous and complicated story of the region into 'us' and 'them' scenarios" (B6; Bloom 70).

Keshavarz, however, in an interview in the same year (Mar. 12, 2007), made some distinctions between *Kite* and *Reading* Lolita *in Tehran* that favored the former: "The works in this category [of 'New Orientalism'] are very different from one another. *The Kite Runner,* for example, is a more effective story and, at least in parts, shows more depth and nuance than *Reading* Lolita *in Tehran.*" Nonetheless, she argued that such books "do share some broad features that explain their popularity to some extent." One such feature was that, whether presented as factual, fictional, or a mixture of both, "they are almost always 'eyewitness' accounts, which speak to the general public's curiosity and deep bewilderment about what seems to be going on in that part of the world." Their readers need no prior knowledge of the contexts of these accounts: "the books themselves do away with bothersome details." Moreover, Keshavarz contended, most "New Orientalist" works "appeal to an ongoing post-9/11 sense of insecurity in the reader" because they reinforce the impression that "the discontented people in the problem-ridden areas in the Middle East [and in Afghanistan] are by and large the monsters that you are afraid of." (In *Kite*, Assef would be the epitome of this monstrousness.) "This quick validation of fears,"

Keshavarz asserted, "brings something of an immediate relief." She did concede, however, that most readers did not swallow such books whole and retained a certain skepticism: they did not believe that these accounts "give them the full picture" and they "continue to search for more" ("Reading More").

As well as these penetrating critiques in articles and an interview, three books on *Kite* appeared between 2007 and 2009. Two were single-authored monographs, the third an anthology.

Breakthrough or Banality? Three Books 2007–09

The first book on Hosseini's debut novel, Judi Slayden Hayes's *In Search of* The Kite Runner (2007), was a short but thoughtful study published in the Popular Insights series, on the margins of the academic mainstream—though its discussion of different concepts of time was rightly included in Harold Bloom's 2009 Guide (67–69) and is considered below. Hayes wrote explicitly as a Christian but, like many of the Amazon responses that Timothy Aubry analyzed (see below), she stressed the novel's universal appeal, the extent to which *Kite* "speaks to all people in much the same way in their deepest needs to deal with their pain and guilt, to find forgiveness, and to do something good or significant with their lives" (loc. 30–31).

Understandably in view of her religious perspective, one matter that interested Hayes was the degrees of religious faith distributed across the characters in the novel. She particularly focused on the moment at the start of Chapter 25 when, waiting in the hospital's "corridor of desperation" (Hosseini 301) after Sohrab's suicide attempt, Amir prays for the first time since, fifteen years ago, he had prayed for the ailing Baba to "a God I wasn't sure existed" (135). At this moment of crisis, Amir experiences a breakdown that is also a breakthrough into an intense commitment to religious faith—in this case, of course, Islam. While acknowledging that Amir's prayer includes an element of "bargaining with God," Hayes affirmed that he is "sincerely praying for another person" and compared him to David in the Old Testament, "praying for God to let his firstborn son live—his child with Bathsheba, the son of his sin" (2 Samuel

12:16)—though David's son does die (2 Samuel 12:18), while Amir's surrogate son will survive. Hayes saw Amir's intense praying as the moment when he "has finally broken free of a conforming faith to one he owns for himself" (locs 810–12).

As already mentioned, Hayes also offers some intriguing observations on time in relation to *The Kite Runner*. Drawing on Edward T. Hall's distinction, in *The Dance of Life* (1983), between "monochronic" and "polychronic" time, she contended that "Western societies tend to be more linear and monochronic. Eastern societies tend to be more cyclical and polychronic" (loc. 1127–28). While this risked sounding like an Orientalizing generalization, it is the case that cultural perceptions and conceptualizations of the nature of time vary and reading *The Kite Runner* in terms of such variations can be fruitful. Venturing another generalization, Hayes suggested that "An Eastern orientation is evident in *The Kite Runner*" (loc. 1128), in that the characters, particularly Amir, repeatedly face situations that present similar challenges; Amir eventually rises to these to a significant extent but in doing so he "simply continues the cycle of life that now includes another generation" (loc. 1130). Approaching the novel through conceptualizations of time, as Hayes did here, offers a different perspective on its use of parallels and repetitions-with-variations.

Rebecca Stuhr's *Reading Khaled Hosseini* (2009) offered thorough coverage of many aspects of *Kite* and also included a substantial discussion of Hosseini's second novel, *A Thousand Splendid Suns*, published the same year. A particularly interesting and useful area of her book is her discussion of the kinds of narrative that can be discerned in both novels. Stuhr highlighted Hosseini's love of storytelling and his aversion to work that departs from narrative progression. She cited an article from 2003 by Ray Conlogue that quotes Hosseini as saying: "I'm not a big fan of hard-core literary fiction. I like stories" (qtd. Stuhr 13; Conlogue, 2003). Stuhr pointed out, however, that storytelling is an oral practice and once narratives take written or printed form they inevitably move away from orality and it is impossible fully to relocate them there. While Hosseini may have seen himself in his fiction as primarily a storyteller, he inevitably, through becoming a published writer, entered into a rich field of work that has been preserved and developed through writing and print, and that tradition would have influenced him.

Stuhr argued that both *Kite* and *Suns* have elements of the epic form, incorporating a hero (female rather than male in *Suns*), a quest that has to be pursued in constraining circumstances, and a crisis that the hero must resolve immediately, without time to think or prepare or plan. These epic elements survive in modified form in the *Bildungsroman*, the formation-novel or novel of "education-by-life," and we can read both *Kite* and *Suns* as *Bildungsromane*. Stuhr contended that we could also see each novel as an historical novel, in that each recreates an earlier era, even if one within living memory, in both Afghanistan and, in the case of *Kite*, the United States. Furthermore, she suggested, we could approach *Kite* and *Suns* as examples of the domestic novel, given that quite a lot of key events in each of them unfold within various kinds of homes and familial arrangements. Moreover, we could also see *Kite*, in its evocation of Afghan American life, as a novel of immigration or ethnicity, although Stuhr felt that "these issues are secondary to the main plot line of Amir's betrayal of his childhood friend and quest to redeem himself" (21–22).

Stuhr highlighted Hosseini's own definition of both *Kite* and *Suns* as primarily "love stories." She quoted from a transcription of a podcast of a talk he had given at a library in Philadelphia, in which he said:

> Both are love stories, they are both stories of love found in the most unlikely places. In [*Kite*] it was these two boys who came from different ends . . . polar ends of society and yet they were like brothers. In [*Suns*] it is the story of this unlikely love between these two very, very different women. (qtd. 203)

Stuhr's own analysis respected but complicated Hosseini's own position. She acknowledged that "Hosseini may be a storyteller and his stories may be at heart love stories" but, she affirmed, "they are squarely stories written within the Western novel tradition." and we enhance our grasp of them "when we consider them within the literary tradition of novels of personal transformation [e.g., *Bildungsromane*]; historical novels providing illumination to readers about country, time, and place; domestic novels providing insight into intimate family relationships taking place primarily within the four walls of the home; or ethnic and immigrant novels exploring the struggle of becoming part of the fabric of a new country" (23). These are all fruitful perspectives to pursue in exploring Hosseini's novels—including the one published four years after Stuhr's study, *And the Mountains Echoed*.

Harold Bloom's collection of short reviews and articles on *The Kite Runner*, which came out in the Bloom's Guides series in 2009, is a slender book, 91 pages in all, which gathered some useful material, including reviews by Kipen, Hower and Noor, and extracts from Hayes and O'Rourke (all discussed above). But Bloom's own introduction marred a book that is supposed, according to the back cover blurb, to "consider [the] work and its significance." Bloom, however, was largely dismissive of *Kite* and failed to engage intelligently or sympathetically with it. He saw the novel as ephemeral, claiming that once US troops withdraw from Afghanistan it would find no readers—not the most prescient of predictions. He called it "a grindingly sincere narrative in the shape of a memoir," (7), a loose and questionable judgment and generic categorization (compare the latter to Stuhr's exploration above of the different generic frameworks that we can apply to *Kite*). While he conceded that *Kite* unquestionably had "redeeming social value," especially for those who, as he patronizingly put it, "cannot absorb serious scholarship about Afghanistan or even responsible reportage" (7), he denied it any literary value, finding it full of clichés (for a reply to this last charge, see the essay "'Avoid them like the plague'" later in this volume).

In this Introduction, Bloom very much gave the sense of an old gatekeeper who is unaware that there are now many other access routes to the property he once thought he was guarding. The era of the magisterial person of letters outside or inside the academy, an Edmund Wilson or Lionel Trilling, whose judgments from on high could significantly shape what and how people read, was largely over by 2009. The Internet made it possible for anyone to be a reviewer or critic and for opinions and judgments to be formed independently of once-dominant academic criteria, for example on Amazon, as Timothy Aubry observed in the first of two important essays that we shall now discuss.

Emotion and Ethics: Two Essays 2009

The two essays, one by Aubry and the other by David Jefferess, first appeared in 2009 and have already become classical points of reference in academic discussions of Hosseini's debut novel. In "Afghanistan Meets the Amazon: *The Kite Runner* in America," published in January of that year, Aubry pointed to the process by which an initial reluctance in American readers to tackle the novel gave way to an enthusiastic endorsement of it, helping to turn it into a runaway bestseller. Posing the question "What does this novel, largely about Afghanistan, offer American readers"? (25), Aubry explored the many responses to it on the website of the online bookseller Amazon, focusing on "the crucial interplay between [two] seemingly contradictory responses" (27). One response stressed the difference of its characters, settings, and themes, while the other response emphasized their likeness despite such differences, their universality. Aubry stressed the emotional and physical intensity in some of the Amazon accounts of readers' reactions, sometimes to the point of real psychological distress and to the wince-making imagining of actual physical pain, which could seem masochistic and could appear, in certain cases to effect a cathartic function, purging the readers of their own sense of guilt and assuaging a desire for atonement.

Kite may also, Aubry suggested, assuage the guilt some Americans might feel about their country's military involvement in Afghanistan, while confirming others in the belief that the invasion was right and showing that those who supported it, caricatured by their opponents as callous and ruthless, also had human feelings. Aubry concluded that "in their own compassionate reaction" to the novel's "tragic narrative," "many readers find a self-validating basis for hope," which offers "participation in a purportedly universal and unifying affective [emotional] response as a nonpolitical solution to the ethnic hierarchies and antagonisms that the novel[. . .] presents as painfully intractable" (37) —and *Kite*'s very representation of intractability elicited this emotional response. This situation cannot be satisfactorily resolved, we may have different views on how to approach it, but we can all, in a sense, share the same intense feelings about it.

David Jefferess, in "To Be Good (Again): *The Kite Runner* as Allegory of Global Ethics," which appeared in November 2009, identified three apparently "contradictory" frameworks for interpreting the novel: "as ethnography, coming-of-age narrative, and/or morality tale" (390). Jefferess saw these as "overlapping, in a way that reflects what [he] interpret[s] as the tensions and limits of current attempts to theorize a global ethics" (390). He explored the way in which "the text's apparent humanizing function reflects current theories of a cosmopolitan ethics" (390) and argued that *The Kite Runner* "seems to present an allegory of the transcendence of national borders in order to affirm contemporary constructions of transnational humanity and benevolence, particularly as articulated in the West" (394).

This idea of transnational humanity, in its "ethic of humanitarianism," calls upon a "discourse of 'goodness'" that "describes and constructs the difference between those who can be constituted as human, or redeemable, and those who cannot." It does so not in terms of race or religion but of "modernity (as encapsulating culture, economics and politics)," which serves as a measure against which those perceived as failing to modernize are judged adversely. But this construction of difference simultaneously "occludes" it "by placing it within the terms of a binary rhetoric similar to those that have served to articulate previous models of radical 'othering'" (399). *Kite* does not acknowledge or grasp this construction of difference.

The three final essays considered in this survey explore, in their respective ways, the intertextual dimensions of *The Kite Runner*: its relations to previous, contemporary and later texts that it cites and/ or resembles, by other writers and by Hosseini himself.

Intertextuality and Ideology: Essays 2011–20

Novelist and education consultant Barbara Bleiman, in "Stories, Novels and Films in *The Kite Runner*" (2011), analyzed the many strands of Eastern and Western storytelling, from literature and movies, in the novel, which Hosseini deploys "to echo the events of the novel, set up interesting comparisons and create a set of symbols for key aspects of the novel, particularly around the theme of heroism and as ways of reflecting on the relationships between Baba, Amir and Hassan." Moreover, Bleiman argued, "these different traditions of storytelling" influence the narrative style of the whole novel, "some parts of [which are] more in keeping with folktale or legend," while others adhere more to "the conventions of the Western tradition of the realist novel."

Bleiman points out the importance to *Kite* of the story of Rostam and Sohrab from the tenth-century Persian epic *Shahnameh*, in which a father unknowingly kills his own son in battle. This relationship has some analogies to Baba's reluctance to acknowledge Amir as a real son. The representation of Baba has a mythic, folkloric quality when father and son are in Afghanistan but becomes more like the kind of characterization typical of a realistic novel when they are in the United States. Amir and Hassan are closely bonded by their passion for the American western movies dubbed into Farsi that they see at the Cinema Park in Kabul such as *Rio Bravo* (1959) starring John Wayne, which they see three times, and *The Magnificent Seven* (1960), their "favorite," which they see "thirteen times" (23). Bleiman suggested that "these films become the measure by which [Amir] judges his own actions," supplying him "with a set of ideas about the nature of heroism in particular." They also provide other templates for action and verbal expression: Bleiman highlighted the adult narrator's rendering of Amir's thoughts when he decides to get rid of Hassan one way or another: "this much had become clear. One of us had to go" (89). This, Bleiman, suggested, "seems to echo the classic Western phrase from the film *The Western Code* (1932)": "This town ain't big enough for both of us." The Western or thriller film, along with Hindi movies and other traditions of Eastern narrative, is also arguably the matrix of Assef, who might seem a stereotype by the standards of the Occidental realist novel and who many of the Amazon readers analyzed by Aubry in his 2009 essay discussed above found unconvincing; but when set in these other literary and cinematic contexts, he emerges as an entirely appropriate figure in the narrative, "the villain who will test Amir's heroism." This is an illuminating analysis of the different genres that mix in *The Kite Runner* and that can sometimes cause critical confusion when an element of the novel employing one kind of generic convention is judged by criteria drawn from another kind.

In "Looking for Home in the Islamic Diaspora of Ayaan Hirsi Ali, Azar Nafisi, and Khaled Hosseini." (2012), Rachel Blumenthal also took up the question of the engagement with other texts and narratives in *Kite*. She pointed out that, while Hirsi Ali, in her autobiography *Infidel* (2007), and Nafisi, in her *Reading* Lolita *in Tehran*, draw mainly on the Western literary canon in their quest for "an ideological homeland" (257), Hosseini's search in his first novel, as Bleiman had observed, takes in both Western and Eastern classics. Blumenthal observed that Amir, as narrator, "cites both Persian poets (Rumi, [Ḥāfeẓ]) and Western authors (Twain, Hugo) as the formation of his intellectual awakening" (258; cf. Hosseini 17). These are not simply allusions but woven into "the structural fabric of his narrative" (258)—"a narrative" that, "on the one hand," "follows in the tradition of the self-made American man"—Amir makes a success of his life and career in the United States—and on the other, uses "Rostam and Sohrab" from the *Shahnameh*," as "a framing device against which" to measure the Amir/Hassan relationship (258). Blumenthal argued that we should see "these dual strands of narrative as a mark of Hossein's hesitancy to privilege one canon," "one set of cultural values" and "one ideological homeland over another "(258). As well as mixing Eastern and Western narrative forms without wholly privileging either, *Kite* also blurs the line between fiction and autobiography, in contrast to Nafisi and Ali, who focus on autobiographical accounts that they offer as nonfictional. Blumenthal contended that it was "difficult to distinguish where *The Kite Runner* functions as autobiography [. . .] and where it functions as fiction" (262). But it is ultimately the novel's "intimate engagement" with "Rostam and Sohrab" that "flags its refusal to settle a textual (or generic) homeland univocally in the West" (262). Both *Kite* and his second novel, *A Thousand Splendid Suns*, "trouble the notion of homeland" (262) and his "diasporic subjects exist, ultimately, in multiple homelands and multiple histories" (263).

Dominic Davies, in "Exploiting Afghan Victimhood" (2013), used the publication in that year of Hosseini's third novel, *And the Mountains Echoed*, as the occasion to highlight what he called "a theme of pervasive injustice" evident in all his novels to date. It is perfectly legitimate, in Davies's view, for Hosseini to focus on "the layers of injustice that have dominated different social groups in Afghanistan over the last half-century"; but Davies also suggested that, in his fiction, the "suffering of Afghans is to an extent commodified, perhaps even exploited, to sell novels to readers in the West who are fascinated by what is, in Western popular consciousness, a war-torn, desolate country." In the context of "the portrayal of Afghanistan by the international media as a country of suicide bombers and female oppression, Hosseini's work does little to add complexity to these discourses." This resembles to some extent Fatemeh Keshavarz's criticisms that we discussed earlier, although Davies did not use the term "New Orientalism." Hosseini, Davies charged, "writes for readers who are detached from any immediate experience of violence and injustice, but who are fascinated by it. He places these subjects a safe distance, framing and describing them at length with exaggeration and proliferation that border on the vulgar." Davies argued that Hosseini thus "taps into a peculiar psychology that refuses the population of Afghanistan, allegorized in the suffering of his protagonists, any form of happiness, hope, or justice" and that provides a justification for Western military intervention.

Davies's construction of Hosseini's intended or actual readership as "detached from any immediate experience of violence and injustice" is a rather sweeping generalization—it would hardly be true of all American Muslims or African Americans, for example— and his disdain for the perceived borderline vulgarity of Hosseini's fiction has a touch of Harold Bloom-like snobbery. Davies did, however, acknowledge that "[a]s literary works, Hosseini's novels do more than this" and he judged *And the Mountains Echoed* as an improvement both aesthetically and representationally: "it is the plurality of the stories, with their shifting interrelations and discrepancies, that gives this novel its power." We might ask, however, whether it could be possible to interpret *Kite* as also offering, beneath and beyond its tightly structured and apparently unidirectional narrative, a "plurality" of "stories" with "shifting interrelations and discrepancies." Hosseini's later fiction may offer a lens, or a gamut of lenses, through which to see his first novel differently.

Conclusion: Critical Catch-Up

It is clear by 2020 that *The Kite Runner* is not an ephemeral work whose success was due to transient historical circumstances and to a degraded culture that lacked literary discrimination. It is also clear that its author is not a flash but emits a steady and broadening beam of light, creating an *oeuvre*, a body of work, that still has time to expand further—Hosseini is only 55. If literary criticism, still locked to some extent in the intellectual and ideological prisons of the past, has been a little slow to catch up with his work and his multitudes of readers, this is likely to change as our twenty-first-century world, in its crises and extremities, starts to look increasingly like a latter-day Hosseini novel and the narrow aesthetic criteria of a bygone age stretch and snap, dissolve and diversify, in response to the multiplicity of fictional modes in many media that now abound. The criticism of *Kite* that has emerged so far provides templates, insights, and intimations to develop, deviate from, and discard in an ongoing critical enterprise to which this volume makes a substantial contribution.

Works Cited

Aubry, Timothy. "Afghanistan Meets the *Amazon*: Reading *The Kite Runner* in America." *PMLA*, vol. 124, no. 1, 2009, pp. 25–43. *JSTOR*, www.jstor.org/stable/25614246.

Bleiman, Barbara. "Stories, Novels, and Films in *The Kite Runner*." EMC, *emagazine*, vol. 51, Dec. 2011. www.englishandmedia.co.uk/e-magazine. [Paywall].

Bloom, Harold. Introduction. *Khaled Hosseini's* The Kite Runner, edited by Harold Bloom. Bloom's Literary Criticism. Infobase Publishing, 2009, pp. 7–8.

Blumenthal, Rachel. "Looking for Home in the Islamic Diaspora of Ayaan Hirsi Ali, Azar Nafisi, and Khaled Hosseini." *Arab Studies Quarterly*, vol. 34, no. 4, 2012, pp. 250–64. *JSTOR,* www.jstor.org/stable/41858711.

Conlogue, R "Afghanistan's Next Chapter." 2003. *The Globe and Mail* [Canada], 2018, www.theglobeandmail.com/arts/afghanistans-next-chapter/article1017245/.

Davies, Dominic. "Exploiting Afghan Victimhood." *The Oxonian Review*, vol. 23, no. 1, 14 Oct. 2013, www.oxonianreview.org/wp/exploiting-afghan-victimhood/.

Hayes, Judi Slayden. *In Search of* The Kite Runner. Popular Insights Series. Chalice Press, 2007.

Hill, Amelia. "An Afghan Hounded by His Past: Khaled Hosseini's Shattering Debut Work, *The Kite Runner*, Is The First Novel to Fictionalize the Afghan Culture for a Western Readership." *Observer*, 7 Sept. 2003. www.theguardian.com/books/2003/sep/07/fiction.features1.

Hirsi Ali, Ayaan. *Infidel*. Free Press, 2007.

Hosseini, Khaled. *The Kite Runner*. 2003. Bloomsbury, 2011.

Hower, Edward. "The Servant. *The Kite Runner* by Khaled Hosseini." *New York Times*, 3 Aug. 2003. www.nytimes.com/2003/08/03/books/the-servant.html. Reprinted Bloom, 2009, pp. 51–53.

Hussein, Aamer. "*The Kite Runner* by Khaled Hosseini: Aamer Hussein Is Entranced by a First Novel of Shame, Honour, Revenge and American Exile." *Independent*, 20 Sept. 2003. www.independent.co.uk/arts-entertainment/books/reviews/the-kite-runner-by-khaled-hosseini-87649.html.

Jefferess, David. "To Be Good (Again): *The Kite Runner* as Allegory of Global Ethics." *Journal of Postcolonial Writing*, vol. 45, no. 4, Nov. 2009, pp. 389– needoc.net/to-be-good-again-the-kite-runner-as-allegory-of-global-ethics.

Keshavarz, Fatemeh. "Banishing the Ghosts of Iran." *The Chronicle of Higher Education*, vol. 53, no. 45, 13 July 2007, p. B6. www.chronicle.com/article/Banishing-the-Ghosts-of-Iran/14693 [Paywall]. Reprinted Bloom, 2009, pp. 70–73.

_____. *"Reading More Than* Lolita *in Tehran*: An Interview with Fatemeh Keshavarz." *MRonline.* 12 Mar. 2007. mronline.org/2007/03/12/reading-more-than-lolita-in-tehran-an-interview-with-fatemeh-keshavarz/.

_____. *Jasmine and Stars: Reading More Than* Lolita *in Tehran.* U of North Carolina P, 2007.

Kipen, David. "Pulled by the Past: An Immigrant Returns to Kabul in Bay Area Author's First Novel." *San Francisco Chronicle*, 8 June 2003, M–1. www.sfgate.com/books/article/Pulled-by-the-past-An-immigrant-returns-to-2611562.php. Reprinted Bloom, 2009, pp. 49–51.

Nafisi, Azar. *Reading* Lolita *in Tehran: A Story of Love, Books, and Revolution.* IB Tauris, 2003. Republished as *Reading* Lolita *in Tehran: A Memoir in Books.* Random House, 2004.

Noor, Ronny. "Reviewed Work: *The Kite Runner* by Khaled Hosseini." Review by Ronny Noor. *World Literature Today*, vol. 78, no. 3/4, 2004, p. 148. Reprinted Bloom, 2009, p. 63. *JSTOR.* www.jstor.org/stable/40158636?seq=1.

O'Rourke, Meghan. *"The Kite Runner.* Do I Really Have to Read It"? *Slate.* 25 July 2005, Extract in Bloom (2009), pp. 64–67, slate.com/news-and-politics/2005/07/do-i-really-have-to-read-the-kite-runner.html.

Smith, Sarah A. "From Harelip to Split Lip: A Few Too Many Parallels Let Down Khaled Hosseini's First Novel." *The Guardian*, 4 Oct. 2003, www.theguardian.com/books/2003/oct/04/featuresreviews.guardianreview15.

Stuhr, Rebecca. *Reading Khaled Hosseini.* The Pop Lit Book Club. Greenwood Press, 2009.

A Tale with Two Centers: Narrative Structure in *The Kite Runner*

Calum Kerr

The narrative of *The Kite Runner* is a seemingly simple one: taking place, for the most part, in chronological order. This belies, however, a very complex interweaving of narratives that revolve around two key events, namely the attack on Hassan in the alley, and the rescuing of Sohrab from the Taliban. These two events act as anchors for the book and, through foreshadowing and retrospection, cast their shadows backwards and forwards through the text in ways that interfere with each other to create several different readings of the text.

In his book, *Narrative*, Paul Cobley takes the more traditional understanding of the structure we see in stories and novels, as used initially by the Russian Formalists—*fabula* (the chronological order of all events that might be included, often translated as 'story') and *sujet* (the ordering and presentation of those events in the text we are given, often translated as 'plot')—and gives us instead a three-part system consisting of plot, story, and also narrative. This is a very useful way for us to understand the complexity beneath the seemingly simple structure of *The Kite Runner*.

In his three-part system, he defines story as "all the events which are to be depicted" (Cobley, 5); plot as "the chain of causation which dictates that these events are somehow linked and that they are therefore to be depicted in relation to each other" (Cobley, 5); and narrative as "the showing or telling of these events and the mode selected for that to take place" (Cobley, 6).

Applying this to *The Kite Runner* allows us, then, to understand that there is one story: all the events from the lives of Amir, his family and his country, that could possibly be inserted into the text; one plot: the ways in which those possible events are linked to each other in a causal relationship; but numerous narratives: the ways in which the two interact to create different strands that can be unpicked and understood by the reader. This multiplicity of narratives comes, then, from the interactions caused by the two key events.

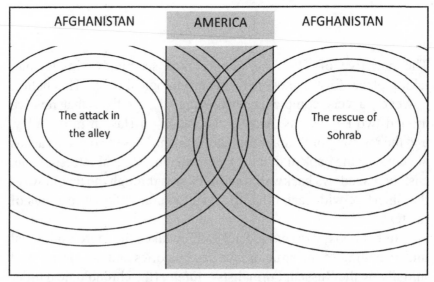

Figure 1. A diagram showing the overlap of interactions from the two main events, and how they emerge from sections in Afghanistan and overlap in the section in America. Diagram by Calum Kerr.

Figure 1 shows an illustration of this idea, with the ripples emerging from each event spreading out and interfering with each other. A true representation, however, would see the ripples from each spreading all the way to each edge, as the overlap is not simply confined to the center section of the book. This can be seen from an examination of the very first chapter.

Chapter 1—*In Medias Res*

As with many texts that wish to grab the reader's attention, the book does not start at the chronological opening of the story which, in this case, would be Amir's birth and childhood. Instead, it starts *in medias res* [in the middle of things], a technique that traditionally places the reader straight into the heart of the action, to create a need to continue reading so they might understand the context of this section of text. The opening chapter of *Kite* does exactly this, taking place towards the chronological end of the story.

However, unlike many uses of *in medias res*, this chapter does not take place in a moment of action. Instead, it takes place in three time periods simultaneously.

The first chapter is headed *"December 2001"* (1). This, we later realize, is toward the very end of the story, after Amir has rescued Sohrab and returned home. Amir is reflecting on everything that has happened to him up to this point. It does still belong in the usual tradition of *in medias res*, in that it is not quite the end of the story, and the connection that forms between Amir and Sohrab over kite flying, and Amir becoming the kite runner for the boy, has yet to occur, but, contrary to the usual tradition, it is not occurring in the center of any action.

Then, with the heading having placed us in one time period, the opening line takes us to another altogether. "I became what I am today at the age of twelve, on a frigid overcast day in the winter of 1975" (1). Although we do not yet know it, this is a direct reference to the first of the key events mentioned above, the attack on Hassan in the alley. It directs us to that moment, again in an instance of *in medias res*, more traditionally used, because that attack is a key moment of action. The rest of the first paragraph keeps us in that moment and gives a little more detail—enough to intrigue the reader, but not enough to provide enlightenment as to its actual nature. As such we can see this foreshadowing as a ripple coming back through the narrative from that key moment and appearing on the very first page.

The next paragraph, however, immediately shifts us to yet another different time period. It opens, "One day last summer. . . " (1), which we know from the title of the chapter is some five or six months earlier. Again, this serves as a moment of *in medias res*, but again not in the traditional sense. It does not take us into the action, into the rescue of Sohrab—although that event has taken place between the aforementioned memory and point of narration—but rather to the threshold moment just before that event. As such, we can see another ripple, this one coming back to us all the way from the second key event.

And then, as the rest of this short chapter continues, we see more ripples. We have references to kite flying, and Hassan, to Baba and Ali and Kabul, and come back once again to the winter of 1975 and the first key event.

This is a complex chapter, especially considering its short length, which takes us on a series of journeys into the past, introduces a number of concepts which will be key to the succeeding text, and introduces some of the key players. It does this while employing, to use one of the terms Barthes coined in *S/Z*, his structural examination of Balzac's 'Sarrasine,' the hermeneutic code, namely establishing an enigma or enigmas that can only be unraveled by reading on through the text (Barthes 19). This is a common technique used to sustain the reader's attention, and the commonest purpose of *in medias res*.

The Narratives in Play

A line-by-line, or even page-by-page analysis of the book would show, as above, these same ripples moving backwards and forwards through the text. With a narrative point of view coming after all of the events, told in past tense, it allows the story, in the discussion of almost any event, to put those events into context of the two key moments.

Here are a few random illustrations:

- Amir finding the book about the Hazara people: a ripple coming back from the attack in the alley (8).
- Baba explaining his atheistic approach to religion and commenting on the Mullahs, the religious leaders, "God help us all if Afghanistan ever falls into their hands" (15): a ripple coming back to us from the rescue of Sohrab, referencing the rule of the Taliban.
- Amir hitting Hassan during a moment of reconnection after the attack (80): a ripple reaching forward this time, creating a reenactment of the attack in the alley, for which Amir feels

responsible, and so becomes the actual antagonist in the reenactment. However, the attack of a Pashtun on a Hazara is also a ripple from the second key event, and the treatment of Hassan and Sohrab by the Taliban and Assef in particular.

- During Amir's return to Afghanistan, giving away his watch, and leaving money under the pillow (211–12): a ripple from the fallout from the first key event, when he achieved the banishment of Ali and Hassan—but with the new perspective that comes as a ripple from the second key moment and his attempt at redemption.

However, while a detailed deconstruction of the way the two key events are linked to almost every moment in the book would be interesting, it would also form a book by itself, and would not tell us much more than we already know. However, if we unpick individual strands, and show how they interact with those key moments, we can see more clearly how the narrative structures of *The Kite Runner* work.

These different narratives can be categorized in a number of ways, but the various possibilities outlined by Christopher Booker in his book *The Seven Basic Plots*, are perhaps the most useful, as they gives us ready-made structures that can be seen emerging in *The Kite Runner*.

In his book, Booker outlines seven basic storylines that underpin, he contends, all narratives. Although perhaps simplistic— and undermined by the later examinations in his own book, as he explores the facts that combination and divergence are key to differentiation—these schema form a classic exercise in narratology and provides us with useful templates for recognizing different narrative arcs.

The seven categories of plot he explores are:

- Overcoming the Monster
- Rags to Riches
- The Quest
- Voyage and Return
- Comedy

- Tragedy
- Rebirth (Booker, 21–193)

While these are exemplified by a range of stories that tackle each type individually—something Booker undertakes exhaustively—they also work in combination to create more complex narratives. Thanks to the interference caused by the two centers of *The Kite Runner*, it is possible to create a reading of the text that fits to any one of them, and in fact, to all of them, with different interactions creating different readings. The following section will unpick these readings and show how *The Kite Runner* achieves its narrative effects.

The Seven Kite Runners

1. Overcoming the Monster

Booker cites many examples of this kind of story, including *Beowulf* (Booker, 25) and *Dracula* (Booker, 27–28). In these kinds of story, the protagonist must face a monster that threatens, if not all of existence, then certainly a large section of it—and, of course, the protagonist's existence too—that cannot be reasoned with and so must be killed or otherwise eradicated.

Beowulf, of course, has Grendel (and his mother) threatening the whole community, and Dracula must be stopped before the whole world is vampirized. Who, then, is the monster in *The Kite Runner*?

The obvious conclusion would be that the monster is Assef. After all, the actual overcoming of the monster must, thanks to the strictures of the hero's journey, be the climactic moment of the plot before the hero's return to normal life. Amir's battle with Assef comes towards the end of the novel and is followed by Amir's literal return home.

While this is true, and Assef is a monster, it is not all of the truth. He is created to be the monster by the narrative surrounding the first key event in the alley. As the perpetrator of that he is shown to be a main antagonist, and his return at the end, threatening Sohrab and Amir's lives, feels poetically correct. Overcoming him is something Amir has been building up to all his life. But Assef is not one man.

He is a symbol, a metonym for the whole of the Taliban, and, if we agree with the attitude expressed by Baba in the early pages, the whole of religion.

So, the monster is the Taliban?

Yes. And no.

For in tales of overcoming the monster, it is not always a physical monster who takes the place of the antagonist. Sometimes it is the self, something inside the protagonist, which must be overcome. This can be seen to be true in the case of *The Kite Runner*, as the attack in the alley creates two monsters. One is Assef, his violence, his bullying, his attitudes. The other is Amir himself, his cowardice, his jealousy, his silence. While the book builds from the first attack to the redemption of the battle with Assef, it also shows Amir building from his callow younger self into a man who can finally defeat his demons—the monster inside himself.

And so, while the battle is about overcoming Assef and freeing Sohrab, the mere fact of entering into the battle is about Amir overcoming and thus freeing himself. This can be seen in the laughter that bursts from him as Assef beats him and, as he says, "for the first time since the winter of 1975, I felt at peace." (252–53) The purpose of overcoming the monster is to achieve a peace that the monster has disturbed, and we can see in this moment that the monster created inside Amir back in the first key event is slain in the second. The ripples of the two work together to create the narrative.

2. Rags to Riches

Cinderella, Aladdin, Oliver Twist, Great Expectations, even *Brewster's Millions*: Booker covers a large number of stories that fit to this mold. (Booker, 51–68)

In this kind of story, the protagonist is often from wealthy or noble beginnings, they lose all of their power and prestige (in some cases, at such a young age that they never knew they had it) and when they regain it, they gain self-knowledge and acceptance. In other cases, they start poor and win their wealth, but it corrupts them, leading to a fall. After the fall, they regain some (or all) of what they have lost, and with it the self-knowledge and acceptance that is always the ultimate aim of these types of story.

In *The Kite Runner*, Amir starts out wealthy. His father is a pillar of the community—the kind of man who builds orphanages—and they live in a large house and are attended to by servants. As is common to the Rags to Riches stories, where the protagonist spends their youth being accustomed to wealth, Amir takes it all for granted. This is the natural order, with him having nice things, the best of everything, a lavish birthday party and expensive presents.

However, it is not long before Amir loses everything, as he and his father have to become refugees and arrive in America all-but penniless and having to reconstruct their lives from the ground up. Now, the purchase of a car is a substantial thing, rather than a natural right, and the ability to pay for a wedding takes all of Baba's savings.

Amir's progression to becoming a writer sees him become comfortable and happy with his life, but he never achieves the levels of wealth that he knew growing up.

However, while this is a material interpretation of this type of story, it runs alongside a more spiritual one.

At the point at which Amir receives his expensive birthday party and gifts, they have already lost their worth—years before the revolution physically removes them from his life—because of the attack on Hassan in the alley. He has already moved from emotional richness to poverty.

After that, with his orchestration of the banishment of Ali and Hassan and his descent into depression, we see him becoming truly emotionally poor. The need to flee and the monetary poverty that follows is a simple reflection of this interior paucity. We then see, through his learning, his relationship with his father, and his marriage, a slow building back to emotional wealth. But it is only in his rescuing of Sohrab, and in the final moments of the book when he becomes the kite runner to the boy, that we see the abandoning of all his self-consciousness, and ingrained feelings of superiority, and a final return to the spiritual richness that he lost through his moment of cowardice in the alley.

Although the Rags to Riches tale is often a very different style of story to that of Overcoming the Monster, we can see again that it is the same two key moments that drive the story, working together, but combining with other plot elements to create a different narrative.

3. The Quest

A classic example of a Quest story would be Tolkien's *The Lord of the Rings*, but it can be traced back as far as the earliest literature in the form of Homer's *The Odyssey*. (Booker, 69) It is an oft repeated tale that gives the protagonist a single goal, in a far away place, and the narrative that unfolds tells the journey that they must go on, and the obstacles they must overcome, in order to reach that goal.

Here, *The Kite Runner* gives us an interesting twist on this tale, in that there is a single goal constructed for Amir—that being "a way to be good again" (168)—but the resolution of it lies in two places and requires two voyages.

The need to reach the goal is, of course, precipitated by the first key event, and resolved, in part, by the second, and is the same goal that the Rags to Riches storyline leads us on, namely the inner peace that Amir loses when he fails to intervene in Hassan's rape, and regains only when he gives himself over wholly to Sohrab.

However, in a Quest story, the goal is very often less interesting than the journey. If it was all about the goal, then Frodo's tale would have involved a quick stroll and a whole load of ring-throwing, and Ulysses would have met far fewer interesting monsters. The journeys that Amir must undertake—first the fleeing from the revolution, and then getting into and out of the now Taliban-held Afghanistan, contain some of the more exciting and thrilling parts of the story, as any good Quest should. They also contain some of the larger pieces of his character development. In the first journey—which is not really part of the Quest, but his removal from the site of the goal, causing the later journey to be necessary —he gains an understanding of his father, and some of the realities of life. But it is in his adult return to and from Afghanistan that he finally understands himself, his country, and his place in his community, the world, and the lives of others.

While the purpose of a quest is often the retrieval, or disposal, of an item, the true purpose of it is always to bring wisdom to the protagonist, and the various encounters Amir has—with the aged Rahim Khan, with Farid and his family, with Assef, with Sohrab himself—are the things that grant him his final goal. It is not just the rescuing of Sohrab that Amir achieves, it is the rescuing of himself.

4. Voyage and Return

Although also containing journeys, Booker makes a distinction between the Quest narrative, and that of the Voyage and Return. He cites *Alice in Wonderland* as a prime example, and describes the plot like this:

> The essence of the Voyage and Return story is that its hero or heroine (or the central group of characters) travel out of their familiar, everyday "normal" surroundings into another world completely cut off from the first, where everything seems disconcertingly abnormal. At first the strangeness of this new world, with its freaks and marvels, may seem diverting, even exhilarating, if also highly perplexing. But gradually a shadow intrudes. The hero or heroine feels increasingly threatened, even trapped: until eventually (usually by way of a "thrilling escape") they are released from the abnormal world, and can return to the safety of the familiar world where they began. (Booker, 87)

In *The Kite Runner* we can see these ideas as being remarkably applicable. His first journey, to America as a refugee, is full of perils and strangeness—travelling inside an empty fuel tanker, for instance—and leads him to a land where everything is strange. Even the things that should be familiar, courtesy of the Afghan diaspora of which they become part, are strange because of their new setting and their lack of context. With this, we can see the first intimations of what Freud referred to as "the uncanny," where what should be familiar becomes unsettling and unfamiliar.

His second journey, back to Afghanistan, is even stranger, and even more uncanny, because of the changes that have happened to the country in his absence. Amir notices the transformation as soon as he crosses the border, but it becomes even more apparent as he enters Kabul. Much that he remembers from his childhood is different, or destroyed, and yet there is still enough identifiable to allow him to see the change, and to feel the discomfort of the difference. The people are similar, but more cowed, and there is a truck full of gun-carrying Taliban roaming the streets, reminiscent perhaps of the Red Queen's guards in this strange, real-life Wonderland, where everything has been turned on its head.

Following the guidelines for this kind of story, he is truly trapped by the Taliban, and Assef, in particular. This is just another reminder of his childhood that is both familiar and unfamiliar: Assef's reappearance in the guise of the new foe fulfils all of the criteria for Freud's uncanny, with Assef becoming his own doppelgänger. Amir does, of course, then effect a "thrilling escape" to borrow Booker's phrase, though it is not as heroic nor as thrilling as he may have wished, involving, as it does, a severe beating, time in a hospital, and his adoptive son's suicide attempt.

However, just as we have seen earlier, the physical manifestation of these plot lines is accompanied by an emotional and spiritual one. As such it can be argued that Amir's voyage commences when he fails to act to save Hassan from Assef in the alley. He moves away from himself, and from the person he thinks he is, and from then on "everything seems disconcertingly abnormal." (Booker, 87) His image of himself is overturned, and the rest of the book consists of his voyage through the world, slowly picking up the broken pieces he requires to reconstruct his image of himself. It is only in the last pages, when he is able to "be good again," that he finally achieves his return, despite having been physically home for some time. Finally, the sense of uncanny dissipates, and home finally feels like home again.

5. Comedy

It may seem strange to apply the term 'comedy' to *The Kite Runner*. It is a text with some moments of levity, but it would be a strange reader who would find themselves laughing along with the story.

However, in more traditional plot formulations, the term 'comedy' is not always associated with humor.

Booker unpicks the history of comedy and the many changes it goes through and catalogues a host of different texts that have been classed as comedy, including some that are distinctly unfunny. However, what these texts share is a story in which the protagonist starts off in a state of equilibrium, where all is right in the world, and then through a series of confusions and unexpected events, finds themselves on the brink of tragedy, only for circumstances to come right again—often through no choices of their own—so the story has a happy ending. Sometimes, but not always, this is a love story, and the happy ending is a marriage.

Amir's life does start in a state of equilibrium, and it can be argued that the key event that upsets this—the attack on Hassan, and more particularly Amir's failure to act—is caused by confusion that is not of his making. If Baba had revealed Hassan's true parentage to Amir earlier on, then Amir would not have harbored the jealousy that caused him to hold back from helping his half-brother. This case of "mistaken identity," especially around a sibling, is common in traditional comedies and was a device used by Shakespeare over and over again.

Amir then undergoes a series of events in his life, many not of his making—he had no control over the collapse of Afghanistan that caused his refugee status, for instance, nor the rise of the Taliban that causes Hassan's death and his own need to return to effect Sohrab's rescue. Even Sohrab's attempted suicide can be seen as arising because of a misunderstanding and does bring the storyline very close to complete tragedy. However, the misunderstanding is corrected, Sohrab is brought home—an act initiated by the second key event, which marks the turn from confusion to resolution—Amir finds peace with his past, and the son he has always wanted. The story does not end with a marriage—one does occur midway through the text, of course, but is not the goal of the comedy arc—but the bonding that occurs between Amir and his nephew/adoptive son is at least analogous.

Even while writing this, and seeing how well it fits, it seems strange to refer to *The Kite Runner* as a comedy. However, because of the series of dark trials that Amir undergoes, the happy ending of the book achieves the catharsis that Aristotle thought should be the goal of comedy. It takes the reader on a journey of fear and worry, only to release those emotions in a gust of relief at the end. It is not a funny book, but in this sense, it is a comedy.

6. Tragedy

Can the same text be a comedy *and* a tragedy?

In this case, yes.

Othello, King Lear, Macbeth, Hamlet. . . What do these four plays have in common? Yes, they are all Shakespearean tragedies. But also, other than the history plays, they are the only plays of his that have the names of the main characters in the titles. It is thus worthy of note, that the book is called *The Kite Runner*, not *Amir*. If we take that as a reference to Hassan (ignoring for the moment Amir's final transformation into the role) then this is his story, not Amir's.

In that respect, then, we can see this as the tragedy of Hassan, a story which results in his death.

However, that is, at best problematic. Traditionally tragedies are about the death of the main character, and that is not the case here. Also, that death is almost always caused by a fatal flaw in the main character—Othello's jealousy, Macbeth's avarice, Hamlet's pride—and it would be hard to ascribe Hassan's death to his own actions.

However, if we look again at the title of the book, and this time take into account its duality—as a reference to both Hassan *and* Amir —then we can start to see how Amir's jealousy and pride lead to Hassan's death; how the actions of Amir during Hassan's attack lead, almost inexorably, to Hassan being in the situation that brings about the end of his life. And so, while Amir's "fatal flaws" do not end his own life, they do kill his literal brother, something that wounds him deeply and fundamentally changes him.

And it is, perhaps, in this fundamental change that we can finally fit *The Kite Runner* into this kind of narrative, for in the final moments, where Amir finally lets go, he is no longer the person that he was—a symbolic death rather than a real one—and this new person is also the kite runner, just as Hassan was. The kite runner is dead, long live the kite runner.

It is, then, perhaps a stretch to claim that *The Kite Runner* is both fully a comedy and fully a tragedy. However, while tragedies do usually end in the death of the main character because of their flaws, it is not too far to claim that the person Amir starts out as, is killed by the events that unfold. Also, while comedies do traditionally have a series of unfortunate events that culminate in a happy ending, those events do not normally go so far as to lead to the death of a main character, which must be seen as tragic. *The Kite Runner* is neither a true tragedy nor a true comedy, but something in between, however, and by using a schema such as this to examine it, we can learn something new about the narrative and the way it works.

7. Rebirth

Booker's final formulation is Rebirth. This can be a literal death and resurrection, but more commonly is the character going into darkness, or a quasi-death—Sleeping Beauty and Snow White, for instance—and then, as he says, "From the depths of darkness they are brought up into glorious light." (Booker, 194)

Perhaps more than any other, this particular story-type can be seen to pertain to *The Kite Runner*, especially when we see how Booker sums up the various permutations of the Rebirth:

(1) a young hero or heroine falls under the shadow of the dark power;
(2) for a while, all may seem to go reasonably well, the threat may even seem to have receded;
(3) but eventually it approaches again in full force, until the hero or heroine is seen imprisoned in the state of living death;
(4) this continues for a long time, when it seems that the dark power has completely triumphed;

(5) but finally comes the miraculous redemption: either, where the imprisoned figure is a heroine, by the hero; or, where it is the hero, by a Young Woman or a Child. (Booker, 204)

Amir's life passes into a veil of darkness after the attack in the alleyway. It seems that everything he loved becomes tainted by his guilt, and he can no longer take pleasure in the things that had previously delighted him. He moves on with his life but carries the darkness with him wherever he goes. A change of location—to America—cannot cure him, although things do seem to improve. The call from Rahim Khan reawakens the darkness, however, and with the news of Hassan's death, it seems that darkness has finally triumphed. It is only, then, in the second key event—when he is rendered almost dead by Assef, even passing into a coma for two days—that redemption arrives. This moment acts like Prince Charming's kiss. It is the point at which his reawakening, his rebirth, starts to occur, and in the last act of the book we see Amir finally emerge from his darkness and into "glorious light,", saved by a child.

Conclusion

Building the narrative around two key story moments—the attack in the alley, and the rescue of Sohrab—allows *The Kite Runner* to develop a multifaceted plot that interweaves many different elements. The attempt above to categorize the novel in various traditional story forms may, at times, require something of a leap, but it does serve as a useful illustration of just how complex the seemingly simple narrative actually is. Amir is a rich character, and the web of relationships, motivations, outside influences, and decisions that form his story lend themselves to a wide range of interpretations.

Booker's seven plots are a useful way to lay bare some of the narrative structures underpinning the book. There would be many other ways to understand what is occurring and how. However, by tying *The Kite Runner* back to the oldest, traditional forms of storytelling, we can see how a book that at times feels like one of Amir's childhood storybooks, achieves the effects that it does on the reader. It is a novel of archetypes and tropes but bound together in a complex web that evokes something new and fresh, something engrossing and surprising, and something that satisfies the reader's need for story.

Works Cited

Barthes, Roland. *S/Z*. 1973. Blackwell. 2002.

Booker, Christopher. *The Seven Basic Plots*. 2004. Continuum. 2005.

Cobley, Paul. *Narrative*. 2001. Routledge. 2001

Freud, Sigmund, David McLintock, and Hugh Haughton. *The Uncanny*. Penguin, 2003.

Hosseini, Khaled. *The Kite Runner*. 2003. Bloomsbury. 2011.

Kite and Scarf: *The Kite Runner* and Mohja Kahf's *The Girl in the Tangerine Scarf*_____

Nicolas Tredell

Published within three years of each other, Khaled Hosseini's *The Kite Runner* (2003) and Mohja Kahf's *The Girl in the Tangerine Scarf* (2006) opened up hitherto unexplored worlds to many readers while offering others, perhaps for the first time, an image of their own worlds. Both novels feature protagonists who are Muslims living in the United States–Amir, in *Kite*, in San Francisco, Khadra Shamy, in *Scarf*, in Indiana and later Philadelphia. Both Amir and Khadra have a sense of possible homelands elsewhere, in the East, that are primarily associated, particularly from a Western viewpoint, with civil war, violence, and disorder: Afghanistan in the case of Amir, Syria in the case of Khadra. But both are divided from those homelands by the conflicts that scar them and by their own American acculturation.

Both start with a return to the past, in memory, and, in *Scarf*, also physically: *Kite* opens with Amir's traumatic recollection from twenty-six years before, when he was twelve, of what he saw "peeking" into an alley in Kabul in winter 1975 (1); *Scarf* begins with Khadra Shamy driving into Indiana, where she "spent most of her growing-up years," and wryly doubting the highway sign that says "The People of Indiana Welcome You" (1). Both make use of the *leitmotif* announced in their respective titles. The kite, in Hosseini's novel, functions as a symbol of freedom, bright color, cooperation between fighter and runner, and a kind of benign competition. In Kahf's novel, the scarf, or more precisely the hijab, is a symbol of identity, commitment, pride, safety, modesty, passion, faith; it is the outward and visible sign of a deep inward spirituality. As the adjective in her title demonstrates, it can also be brightly colored. *Scarf* vigorously and vividly contests any construction of the hijab as primarily oppressive.

Both novels have the form of the *Bildungsroman*, the novel of "education by life," and as *Bildungsromane* generally do, both offer modern versions of one of the most ancient forms of storytelling, the quest narrative, showing their chief characters searching for identities that will enable them to live with their often conflicting allegiances, gratify their desires, and assuage the various guilts and tensions they feel. Both novels have an autobiographical aspect in the experiential if not empirical sense, but they clearly offer themselves as fictional rather than real-life accounts, even if, in part, they are implicitly based on "true events." The styles of both novels are studded with transliterated words from Eastern languages, including Arabic, Dari, Farsi, and Pashto.

There are also, however, significant contrasts between the two novels. *Kite* has a first-person narrator-protagonist in the shape of Amir, *Scarf* a third-person narrator with Khadra as the main viewpoint character. *Kite* has twenty-five numbered but untitled chapters whereas *Scarf* has 66 chapters and one final epigraph. The chapter names are given in the Contents list rather than at the head of each chapter; but each chapter head has an epigraph, and it is from the first word or words of these epigraphs that the chapter names in the Contents list come. They range widely: examples include Chapter 3, "Go Forth Lightly and Heavily" (41), from the Quran 9.41; Chapter 6, "The Presence of the Heart with God" (30), from the Muslim philosopher al-Ghazali; Chapter 14, "I Was a Hidden Treasure" (78), "attributed to God in a Hadith Qudsi"; Chapter 19, "When Your Daughter's Menarche Comes" (108), supposedly "a Damascene custom of unknown origin (now nearly defunct)"; Chapter 43, "When the Silverfish Is About to Molt" (261), which comes from *Broadsides from the Other Orders: A Book of Bugs* (1993) by the American author Sue Hubbell (1935–2018); and Chapter 64, "The Heart A Sudden Rose" (427), from the American Muslim poet Daniel Abdal-Hayy Moore (1940–2016).

Kite has a strong masculine focus and concentrates on male bonding and experience; *Scarf* has a strong feminine focus and concentrates on female bonding and experience. Both novels are rich in event, incident, evocation; but *Kite* is organized around one traumatic moment—the rape of Hassan—that drives Amir's quest for some kind of atonement; all the other events in the novel center around that rape, like iron filings around a magnet. *Scarf* offers a proliferation of events that represent many different aspects of Khadra's experience and self-configuration, so that the novel resembles a kaleidoscope with constantly changing patterns that never quite settle into a fixed or final shape.

Islam matters a lot in both novels, but in *Kite* it is loaded mainly into one scene in Chapter 25 in which, in extremity, Amir returns to and deepens his Muslim faith (301–02). In *Scarf*, Islam is an almost constant presence, in its strength, its reach, its varieties, its internal debates, its protections, its oppressions, its liberations and its spiritual exaltations. Amir in *Kite* is beset by guilt and this sets the dominant tone of the novel, which is somber even in its positive moments, such as the wedding ceremony of Amir and Soraya in Chapter 13, where Amir cannot help wondering whether Hassan had ever married and if so, to whom (149). Khadra in *Scarf* suffers guilt along with many other painful emotions, but the style of the novel has an energy, an exuberance, a *brio* that counterpoints, without cancelling, its darker moments. *Kite* is rarely comic; *Scarf* generates much laughter, even, or especially, at difficult moments. But both novels have a resilience that does not cancel the traumas they depict but demonstrates the point that Edgar makes in Shakespeare's tragedy *King Lear*: "The worst is not, / So long as we can say 'This is the worst'" (84; 4.1.27–28)—that is, as long as we are still alive and can grasp and articulate our condition, we have not reached a nadir of hope.

Both novels portray marriages in which husband and wife quickly come under pressure to have children; Amir and Soraya are unable to have a child, but Khadra conceives all too quickly and at the worst time, when her marriage is almost over. *Kite* offers a portrait of an enduring marriage without direct biological issue that expands to encompass a surrogate son who is, in fact, a nephew. Both novels deal frankly, though not sensationally, with rape and murder, and other forms of killing that would not legally count as homicide but come very close to forms of it that are legitimized by war or a particular penal system. In *Kite*, these crimes are concentrated in the figure of Assef who, as a teenager, rapes Hassan, still a boy, and, as an adult, and a powerful Taliban official, systematically abuses Hassan's young son Sohrab. Assef also relishes killing, joyously casting the first stone to begin the public execution of an adulterous couple in the football stadium in Kabul. In *Scarf* there is a range of male violence toward women, from the rape, murder and mutilation of Zuhura, an able, feisty young militant, a force of life, whom Khadra much admires, to Khadra's discovery at the end of Chapter 44, via her Aunt Razanne, that her own mother, in her early-to-mid teens, was raped by her history teacher (289).

Kite ends with the kind of settlement often found in the traditional *Bildungsroman*, in which the protagonist, after many vicissitudes, achieves a reasonable degree of happiness and success in his personal and professional life; Amir becomes a successful novelist; and he, Soraya, and Sohrab form a family unit, with Sohrab as the traumatized child whom they seek to nurture and heal. *Scarf* shows Khadra becoming a successful photographer but staying single and continuing to wear the hijab in a positive, affirmative way.

We shall now compare and contrast these two novels in more detail, focusing on four main areas: their representation of racism and prejudice; their treatment of rape and murder; their portrayal of marriage and procreation or its absence; and their exploration of religion and spirituality.

Racism and Prejudice

In *Kite*, the key prejudice that is crucial to the whole action of the novel is the prejudice of Pashtuns against Hazaras; and this is clearly racist, directed against visible markers of ethnic difference rather than of religious difference. It is concentrated in Assef, but it is worth underlining the fact that Assef is half-European, with a German mother, as we learn in Chapter 5. Assef's mother, like Amir's father, condemns Hitler as insane and a killer of many innocent people, but Assef disagrees. In Chapter 5, mocking Hassan with racist abuse, Assef calls Hitler a "great leader," a visionary who, had he been allowed to "finish what he had started," would have made the world "a better place" (35). In Chapter 8, Assef gives Amir "a biography of Hitler" as a birthday present (85). To highlight Assef's German mother in this essay, even if she is anti-Hitler, might appear to risk reanimating another prejudice lingering from the world wars of the twentieth century, against Germans; but the wider point the mention of Assef's mother makes in the novel is that racism is not confined to Pashtuns or any other ethnicity or region of the world. It can occur in supposedly "advanced" countries, like Germany, as well as "underdeveloped" ones, like Afghanistan. As Marlow says in Joseph Conrad's *Heart of Darkness* (1902), speaking of the idealistic Mr Kurtz who descends into sensual and sadistic self-indulgence and gratuitous cruelty in Africa: "All Europe contributed to the making of Kurtz" (71). It could likewise be said that all Europe not only contributed to the making of Hitler but also played its part in the making of Assef—and of Afghanistan.

Assef justifies his prejudice against Hazaras with a nationalist ideology whose structure and components are familiar. Pashtuns "are the true" and "pure Afghans" and the land of Afghanistan is theirs. Hazaras, marked by their distinctive features (hence the abusive term Assef uses of Hassan, "Flat-Nose") are perceived as polluting the Pashtun's "*watan*," their "homeland" and dirtying Pashtun "blood" (35). Assef sees Amir, because of his friendship with Hassan, as "a disgrace to Afghanistan" (36). Substitute other ethnic and national names for "Pashtuns," "Hazaras," and "Afghanistan" and this could be any nationalist ideology anywhere in the world. It is this ideology which, in Chapter 7, Assef uses to justify his rape of Hassan when his crony, Kamal, has doubts: "It's just a Hazara" (66). Amir, as he is all too painfully aware, is complicit with this denigration of Hassan.

The Pashtun prejudice against Hazaras is carried into the United States, embodied most dramatically in the expatriate General Taheri, Amir's father-in-law. In Chapter 25, Taheri asks Amir why he brought Sohrab from Afghanistan to live with Soraya and himself. Significantly, he justifies the question on grounds of communal rather than individual prejudice: "I have to deal with the community's perception of our family. People [. . .] will want to know why there is a Hazara boy living with our daughter" (315). Amir replies frankly: "my father slept with his servant's wife. She bore him a son named Hassan. Hassan is dead now. That boy [. . .] is Hassan's son. He's my nephew." (315). He then ventures to lay down the law to Taheri with unusual firmness: "You will never again refer to him as 'Hazara boy' in my presence. He has a name and it's Sohrab" (315).

This is a complex moment. On the one hand, Amir has stood up for Hassan's son against Pashtun anti-Hazara prejudice in a way that he was never able to stand up for Hassan himself against Assef and his own internalized racism. On the other, his revelation of the true identity of Sohrab's father dilutes the boy's Hazara identity; he is no longer wholly Hazara and thus, despite the illicit manner of his conception, subtly more acceptable to Pashtuns than a "pure" Hazara boy might have been. Moreover, Amir's injunction never to refer to him as 'Hazara boy' is, on one level, positive, asserting that Sohrab should be spoken of as a named individual rather than contemptuously consigned to a general category with negative connotations. Conversely, it can be seen as making him more acceptable to Pashtuns by not mentioning a key component of his ethnic identity.

This portrayal of Afghani anti-Hazara racism within America is not complemented, however, by any portrayal of racism or prejudice in non-Muslim Americans in *Kite*. As Timothy Aubry observes, Amir "never reports any encounters with racism" in America and "depicts the United States as a remarkably hospitable place for Muslims." (35). This remains the case even in the immediate aftermath of 9/11, as "Jennifer M-R," an Amazon reviewer whom Aubry quotes, points out. In Chapter 25, Amir records how, after the fall of the Twin Towers, the "American flag suddenly appeared everywhere" and how "[s]uddenly, people were standing in grocery store lines and talking about the cities of my childhood, Kandahar, Herat, Mazar-i-Sharif" (316). But there is no mention of any verbal or physical hostility in the United States to Afghans and Afghanistan, or to Muslims. This absence of any portrayal of American racism or anti-Muslim prejudice doubtless helped to increase *Kite*'s popularity with many US readers. It enhances the contrast between a "bad" Afghanistan and a "good" America. It is, of course, both credible and understandable that refugees from a war-torn Afghanistan in which they have been in extreme peril might find California an agreeable place by contrast, even if they are unable to enjoy anything close to their previous lifestyle, as happens with Baba, reduced from a member of a wealthy elite in Kabul to a gas-station worker in San Francisco (even if he does rise to become a manager). Moreover, the Muslim identity of Baba and Amir is not strongly marked at this stage by clothing or religious practice: Baba is a skeptic and Amir's embrace of Islam, temporarily when Baba is very ill, and fervently when Sohrab seems to be hovering between life and death, does not manifest itself in any marked change in his public appearance and behavior.

Khadra, growing up in Indiana from early infancy, has a different experience. She is aware that she belongs to a minority in the United States. In Chapter 6, she mentions "a map captioned 'The Muslim World'" (32) in the back hallway of the Masjid Salam mosque in Indianapolis, where she and other girls went for "weekend Islamic school" (31):

> The countries that were mostly Muslim were dark green. Light green meant they had a lot of Muslims, yellow-green and yellow meant they had some, and the pink and dark pink countries had next to none. The USSR, Khadra was surprised to see, was light green. China was yellow. The United States was only pink. Muslims did not count for much here. (32)

There is an intertextual echo here of Conrad's *Heart of Darkness*, where Marlow looks at a map of Africa in the waiting-room of a Belgian company and sees "a vast amount of red" (14)— the cartographic color of the British Empire. This confirms him in his sense, as an Englishman, of being a member of a dominant imperial nation, even if the novel goes on to offer a general critique of Imperialism that could apply to Great Britain as well as its most obvious though unnamed target, the Belgian Congo. In contrast, the map Khadra sees unsettles any easy settlement into a sense of

American identity, showing that her religious orientation makes her part of a relatively small minority. At the same time those dark green and light green countries remind her that there are other places in the world where she would be in the majority.

In Khadra's narrative, Muslims in Indiana have to contend with organized local prejudice. In Simmonsville, the small town adjoining the house on the southern edge of Indianapolis where she and her parents live, a Muslim outreach center known as the Dawah has been created. This arouses the ire of an army veteran called Orvil Hubbard, who has a prosthetic leg after stepping on a landmine in Korea, and who likes to don his old army uniform and sport his Congressional Medal of Honor when protesting the Muslim presence. In Chapter 7, Hubbard forms "the American Protectors of the Environs of Simmonsville" (42), known more simply as "the Protectors" (42–43), and later, in Chapter 16, acronymized as "APES" (97) to guard against what they see as Muslim "incursions" (42). He says quietly "I'm not speaking from ignorance [. . .] I've lived in their countries, and I know. They *will* destroy the character of our town" (42, italics in original). The Protectors tell the Immigration and Naturalization authorities that the Center is a refuge for illegal immigrants, though a search reveals nothing. They then try to use "zoning ordinances" against the Center (43). Though these attempts to shut down the Center are unsuccessful, there are hints that the Protectors may have been responsible for, or contributed to a cultural climate that encouraged, a particularly brutal crime against a young Muslim woman.

The narrator does point out, however, that those Muslims who run and frequent the Dawah Center know "next to nothing" (45), and do not trouble to find out anything, "[a]bout the lives of the small-town residents of Simmonsville and southern Indianapolis," "the shopkeepers and schoolteachers, the beer-and-peanuts crowd and the country club set, much less the outlying landscape of central Indiana with its farmers in crisis, many facing foreclosure in the 1970s" (44–45). There is thus a sense of two enclosed communities whose interactions with each other are limited and seem inadvertently or deliberately hostile.

In *Kite*, the expatriate Afghan community in California is also shown as an enclosed one. As we have already observed, it carries its anti-Hazara prejudices from its native country. Baba also carries his anti-Russian prejudice from his native country. In Chapter 12, when Baba falls ill with cancer, Amir goes with him to see a pulmonologist whose surname is Schneider. Baba has already discovered, however, from reading Schneider's biography in the waiting room, that the doctor, though born and raised in Michigan, has Russian parents— he is, as Baba puts it with a grimace "like it was a dirty word," "*Roussi*" (135), Amir's attempts to reason him out get short shrift. Baba declares "I'll break his arm if he tries to touch me" (135). It is, of course, understandable that a native of an invaded country might feel anger toward those who seem to represent the invaders, but Baba takes it too far. It is structurally similar to holding any German responsible for World War II or any Afghan American responsible for 9/11. Amir, however, aims to explain it primarily in terms of patriotism. "Sometimes I think the only thing he loved as much as his late wife was Afghanistan, his late country" (136).

In Chapter 13 of *Kite*, Amir describes the success of his first novel, "a father-son story set in Kabul" (159), a narrative that obviously bears some structural resemblance to the Kabul sections of *Kite* itself but does not appear to engage with expatriate issues. He goes on "a five-city book tour" (160) but *Kite* does not mention any interactions with non-Afghan Americans that might have occurred during this excursion. Rather, Amir focuses on the fact that he becomes "a minor celebrity in the Afghan community" (160). He engages in other activities that might have given openings for the description of such interactions. For example, as he also mentions in Chapter 13, he attends San José State University as an English major (158) and, as he mentions in Chapter 15, he takes a creative writing class there (172), but again there are no accounts of encounters on this course with non-Afghans. When he marries, he does so within the American Afghan Pashtun community. To highlight the extent to which the narrative stays within that community is not in any way to criticize *Kite* but to define the areas within which it works.

The only mildly abrasive encounter that Amir has with American culture is described in Chapter 25 of *Kite* when he recalls a minor incident at a video store in Fremont in 1983 or 1984. He is in the Westerns section and a man points to *The Magnificent Seven* and asks if he has seen it. This movie was, of course, the favorite of Amir and Hassan when they used to go to the Cinema Park in Kabul together as boys, the movie he had then seen thirteen times, as Amir mentioned back in Chapter 4 (23). Amir tells his questioner how many times he has seen it but then makes the mistake of revealing who gets killed in the movie (311). With a "pinch-faced look" and an ironic "Thanks a lot, man," his interlocutor shakes his head, mutters, and walks away. Amir regards this as an uncomfortable lesson in cultural difference. "That was when I learned that, in America, you don't reveal the ending of the movie, and if you do, you will be scorned and made to apologize profusely for having committed the sin of Spoiling the End" (311). Amir's take on this incident is wryly humorous; it is a small *faux pas* that might be a minor incident in a comedy of manners. In *Kite*, the disturbing prejudice and racism are largely confined to Afghanistan and expatriate Afghanis. America, in those respects, is a great good place. In *Scarf*, the great good place itself is shown as harboring and encouraging racism and prejudice, and rape and murder.

Rape and Murder

Rape features significantly in both *Kite* and *Scarf*, though it is more continuously present in the former, since, as we observed at the start of this essay, the whole plot and narrative of Hosseini's first novel turns around Assef's rape of Hassan, which is reproduced and systematized in Assef's abuse of Sohrab, Hassan's son. In *Scarf*, rape does not function in this way but it punctuates the narrative powerfully, especially in relation to Khadra's heroine Zuhura, the daughter of "a very pale white man," a Muslim convert, and a "darkest blue-black" mother from a family in the Kenyan city of Mombasa in Africa (28). Almost a grown-up to Khadra as a girl, Zuhura is eloquent, educated (at Indiana University, Bloomington), and a fighter for her community. She keeps a watchful eye on

Orvil Hubbard and challenges the white building inspector whom Hubbard has called in to inspect the Dawah Center, contending that "zoning law" has frequently been employed as a means of racial exclusion (43). She hopes to be a lawyer and already shows signs of having the skills for that profession, but, as the narrator points out, these are not "the best skills for getting along as a foreign newcomer in Simmonsville, or as a black woman in the social landscape of central Indiana" (44). She increasingly emerges as a community leader while at the same time getting engaged to a man whom she realizes might cramp her militant style.

As the activities of a revived Ku Klux Klan become increasingly threatening, Zuhura disappears, and it looks ominous. In Chapter 16, Khadra's Uncle Abdulla laments that, even if Zuhura is found alive, she will be, as a single Muslim woman, socially "ruined" (92) because of the suspicion that she may have been involved in some sexual impropriety, which will make her a very doubtful prospect for marriage, like Soraya in *Kite* who, as she tells Amir in Chapter 12, ran away at the age of eighteen with an Afghan man and stayed with him for nearly a month (143). Zuhura, however, does not survive even as a doubtful marriage prospect. Some days later her "body [is] found in a ravine:" in a condition summarized in staccato prose that drives home the brutality of her death: "Murdered. Raped, Cuts on her hands, her hijab and clothes in shreds" (93). The desecration of her hijab, a leitmotif of the novel and a key symbol of Muslim female identity, compounds the horror of her violation and slaughter.

In another kind of novel—one more like *Kite*, perhaps—this brutal murder would become the central narrative driver. Indeed, the first-time reader of *Scarf*, with no prior knowledge of the whole novel, might well expect the story, after the discovery of Zuhura's body, to concentrate on the quest for her killer(s), first of all among the Protectors and the Klan. But as we learn later in Chapter 16, the police, insofar as they pursue the matter at all, question her fiancé rather than the Protectors or Klan and finally let him go without charge but deport him "on a technical visa violation" (97). The investigation then concludes. As the narrator says, "Zuhura's murderer was never caught" (97).

Khadra has recurrent memories of Zuhura, however. On one occasion, she even returns to the spot where Zuhura's mutilated body was found. Much later on in *Scarf*, in Chapter 56, she tries, in light of her own later experience, to answer the question "Who had Zuhura been, really?" (357) Those at the Dawah Center had constructed her as a "martyr," and for many years Khadra had believed this (357). But she considers another possibility: that Zuhura may have "been just a regular Muslim girl trying to make her way through the obstacle course—through the impossible, contradictory hopes the Muslim community had for her, and the infuriating, confining assumptions the Americans put on her? A girl looking for a way to be, just *be*, outside that tug-of-war?" (358, italics in original).

In a sense, Khadra is defining her own quest here. She too is "looking for a way to be," "outside that tug-of-war," while also realizing that she is, necessarily, involved in the latter, with conflicting allegiances to Islam, to the Muslim community, and to America. There is a clear difference in this respect between Khadra in *Scarf* and Amir in *Kite*. Khadra is "looking for a way to be" throughout Kahf's novel and in a sense she is still searching for that at the end of it. Amir's identity has, in a sense, been fixed since early adolescence, as he announces in the very first words of novel: "I became what I am today at the age of twelve" (1). Amir's life-task is to work out a way in which he may live with an identity that, in a sense, he already has; Khadra's task is to find or fashion an identity from the various components around her. But just as Amir has to work through his trauma and grief over Hassan, Khadra has to work through the trauma and grief of Zuhura's slaughter, even if this is less central to her life that Hassan's loss is to Amir. It is only in Chapter 64, very near the end of *Scarf* that Khadra is able, at last, to cry for Zuhura (429).

Two ways of confirming or constructing human identity are through marriage and procreation, major rites of passage in many human lives. We can compare and contrast how *Kite* and *Scarf* deal with this.

Marriage and Procreation

In *Kite*, Amir's marriage lasts; in *Scarf*, Khadra's marriage soon ends. Amir marries within the expatriate Afghan community in California, as already mentioned; Khadra likewise marries within her community, "to a nice Muslim guy" (16). Amir marries Soraya, the daughter of General Taheri; Khadra marries Juma al-Tashkenti. Both Soraya and Juma are good looking and intelligent. In both novels, the wedding ceremony is evoked vividly (see Kite, Ch. 13, 147–49; *Scarf*, Ch. 36, "In Islam It Is Said," 213–16). The marriage of Amir and Soraya is happy from the first: as he puts it in Chapter 13, we "settled into the routines—and minor wonders—of married life" (158). Despite the mention of "wonders," however, the sense of "routines" predominates already; Amir and Soraya rather quickly settle down into behaving like an elderly married couple, and there is little sense of erotic passion or indeed of much passion of any kind. The early days of the marriage of Khadra and Juma are evoked with more intensity in Chapter 38 of *Scarf*. Khadra at first loves matrimony, which gives her a sense of identity and belonging:

> To be a married woman of your very own, on equal terms with married women and other real people—in the community, only married people had prime status. Married life was bliss. To have a friend always, a built-in friend. To pray fajr [the first of five daily prayers by practicing Muslims] beside him in the dark misty dawn and then sleep beside him in your full-sized bed—your very own *man*. (221–22, italics in original)

The narrator also makes it clear, without over-explicitness, that the marriage is erotically charged. Juma is attracted to her in this way and in others. Indeed, we are told in Chapter 38 that "[s]he fit the profile of the wife Juma always knew he'd have. An observant Muslim, of course, but also a modern, educated woman, not old-fashioned and boring" (222).

Both couples are under strong pressure to have children quickly. As the narrator of *Scarf* says, "In the months after the wedding, not a week went by when someone didn't ask Khadra if she was pregnant" (225). As she observes to Juma after refusing his erotic overtures, "It's like they're all here in bed with us, going 'Have babies!'" (227). Amir and Soraya are unable to conceive a child by the traditional means or with IVF, and medical investigations finally attribute this to "Unexplained Infertility" (162). Khadra has the reverse problem. As the prospect of relocating to Kuwait with Juma looms—one she had accepted before their marriage—she feels increasingly entrapped, not only by the pressure to bear children but also by an increasing sense of constriction in her life with Juma. In Chapter 40, she asks herself: "Was this what marriage amounted to, compromise after compromise, until you'd frittered away all the jewels in your red box? She woke up one morning and felt as if the future were closing in, the horizon shrinking smaller around her" (244). At that point, she vomits, signaling not only her disgust with her deteriorating matrimonial state but also the biological fact that she is pregnant. She procures an abortion, ends her marriage, gives up her college degree, and leaves Indianapolis for Philadelphia. It is clear that the traditional kind of narrative settlement for a rebellious woman protagonist—as in Charlotte Brontë's *Jane Eyre* (1847), for example—is not for Khadra, at least at this point.

In *Kite*, there is no sense of any threat to the marriage of Amir and Soraya, despite their inability to have children. In a sense, of course, this is necessary to the demands of the plot of the novel; if they did have children of their own, Amir's obsessive devotion to saving Sohrab in an attempt to atone for his failure to try to prevent Hassan's rape twenty-six years before would seem more like an obsession in the negative sense, an unbalancing preoccupation that might sap his attention to any direct biological progeny. Moreover, introducing a traumatized child into an already existing family with children would raise a whole host of extra questions that would disturb the neat symmetry of the conclusion as it exists, where Amir and Soraya can focus wholly on Sohrab. *Scarf* is not as strongly plotted a novel as *Kite*—it allows in more of the redundancy, the excess, of real life—and the eschewal of the marriage/family resolution is necessary to its open-ended, loose-at-the-edges narrative, which matches Khadra's existential trajectory throughout the novel.

Kite also incorporates another kind of settlement: a commitment to religious faith. Such a commitment recurs, in a sense plays through, *Scarf*. We shall now consider how each novel handles this theme.

Varieties of Religious Experience

It is possible to play down the Islamic religious experience in *Kite*. In 2005, Meghan O'Rourke asserted that of the "631 Amazon reviews" and many newspaper pieces on Hosseini's first novel, "most fail to mention that the narrator converts from a secular Muslim to a devoutly practicing one." The narrative encourages this, in O'Rourke's view, by presenting "Amir's conversion [not as] a sign of his adherence to a particular set of theological beliefs, but of a generalized spirituality reflecting his moral development over the course of the novel." If we look at the "conversion" passage in Chapter 25 of *Kite*, when Amir is desperately praying in the hospital corridor for Sohrab to survive, the language sometimes specifically references Islam—for example, when Amir says "*La illaha il Allah, Muhammad u rasul ullah.* There is no God but Allah and Muhammad is His Messenger." (301). At other times it could be a Christian prayer—for instance, "I will pray that He forgive that I have neglected Him all of these years" (302). Moreover, the situation in which he is praying recalls the phrase "There are no atheists in foxholes"—that is, in circumstances of extreme peril to oneself or one's loved ones, for example in wartime combat, even non-believers might pray. Any belief this produces can be dismissed as being coerced by circumstances rather than freely chosen—rather like making a profession of belief in a particular faith in which one does not, in fact, believe under torture—and it will not necessarily endure. Sometimes, indeed, it may be quickly or almost instantly forgotten once the mortal peril has passed. It is a suspect rather than sound conversion. It is true that the novel gives some indication that Amir's renewed faith will prove enduring: later in Chapter 25, very near the end of the novel and the slight signs of a breakthrough in the psychological healing of Sohrab, Amir recites prayers "morning *namaz*" and can now recite the verses "naturally" and "effortlessly"

(318). But Amir's tendency to obsessiveness prompts the question as to how far this is genuine spirituality and how far a neurotic practice.

If Muslim spirituality is a largely peripheral and not wholly convincing aspect of *Kite*, it features much more centrally and strongly in *Scarf*, as a key element in the rich tapestry of Khadra's life. In a sense, *Scarf* is an Islamic equivalent, in the form of a novel, of William James's classic psychological study *The Varieties of Religious Experience* (1902). As with Amir's "conversion" in *Kite*, and many of the experiences James describes, it would be possible to interpret the religious moments in *Scarf* in terms of religions and belief systems other than Islam, or in terms of what O'Rourke calls "a generalized spirituality," Islam is in the foreground for Khadra who has been, as Chapter 34 tells us, "steeped as she was since earliest childhood in the words of Quranic and Prophetic traditions" (194). But Islam, like Christianity, is monotheistic but not monolithic; Chapter 39 records her realization that "the belief system of her parents and their entire circle, including the Dawah Center, was just one point on a whole spectrum of Islamic faith. It wasn't identical to Islam itself, just one little corner of it" (232). She finds it "difficult to accept" (232) that "these other paths had always existed beyond the confines of her world, and yet were still Muslim" (232–33). Indeed, for a time, she "[h]eroically" resists this (233). Her encounter with it is, however, an important part of her intellectual and spiritual development.

Scarf traces Khadra's intricate, impassioned negotiations with varieties of Islam and with religious experience. She comes to recognize the elusiveness of what she is trying to grasp, using imagery drawn from her successful adult career as a photographer. In Chapter 63, near the end of the novel, she reflects on "the strange ways of the heart in its grasp of things, the way Reality unveils itself for an instant and then just when you think you've got a shot at it, the shutter goes down, and the light has evaporated" (421). The only thing to do is to keep "hoping for another glimpse, and meanwhile working patiently at your little given task, just working at developing the picture, whatever you've been lucky enough to get in that instant." (421).

Conclusion

Kite and *Scarf* are two remarkable novels that introduce new topics and concerns into Anglophone American and global fiction. *Kite* has enjoyed bestseller status and a huge readership, in English and in translation into many languages, around the world. *Scarf*, while it gained an enthusiastic readership, not least among young American Muslim women who felt they could identify with Khadra's experiences and dilemmas, has made less impact. This may be partly due to the fact that Kahf has not published another novel since then, turning to poetry, while Hosseini has published two more that have also won much acclaim and a host of readers. But it is also due to the fact that *Scarf* is a harder-edged novel, in its engagement with Islam, in its criticisms of America, in its eschewal of easy settlements. This is not to say that it is better than *Kite*, or vice versa; each novel accomplishes much in the terms that it establishes and the implicit aims it sets for itself; but it is enjoyable, enlivening and, yes, sometimes harrowing, to compare and contrast them, to read them against each other in a way that helps to highlight more fully what each has to offer and to suggest future possibilities for Afghan American, Syrian American, North American and global world fiction.

Works Cited

Aubry, Timothy. "Afghanistan Meets the *Amazon*: Reading *The Kite Runner* in America." *PMLA*, vol. 124, no. 1, 2009, pp. 25–43. *JSTOR*, www.jstor.org/stable/25614246.

Conrad, Joseph. *Heart of Darkness*. 1902. Penguin Modern Classics series. Penguin, 1973.

Hosseini, Khaled. *The Kite Runner*. 2003. Bloomsbury, 2011.

Kahf, Mohja. *The Girl in the Tangerine Scarf: A Novel*. 2006. PublicAffairs, 2007. Kindle Edition.

O'Rourke, Meghan. *"The Kite Runner.* Do I Really Have to Read It"? *Slate.* 25 July 2005, slate.com/news-and-politics/2005/07/do-i-really-have-to-read-the-kite-runner.html.

Shakespeare, William. *King Lear,* edited with a commentary by George Hunter, introduced by Kiernan Ryan. Penguin Shakespeare series. Penguin, 2005.

CRITICAL READINGS

"Ask him where his shame is": War and Sexual Violence in *The Kite Runner*

Georgiana Banita

Readings of *The Kite Runner* tend to foreground the personal "past of unatoned sins" (1) that drives the narrator's desire to undo unforgettable wrongs. In this essay, I focus on the precise nature of these sins in the context of sexual violence as a weapon of war. Instances of sexual violence play an important part in *The Kite Runner*'s carefully patterned structure. Paying attention to these decisive moments affords a nuanced perspective on the kind of abuse that forms the lynchpin of the novel. After all, it is the rape of a young Hazara (Hassan) by an aggressive Pashtun (Assef) that largely determines the course of the story, precipitating the return of the protagonist, Amir, to his homeland in a desperate attempt to atone for having witnessed this sexual crime without intervening. This and other similar episodes in the book are best understood against the background of widespread and indiscriminate sexual abuse used as a war tactic during the conflicts sweeping across Afghanistan over the past 40 years. All warring factions (the Soviets, the mujahideen, the Taliban, the Northern Alliance, and local warlords) were guilty of such violations, though the victims were primarily women and members of the persecuted Hazara community.

Sexual violence during armed conflict serves purposes linked to the conduct of the hostilities themselves, such as torture or the humiliation of the opponent. Many historical conflicts were accompanied by mass rapes and other forms of sexualized violence, including several in the twentieth century: the 1915 Armenian genocide, the Japanese invasion of Nanjing in 1937, World War II (during the Holocaust and in the streets of Berlin after 1945), the Korean War, and the Vietnam War. Despite being committed on a massive scale, sexual violence in these instances was considered an inevitable part of military aggression and even in the cases where war trials were held, it was not prosecuted on its own grounds.

It was the acts of sexual violence committed during the highly mediatized Balkan wars and the genocide in Rwanda in the 1990s that finally drew attention to women's rights during warfare and sparked demands for accountability. The resulting image of sexual violence as a strategy of war enabled an understanding of such violence as a serious security issue, which in turn facilitated its criminal prosecution (Crawford, Hirschauer). It also galvanized the efforts of the international community to condemn the perpetrators, assist the victims, and take preventive measures.

By taking a closer look at *The Kite Runner*'s representation of sexual violence during armed conflict, I hope to show that Hosseini acts from a position of humanitarian sympathy with the victims and faith in the ability of fiction to do its part in investigating the complex causes and victimology of this vile crime. The novel takes a complex view of the issue by attending to its significance within Afghan culture in several interrelated ways. First, Hosseini correlates the violence experienced by Hassan and others with the wars unfolding in the background of the novel's family drama. Second, he scrutinizes the gender dynamics in the families at the core of the book (Amir's and Hassan's) to account for the shame that overwhelms Hassan after his experience of rape. Third, he draws together a series of abuse narratives to show that sexual violence is not an isolated occurrence, but very much a commonplace aspect of armed conflict, irrespective of individual circumstances. And finally, in picturing sexual violence Hosseini also explores the reasons why the brutal violation of the victim's personal identity leaves lasting scars, especially in the context of Afghanistan's patriarchal culture. In a nutshell, I suggest that exposing sexual violence in this way illuminates the role of sexuality and gender in the shaping of modern conflict while also highlighting the ability of literature effectively to expose and denounce human rights atrocities carried out beyond the gaze of international observers.

Sexual Violence as a Weapon of War in Afghanistan

The Kite Runner is in many ways a war novel. Even the kite-fighting tournament, the centerpiece of the narrative's symbolic world, is a

---

metaphor of armed conflict: "In Kabul, fighting kites *was* a little like going to war" (53), Hosseini writes. Kite runners like Hassan exhibited a level of dedication and submission comparable to the honor and valor codes of the armed forces. The novel spans thirty years of Afghan history, marking the beginning and end of various hostilities from the summer of 1973, when the king's cousin, Daoud Khan, put an end to the constitutional monarchy in a bloodless coup (39), followed by the communist coup of 1978 and the Soviet invasion of 1979. The opening chapters document the moment the rule of law starts to erode, as the sound of rocket and artillery attacks percolates through the pages in a harbinger of worse things to come. When Amir and his father leave Kabul, they do so as a last resort, eager to escape the bombed-out ruins, the curfews, the patrolling Russian troops, and the "tanks rolling up and down the streets . . ., their turrets swiveling like accusing fingers" (119). Throughout the book, whatever conflict may be unfolding, we are presented with the same "gray, barren canvas" (130) that life in Afghanistan has become.

The year 1989 brings with it the publication of Amir's first novel and the withdrawal of the Soviets from Afghanistan, yet the war continues, pitting the mujahideen against the Soviet puppet government. The Northern Alliance transforms Kabul into a warzone between 1992 and 1996, leaving a trail of destruction even greater than the one for which the Soviets were responsible. Just going about your daily life—as Amir's childhood mentor, Rahim Khan, remarks in the book—"you risked getting shot by a sniper or getting blown up by a rocket" (209). The Taliban make matters even worse: "They don't let you be human" (209), as Rahim Khan puts it. And Hosseini pulls no punches in describing the aftermath of rocket hits. While "sifting through the rubble" of a bombed-out orphanage, one built by Amir's father (Baba), survivors find "body parts of children" (211). "Is there a more Afghan way of dying" (217) than being blown up, Rahim Khan eventually asks, rhetorically and resignedly, after telling Amir that Hassan's father, Ali, was killed by a land mine. The Taliban also ban kite fighting and carry out massacres of the Hazara community. By the time Amir returns to Kabul to rescue Hassan's son, the city has been almost completely wiped out, reduced in essence to "the heading of an AP story on page 15 of the *San Francisco Chronicle*" (253) rather than a real, habitable place. Importantly, each of the conflicts and peaceful interregnums have significant ramifications for the safety and welfare of Afghan women.

It comes as no surprise that Afghanistan, a nation subjugated by fundamentalist regimes and often a pawn between global superpowers, poses unique challenges to a gendered human rights discourse. "The experience of war and external occupation," international relations scholar Janie L. Leatherman writes, "has made Afghan women's bodies 'globalized property' over which they have limited control" (2). Due to legal barriers to women seeking justice and the rampant sexism stigmatizing survivors of sexual violence, incidents of rape were underreported in Afghanistan in the timeframe covered by the novel. And because perpetrators could act without fear of punishment, sexual violence reached epidemic proportions. Replacing the monarchy with a republic initially promised substantial positive changes: "People spoke of women's rights and modern technology" (47), but their hope was short-lived. Under the mujahideen, Afghanistan became a failed state that could no longer protect its citizens, and least of all its women. "Not only had they been unable to bring about peace in their war-ravaged country, but what was worse was that many of them had begun to engage in unsocial activities" (Matinuddin 23), including extortion, looting, drug trafficking, and rape. And yet whatever sexual atrocities one regime was responsible for, the next managed to exceed them. It was after the fall of the Soviet-installed leader Najibullah that "for the first time in the history of Afghanistan . . . rape became a regular feature of war" (Rubin 135). In an attempt to cleanse the nation from the moral sins that had fueled civil war, "the Taliban instituted a regime of draconian purity the likes of which the world had never witnessed" (Gopal 7). The novel accurately captures the wasteland into which the Taliban turned Afghanistan, a lawless place where warlords and various groups aided by foreign powers were preying on women, girls, and boys.

The Kite Runner is a rare example of a novel that depicts sexual violence perpetrated against boys. The bulk of statistical and academic research on sexual violence focuses, of course, on violence against women, because gender has often been conflated with women and girls. Consequently, sexual violence experienced by men and boys has been under-analyzed. There are other factors that obfuscate the extent of the problem and contribute to the culture of silence around male victims in Muslim cultures. For one thing, men are more reluctant to acknowledge their experience of abuse, since it is perceived as incompatible with the idea of masculinity; they also fear being seen as homosexuals, which would result in being stigmatized by their communities. And yet in a society like Afghanistan, where gender is used as a means of social stratification, hierarchical distinctions separate not only masculinity from femininity, but also forms of masculinity deemed inferior to dominant masculinities. Even though the sexual violence depicted in the novel affects a boy rather than civilian women, it is important to note that it nonetheless rests on male/female gender hierarchies.

Despite the fact that the underlying motivation for the assault is the symbolic destruction of Hassan's ethnic group, the precise nature of this destruction is informed by gendered patterns; specifically, the attacker seeks to emasculate the opponent as a means of deciding the conflict in his favor. At first glance, it might appear that targeting men and boys betrays the intention to suppress another ethnic group more clearly than attacks against women, which could be dismissed as acts of lust. At the same time, by using sexual violence to force men into passivity, the perpetrator ultimately also confirms the negative characteristics associated with the female gender in the respective culture. As a tactic of political violence, rape, therefore, is experienced individually, but has ramifications for the entire community, serving as an instrument to maintain hierarchical relations. In the words of the international security scholar Sara Meger: "When perpetrated against men, then, sexual and other forms of gender-based violence represent a form of 'othering' through which the victimized men are made into gender 'decoys,' enforcing a differentiation between categories of men and a hierarchy of power based on gender" (177). Hassan's rapist wants to treat him like a woman in order to rob him of his virility and hence of his humanity. In this way, Hosseini shows that the power dynamic of wartime rape in Afghanistan is premised on local gender norms, namely the socialization of men to disrespect women. This disparagement surfaces across multiple sites of female representation in the novel, from sexual activity to birth and motherhood.

Gender and Sexuality: Sex, Birth, Motherhood

Female characters stand out through their prolonged absence from the main narrative strand of the novel. Mothers and wives, for instance, play second fiddle to the male protagonists, though not by any conscious decision of their own; rather, it is Afghan society itself that marginalizes them and impedes their personal development. Amir's mother, Sofia Akrami, "hemorrhaged to death during childbirth" (6). Hassan lost his mother "to a fate most Afghans considered far worse than death: She ran off with a clan of traveling singers and dancers" (6). In the case of Amir's mother, the neglect of women's reproductive health and poor access to life-saving medical care turns pregnancy into a possible death sentence. Far from being rare, this tragedy accurately reflects the fact that maternal mortality remains the leading cause of death among women of childbearing age in Afghanistan. Hassan's mother, Sanaubar, survives the birth of her baby by sheer luck, since she enjoys none of the prenatal medical benefits Western women take for granted: "No obstetricians, no anesthesiologists, no fancy monitoring devices. Just Sanaubar lying on a stained, naked mattress with Ali and a midwife helping her" (11). The suggestion that death would have been a better fate for Sanaubar than running away with a lover signals the restricted sexual freedom of Afghan women in the 1960s, who were unfairly stigmatized as promiscuous at the same time that countless Western women were eloping with counterculture transients in the name of democratic ideals like individual freedom, feminism, and sexual liberation.

The boys are affected differently by the absence of their mothers. Hassan never talks about his, "as if she'd never existed" (6); Amir, in contrast, longs to have met and known her (7). It is a telling difference because it has to do with the different ways in which the two women—one Pashtun, the other Hazara—were treated by a bitterly divided society. Sofia Akrami, "one of Kabul's most respected, beautiful, and virtuous ladies" (16), was a university instructor in classic Farsi literature and a descendant of the royal family. Amir would often retreat into his mother's books, reading Arabic, European, and American writers (21). Sanaubar was not only forbidden to obtain an education, she was also at the mercy of military personnel patrolling the streets of Kabul. "I knew your mother," a soldier boasts to Hassan; "I knew her real good. I took her from behind by that creek over there" (7). In the eyes of this soldier, Sanaubar (though he never even mentions her name) is only worth remembering for her "tight little sugary c[***]" (7). Everything we learn about her in the novel is second-hand information based on rumor and innuendo. She was, allegedly, "a beautiful but notoriously unscrupulous woman who lived up to her dishonorable reputation" (8). Yet this suspicion is grounded solely on her effect on men. Her "brilliant green eyes and impish face had, rumor has it, tempted countless men into sin," while her "suggestive stride and oscillating hips sent men to reveries of infidelity" (8).

Many of the other family stories shared by the novel's central and supporting players suggest that women are treated as second-class citizens. Above all, they are disposable; when they are removed from their roots, as Rahim Khan's Hazara lover Homaira is, at first glance it appears to be for their own good. "She would have suffered," Rahim Khan opines, "You don't order someone to polish your shoes one day and call them 'sister' the next" (105). Yet this kind of mentality shift is exactly what any type of progress toward greater ethnic and gender parity requires. Most of the Pashtun men that feature in the novel, apart from Amir himself, have internalized the double standard that prescribes chastity for unmarried women yet sanctions sexual experience for unmarried men. Even Amir's father expresses reservations about the Afghan woman that Amir sets his sights on in California. When he reveals to Amir that Soraya is no stranger to love, he does so somberly, as if she were suffering from a grave illness (149). Soraya's mother, too, firmly believes that every woman ought to have a husband and child, even if family life "did silence the song in her" (187).

Amir, however, looks critically on the advantages afforded by his status and on "the sin-with-impunity privileges that came with them" (317). The novel questions Afghan gender norms through Amir's thoughtful, self-reflective observations. "I was fully aware," he remarks, "of the Afghan double standard that favored my gender" (155). He also understands that his special status is nothing but a lucky win "at the genetic lottery that had determined [his] sex" (157). Amir even shares Soraya's frustration that Afghan men are permitted to "go out to nightclubs looking for meat and get their girlfriends pregnant" (188) while she can never live down a single youthful indiscretion. Much like his father, in other words, Amir lives by his own rules, disregarding social custom and embracing liberal views. Yet very much unlike his father, he tries to live by his own principles and refuses to share the illusion that his immunity is natural or incontestable. Throughout the novel, whenever we are confronted with sexual violence, our perspective coincides with Amir's, so we always feel his outrage at the dissolution of state protections for women and children as well as his self-critique. Three instances stand out among the horrors that he witnesses or is aware of: the rape of Hassan by Assef, a Soviet soldier's attempt to rape a female refugee, and Sohrab's sexual captivity.

Three Stories of Sexual Violence

Echoes of the sexual violence we encounter later in the book already resonate in an early passage that details Amir's frustration with his father's decision to have him circumcised at the age of ten; "it felt like someone had pressed a red hot coal to my loins" (50), he recalls. Here and increasingly after Hassan's rape by Assef, Hosseini ascribes to his protagonist a deep suspicion of all things sexual. Whatever aspects of his life it may touch, for him sexuality holds violent, cheerless connotations. In a rare instance in which he briefly refers to the tragedy of his birth, he even expresses a desire to be "pardoned for killing [his] mother" (60). But it is the rape of Hassan that serves as a pivotal lens through which the reader is asked to understand the gender and ethnic dynamic of Afghan culture and to gauge the impact of the abuse. Assef's attacks conform to the definition of sexual violence as a war tactic to the extent that they are meant to humiliate an opponent in the context of an ethnic conflict. Assef holds his blood to be purer than that of the Hazaras, who in his view "pollute" (43) the country of Afghanistan. To see another Pashtun, like Amir, play with a Hazara boy simply repulses him. As the literary scholar Rebecca Stuhr has argued, prejudices in Afghan society support a power structure that both "makes it possible for Amir to treat Hassan as an inferior" and "allows Assef to rape Hassan without fear of reprisal" (42). The two forms of abuse—ethnic disrespect and sexual humiliation—are entwined and interdependent.

The rape scene is given a brutal, explicit treatment in the book. When Assef and two other boys attack Hassan, they do so with an indifference and brutality that reduce the boy to the status of a "wild animal" or "ugly pet" (76, 77). After the assault, Hassan and his brown corduroy pants are discarded like garbage amid "Worn bicycle tires, bottles with peeled labels, ripped up magazines, yellowed newspapers, all scattered amid a pile of bricks and slabs of cement" (80). Hosseini also makes a point of describing "the dark stain in the seat of his pants" and the "tiny drops that fell from between his legs and stained the snow black" (84), as well as "Assef's buttock muscles clenching and unclenching, his hips thrusting back and forth" (122). It is a shockingly graphic portrayal of rape for a book that has sold millions of copies the world over. It also powerfully illustrates the meanings and effects of a rape committed for the benefit of witnesses, in this case the other boys, who decline to participate in the crime. In visibly flaunting his physical dominance, Assef shows the others that he wants to strip the Hazara boy of his manhood and thereby reduce him to the status of women and homosexuals in the gender hierarchy of Afghan society. In the process, he aims to instill fear among the wider Hazara community and a sense of entitlement in fellow Pashtuns.

The abuse is not complete when the perpetrators have left the scene. Hosseini actually locates the weapon of war not simply in the act itself, but in the feelings of guilt, helplessness, unworthiness, and dishonor that rape brings forth in the victim. Sexual violence is, of course, especially effective due to the stigma that attaches to sexual victimization. It is an unspeakable crime, both in the sense that it places the victim's human dignity in jeopardy and because for those who experience or witness it, it is a painful taboo that they cannot easily divulge or discuss. With their emotions bottled up and their mind poisoned by self-hatred, survivors of sexual abuse will typically keep to themselves and exhibit symptoms of posttraumatic stress disorder (PTSD) and depression. Hosseini's predilection for clichés and his medical training serve him in good stead here, because it turns out that in the aftermath of the sexual attack Hassan's behavior and state of mind bear all the telltale signs of PTSD. The former California physician registers all the key symptoms: the boy is physically drained ("Lines had etched into his tanned face and creases framed his eyes, his mouth," 97–98). He hardly speaks anymore, shuns company, and generally withdraws into himself as if waiting for a wound to heal. The traumatic incident leaves traces on Amir as well. Memories of the attack follow him everywhere, long after the scene in the alley. When he is given a brand-new Stingray bicycle for his birthday, its red steel-frame body conjures up memories of blood (107). The remainder of his life in Afghanistan will be saturated in the color of this memory.

After he fails to save Hassan, Amir is given a second opportunity to redeem himself during his clandestine journey out of Afghanistan. On their way out of Kabul, the group of refugees that Baba and Amir have joined is stopped at a checkpoint and forbidden from continuing their journey unless a Russian soldier is permitted to spend half an hour with a female refugee handpicked from the desolate group. Amir's father valiantly objects, doing so on the grounds that far from precluding any notion of shame, as the soldier would have it, war in fact "*demands*" (122) decency even more than peacetime does. Apart from Baba, no one dares to express outrage or attempts to hinder the rapist. Even when another, more senior Russian soldier intervenes, he offers a feeble apology that simply blames the younger, hot-headed comrade's behavior on his inexperience and drug habit. Hosseini dwells on this incident for the same reason that I use Baba's reproach, "Ask him where his shame is" (121), in the title of this essay: Because it demonstrates the use of sexual violence as a strategy of war, one that humiliates, terrifies, and tortures innocent civilians. The arbitrary, seemingly haphazard nature of the soldier's demand suggests that he is merely a sexual opportunist motivated by sheer whim and lust. Yet the self-righteous, calculated manner in which he makes his proposal to trade free passage for sex, alongside his pre-prepared argument about the shamelessness of war, point to a widespread practice of sexual violence committed with total impunity. The female refugee is lucky to escape unscathed; other women in the novel fare much worse, including Sanaubar. On being reunited with her family, she cannot hide the scars of a brutal attack: "One of the cuts went from cheekbone to hairline and it had not spared her left eye on the way. It was grotesque" (221). Hassan's wife, Farzana, is beaten with a wooden stick by a young Talib because she raises her voice when asking a vendor about the price of potatoes, suspecting he might be hard of hearing (228). Though surely reprehensible, none of these attacks or attempted attacks are quite as terrifying as Sohrab's month-long sexual slavery.

The shocking nature of the crime against Sohrab is further compounded by the fact that it is carried out openly—much more so than the assault on Hassan—without any shame or fear of consequences. After his parents are executed in the street by the Taliban, Sohrab finds temporary shelter in an orphanage. Every month or two, a Talib official—later Amir recognizes him as Assef—pays the orphanage director a fee for the permission to abduct a child, mainly girls but boys too, on occasion, including Sohrab. Hosseini is quite charitable with this man, who reluctantly turns a blind eye to the Talib's abuse of power in order to secure an income and keep the orphanage afloat. Though visibly tormented by the nefarious exchange, he appears at peace with the compromise he is forced to reach. "If I deny him one child," he reasons, "he takes ten. So I let him take one and leave the judging to Allah" (270). The scenes that feature Assef in his den make it clear, however, that any judgment of this particular man must result in a brutal sentence commensurate with his crimes. Assef's abuse of the boy operates in a similar manner to the other forms of sexual domination he engaged in before, namely along gender lines. That sexual violence rests on the feminization of its victims is confirmed by Sohrab's physical transformation while in Assef's captivity: "His head was shaved, his eyes darkened with mascara, and his cheeks glowed with an unnatural red. When he stopped in the middle of the room, the bells strapped around his anklets stopped jingling" (293). The intended degradation requires that the Hazara boy be endowed with both feminine and animal attributes. The shaving of the head conveys his emasculation and the makeup softens his appearance, while the tinkling of the ankle bells accentuates his subordination to his master.

The abuse affects Sohrab much like it did his father before him. He feels uncomfortable with Amir's attention and flinches when touched, going for a whole year without speaking to either of his adoptive parents. "I'm so dirty and full of sin" (335), he insists between bouts of crying and torpor. When Amir finds him with his eyes "still half open but lightless" (366) in a bath of bloodied water, it is clear that despite having survived this suicide attempt, something inside him is irreparably damaged. The final chapters of the book painstakingly chronicle the stages of Sohrab's trauma. A blend of fear and shame makes it impossible for him to live a normal life or simply accept himself as a member of society and of a new family in the United States: "He walked like he was afraid to leave behind footprints. He moved as if not to stir the air around him" (381). In short, he displays the caution and paranoia of a prey species that expects to be attacked again, viciously and without warning, by its natural predator. All the abusive situations Amir personally witnesses or hears about are filtered through his disapproving point of view, so the novel's overall depiction of sexual violence takes on a similarly accusatory tone. Hosseini's attention to the power politics of sexual violence in war, the gender inequality that it feeds on and perpetuates, and the enduring trauma of physical abuse cast a much-needed light on a tactic of war that is too often and too easily elided from literary representations of warfare.

Sexual Violence as Metaphor and Allegory

However specific Hosseini's accounts of sexual violence in this novel may be, the central rape scene can also be understood at a more abstract level as a symbol for acts of violence that play themselves out on a larger scale. Hosseini himself has suggested a reading of this kind against the backdrop of international indifference to Afghanistan's problems: "For me, the scene in the alley has always had a metaphoric quality to it. . . . A lot of fellow Afghans feel like that's what happened to their country, if you substitute Afghanistan for Hassan" (Hosseini). But the scene invites a plurality of interpretations, depending on the context to which it is transposed. On one hand, as I have argued elsewhere, the novel was successful partly because it uncovered "parallels between Afghanistan's struggles for political and cultural autonomy and a shaken US national consciousness after 9/11" (Banita 336). On the other hand, the sexual violence described in *The Kite Runner*, which was published just as the 9/11 wars were expanding across the Middle East and Central Asia, can also be seen as emblematic of the physical and psychological toll of the war on terror. The release of the Abu Ghraib images only one year later confirmed that sexual violence was being used by all warring factions, including the US military. Sex, the torture images suggest, is inseparable from the power dynamics of the war on terror much the same way that the conflicts in Afghanistan derived their viciousness from the transgression and taboo of forcible intercourse.

Hosseini's unabashed dramatization of sexual violence is not without its hazards, however. At an early stage of cultural awareness regarding US military entanglements in the country, *The Kite Runner*'s approach through the prism of intimate violence arguably helped position Afghanistan "as a generalized zone of suffering in need of

Western protection and rescue" (Ivanchikova 3). When he doubles down on the subject by portraying Sohrab's similar experience with the same sexual predator, Hosseini opens himself to the accusation that he might be catering to an Anglophone reading public's prurient "appetites for cultural otherness and curiosity about a distant war" (Ivanchikova 5). What is more, in the aftermath of 9/11, public figures who voiced concerns about human rights—especially the rights of women—in Muslim-majority countries were suspected of trying to "manufacture consent for international engagements across the Muslim world" (Abu-Lughod 81). Certainly, writing about the suffering of the Hazaras in Afghanistan in a way that resembles the narratives of class or racial injustice in Western fictions by Mark Twain or Victor Hugo encourages American readers to assume the moral high ground and endorse the rationale of the war on terror. After all, how could anyone sympathize with the barbarian norms of this medieval society?

While this criticism has at least some partial validity, Hosseini's frank and courageous depiction of rape is important in light of the strong barriers to reporting sexual violence in Muslim-majority states. At the same time that it seems degrading to members of the Hazara community to dwell on this episode, portraying sexual attacks against Hazara children in a book aimed at a mass audience is a fundamental step in recognizing the illegitimacy of wartime rape. By naming and shaming a rapist, Hosseini makes clear that sexual violence is an affront to social order and human rights that deserves global scrutiny as an issue of principle. Moreover, as the political ethnographer Torunn Wimpelmann points out, "naming an act as a violation against someone other than the family sovereign signifies a challenge to absolute sovereignty, as it names other people as holders, or partial holders, of rights" (5). Seen in this light, the novel's condemnation of the Pashtun rapist underscores Hassan's rights and entitlements as a legal person, while challenging the ethnic divide that elevates the Pashtuns above the Hazara—across the nation and within the pecking order of Amir's extended family. Hosseini, who would later become a UNHCR Goodwill Ambassador, probably did more than anyone, at a time when Afghanistan was an enemy nation on the news channels, to help Americans understand the roots and manifestations of inequality in a place deeply scarred by never-ending bloodshed.

Works Cited

Abu-Lughod, Lila. *Do Muslim Women Need Saving?* Harvard UP, 2015.

Banita, Georgiana. "The Kite Runner's Transnational Allegory: Anatomy of an Afghan-American Bestseller." In *Must Read: Rediscovering American Bestsellers: From Charlotte Temple to The Da Vinci Code*, edited by Sarah Churchwell and Thomas Ruys Smith. Continuum, 2012, pp. 319–39.

Crawford, Kerry F. *Wartime Sexual Violence: From Silence to Condemnation of a Weapon of War*. Georgetown UP, 2017.

Gopal, Anand. *No Good Men among the Living: America, the Taliban, and the War through Afghan Eyes*. Henry Holt and Co., 2016.

Hirschauer, Sabine. *The Securitization of Rape: Women, War and Sexual Violence*. Palgrave Macmillan UK, 2014.

Hosseini, Khaled. *The Kite Runner*. Anchor Canada, 2004.

_____. "'The Kite Runner' Soars into Theaters." Interview by *Beliefnet*. *Beliefnet*. n.p., 30 June 2016, www.beliefnet.com/entertainment/movies/2007/12/the-kite-runner-soars-into-theaters.aspx.

Ivanchikova, Alla. *Imagining Afghanistan: Global Fiction and Film of the 9/11 Wars*. Purdue UP, 2019.

Leatherman, Janie L. *Sexual Violence and Armed Conflict*. John Wiley & Sons, 2013.

Matinuddin, Kamal. *The Taliban Phenomenon: Afghanistan 1994–1997*. Oxford UP, 2002.

Meger, Sara. *Rape Loot Pillage: The Political Economy of Sexual Violence in Armed Conflict*. Oxford UP, 2016.

Rubin, Barnett R. *Afghanistan from the Cold War through the War on Terror*. Oxford UP, 2015.

Stuhr, Rebecca. *Reading Khaled Hosseini*. The Pop Lit Book Club. Greenwood Press, 2009.

Wimpelmann, Torunn. *Pitfalls of Protection: Gender, Violence, and Power in Afghanistan*. U of California P, 2017.

Hidden in Plain Sight: Caste and Sexuality in Khaled Hosseini's *The Kite Runner*_____

Lucky Issar

In Khalid Hosseini's *The Kite Runner,* Ali is a marginal but fascinating figure who seems to epitomize certain facets of Afghan society and its culture. Men and young boys mock him for things over which he has no control. Ali's walk, anatomy, and inability to produce a child generate anger in other men. Pashtun boys "chased him on the street and mocked him when he hobbled by. Some had taken to calling him *Babalu,* or Boogeyman. "Hey, Babalu, who did you eat today? [. . .] you flat-nosed Babalu"? (Hosseini 8). I stress "men and boys" because women hardly appear in the text, and when they do, they remain either silent or peripheral to the novel's main plot; or they emerge only to highlight some aspect of the novel's male characters. In Hosseini's novel, the role of women is seemingly played by men. Afghan society's collective rage against Ali is complicated because this rage leaks into children's play, indicating the damaging impact of societal norms on individuals. For instance, boys humiliate Ali as if he were "less." Ali is "unique," but the way men act toward him reveals society's unruliness. Every major male character who appears in the novel shares some aspect of Ali's life, and thus, despite being marginal, Ali surfaces as a significant figure. Keeping Ali's character in mind, I propose to examine other male characters to understand what they may reveal about Afghan society and its dominant socio-cultural norms. I argue that the Hindu "cultural" practice of untouchability plays a pivotal role in shaping Afghan society's attitude toward non-normative sexualities, gender roles, and women.

The Indian caste system is a system of social stratification of society based on the hereditary division of people into Brahmins (priests), Kshatriyas (warriors), Vaisyas (farmers and merchants) and Sudras (laborers and domestic servants). Those who do not fall in the domain of caste are called "Untouchables" or Dalits—the most marginalized and exploited people in India. Upper-caste people practice untouchability against Dalits. Caste is embedded in Hinduism, but culturally it is practiced across all religions throughout the Indian subcontinent (Roy 24). Although present-day India came into existence on August 15, 1947, its historical and cultural geography exceeds India's national boundaries. For instance, people in the north of India are culturally and ethnically more like people in Pakistan and Afghanistan than people in Kerala. Also, the Vedic civilization and its early literatures flourished along the river Saraswati in the region of the Punjab. Two seminal Hindu epics, *The Ramayana* and *The Mahabharata*, were not only written in the Vedic period but also refer to several places that exist in modern-day Pakistan and Afghanistan. Simply put, many do not realize that mainstream Indian cultural practices have a strong impact on countries surrounding contemporary India. For instance, the more than 2000-year-old Indian caste system has influenced communities and people across religions and beyond India's national boundaries. In addition to Hindus, elite Indian Muslims, Sikhs, and Christians all practice caste discrimination although their scriptures forbid the practice of untouchability (Chughtai 164).[1] Pakistan, Bangladesh, and Nepal all have their own communities of Untouchable sweepers. Also, since Hinduism is older than any other religion that is practiced in the Indian subcontinent, the Hindu practice of caste lurks underneath religions that emerged later such as Christianity, Sikhism, and Islam. One striking example of caste in Islamic societies was seen when India was partitioned; Hindus and Sikhs came to the Indian side and Muslims went to what then became Pakistan. On both sides people were butchered. Pakistan declared that Untouchable municipal sweepers were part of the country's "essential services" and impounded them, refusing them permission to move to India (Ambedkar 369–75). Even today in Pakistan and Afghanistan, while various Islamist sects slaughter each other over who is the more faithful Muslim, they hardly seem to question the very un-Islamic practice of "untouchability." In other words, caste functions in Indian society not only to create "inequality," but also to repress people sexually. In order to maintain caste "purity," members of upper-castes marry within upper-caste communities.[2] Likewise, in Afghanistan, "the most common marriage is an arranged marriage in which the bride and groom share the same ethnicity, social class, and level of reputation." (See *Afghan Women*). I will next examine how ideas of caste "purity" and caste's interface with sexuality unfold in an Afghan society whose history in terms of both its religion and culture intersects with Indian culture.

Toxic Masculinities and Male Friendships

Only on the surface do all the male friendships in *The Kite Runner* seem familiar, and even admirable. In addition to Amir and Hassan's friendship, we see two other male friendships: Baba (Amir's father) and Rahim Khan's; Baba and Ali . While Amir and Hassan's friendship is central to the main plot, the story is told from Amir's point of view—a wealthy Pashtun boy. These seemingly conventional friendships, when probed, not only give "surprising" clues about Afghan society but also explain that society's complex relationship with "desire," and societal violence against sexual and caste minorities. Before examining Amir and Hassan's friendship, I begin with Baba's two friends, Ali and Rahim Khan, to demonstrate how sexual repression generates violence and cruelty, and shapes Afghan society.

Ali and Baba grew up as friends in Baba's wealthy household (Baba's parents raised the destitute Ali). As adults, Ali remains poor and turns physically deficient; Baba stays rich and becomes hypermasculine. Ali is the antithesis of Baba. Unlike Ali, Baba Sahib is a man of the world. Despite these significant differences, they also share some similarities. For instance, Ali's "unruly" body and Baba's hypermasculinity come to suggest their queerness. While Ali's queerness is visible, Baba's queerness remains hidden behind his wealth and gated mansion. Both are men without women. After giving birth to Hassan, Ali's wife runs away, making her dissatisfaction with Ali clear. Likewise, Baba, despite his wealth and masculinity, never remarries after his wife dies in childbirth. Ali and Baba not only live in the same house but also raise their boys, Amir and Hassan, as single fathers. It seems a highly unlikely arrangement in a culture where, unlike women, remarriage for men is an easy option. Unlike Ali, Baba's single status seems odd and unconvincing considering his class status and his hypermasculinity. Also, Baba pursues a lavish lifestyle: he socializes aggressively with his male friends, offers food and drink without reserve, and thus shows a desire for a good life. Amir describes his father's lifestyle thus:

> Baba's room, and his study, also known as "the smoking room," [. . .] perpetually smelled of tobacco and cinnamon. Baba and his friends reclined on black leather chairs there after Ali had served dinner. They stuffed their pipes [. . .] and discussed their favorite three topics: politics, business, soccer. Sometimes I asked Baba if I could sit with them, but Baba would stand in the doorway. "Go on, now," he'd say. "This is grown-ups' time [. . .] He'd close the door, leave me to wonder why it was always grown-ups' time with him. I'd sit by the door, knees drawn to my chest. Sometimes I sat there for an hour, sometimes two, listening to their laughter, their chatter. (4–5)

Baba loves the company of his male friends and guards his "grown-ups' time." He banishes his son from the adult talk that includes "politics, business, soccer." While the son sits and cries outside, Baba entertains his friends. However, although Baba seems like a pleasure seeker, he does not seek women. On the contrary, he has two close friends: Ali and Rahim Khan, with whom he shares a close bond. (He spends many evenings behind closed doors with Rahim Khan, where Amir is not allowed; and since Rahim Khan, unlike Ali, shares Baba's class status, he is frequently seen socializing with Baba.) Ali's humble and almost ascetic and Baba's hedonistic lifestyles only emerge to suggest their queerness.

Baba's attitude toward queerness is messy—he admires male aggression and hypermasculine environments, but he resents passivity in men. While he lives an astonishingly privileged and self-gratifying life, he worries about his son's (Amir) reading habits and his submissiveness—both attributes make Amir less worthy in Baba's eyes. He keeps harping on the idea that "there is something missing in that boy" (21). Although Baba does not explicitly show his contempt for Amir's timidity, his subtle disapproval has a corrosive impact on the boy. He desperately seeks his father's approval and affection and looks for ways to impress him. While he craves his father's attention, he hardly speaks about his mother. (Neither Baba nor his sensitive son, Amir, mentions her.) Moreover, Baba expects Amir to be a certain kind of boy, and not the way Amir is. Implicit in such expectation is Baba's disdain for non-normative bodies and forms of behavior that conflict with Afghans norms.

Within the domain of home, Amir learns that certain kinds of bodies and behaviors are to be despised, and thus he internalizes a certain kind of hatred for himself. He wants to be the sort of Amir that his father can be proud of, but eventually he gives up trying to transform himself, and his father also stops trying to mold him. However, this internalization of (homo)phobia affects Amir and those closest to him such as Hassan—who Amir thinks is Ali's son; both Ali and Hassan live in the servant quarters on the grounds of Amir's house. After Assef, a Pashtun boy, rapes Hassan, Amir changes completely toward Hassan. In a way, Hassan's rape ends their relationship. Although the text frames Amir's distancing as an articulation of his guilt for not standing up to help Hassan, I argue that it is homophobia and fear of non-normative sexualities that makes him discard Hassan. Here Amir, with far more intensity, mimics his father's behavior. For Amir, Hassan's rape is Hassan's death. Amir shows a great degree of discomfort, disgust, and fear toward what happens to Hassan. Amir's changed—and anxious— behavior toward Hassan reflects Baba's attitude toward Amir. Amir wants to disassociate himself from Hassan because he does not want to inhabit a negative social space—that may distance him further from his father—that is considered unworthy of a man in Afghan society. A space to which Hassan, now, as a rape victim, belongs. One can also argue that Baba's anxiety about his son, and Amir's active avoidance of Hassan are "unexamined" reactions to their own repressed sexualities

With regard to his friendship with Hassan, Amir shows how heteronormative norms run through him. Amir's giving up on

Hassan may have other reasons that the text, perhaps by default, evades. Since Hassan has been publicly defiled, Amir thinks of him as unworthy of his friendship, and more momentously fears that any association with him may tarnish his own image in society. One can also argue that the whole idea of generous, sacrificial, and ever-smiling Hassan is a creation of Amir's mind. Despite his marginalized background and with no access to education—as Amir reminds the reader, "[t]o [Hassan], the words on the page were a scramble of codes, indecipherable, mysterious" (26)—Hassan emerges in the text as a philosopher who says the most profound things. Consider his response to Amir's story of a man who finds a magic cup that can turn his teardrops into pearls, devises "ways to make himself sad" so that he will cry and get more pearls, and who we finally see "sitting on a mountain of pearls" (27) with a knife in his hand and the slain body of his wife, whom he has killed in order to make himself cry more: Hassan gives an astute critique: "[w]hy did the man kill his wife? In fact, why did he ever have to feel sad to shed tears? Couldn't he have just smelled an onion"? (29). Throughout the story, Hassan acts in an extremely cultured and nuanced manner. Such extraordinary traits in Hassan are highly unlikely if not impossible. Only as Amir's double does Hassan make sense.

In this perspective, I suggest that Hassan's rape could actually be Amir's rape; his intense reaction to the post-rape Hassan is a sign of self-hatred. If for a moment we assume that instead of Hassan, Assef has actually raped Amir, Amir's character not only seems less vague, it suddenly gains coherence. Since the stakes of accepting and telling his father about "an incident involving rape" amount to losing his father forever, he withholds telling it. Also, as a narrator, the story can be easily handled if the pain and humiliation of rape could be outsourced to Hassan, who is a Hazara and, therefore, a dumping ground for Pashtuns on which to deposit whatever they find unpalatable to themselves.[3] In addition, as a storyteller, on several occasions, Amir has proved himself to be an unreliable narrator with regard to Hassan. Some of Amir's lies Hassan knows but the ones he does not know are perhaps the most dangerous in the epistemological sense. Once, while narrating a story to Hassan, Amir changes the plot on a whim. Bearing these strands of Amir's personality in mind, one can assume that Amir's guilt and inability to protect Hassan, which gnaw at him, could be the result of his inability to stand up for himself and to expose Assef.

Sometime after Hassan's rape, when Amir and Assef face each other at Amir's birthday party, the meeting evokes a range of negative emotions in Amir. His intense, hallucinatory rage suggests him to be the rape victim. Here, Amir's father feels that Amir is acting weirdly, and Rahim Khan offers him help—all this subtext adds to the confusion. The narrative suggests that Amir feels all this inner turmoil because of Hassan's rape, but Amir has acted worse than Assef toward Hassan. (While Assef's hatred toward Hassan is straightforward—Hassan is an "inferior" Hazara to him—Amir's abrupt change and active cruelty toward Hassan must have been "unsettling" for Hassan.) Post rape, every time Hassan asks Amir to join him, he refuses. One day suddenly Amir wants Hassan to join him for a mountain walk. Here, something completely strange happens. While Hassan being a rape victim acts normally, it is Amir who reveals signs of post-traumatic stress (here, Amir acts like his father; like his father who wants a certain kind of Amir, Amir wants a certain kind of—the unsullied, pre-rape—Hassan). He hits Hassan with pomegranates one after the other, drenching him in their blood-like juice. How could Amir's act be any different from what Assef does to Hassan? Amir's act involves rage, anger, hurt, and bodily intrusion, which also marks Assef's aggression on Hassan's body. After hitting Hassan for no reason, Amir dares Hassan to hit him back:

> "Hit me back!" I spat. "Hit me back, goddamn you!" [. . .] [b]ut Hassan did nothing as I pelted him again and again. "You're a coward! I said. Nothing but a goddamn coward!" [. . .] Then Hassan *did* pick up a pomegranate. He walked toward me. He opened it and crushed it against his own forehead [. . .] "Are you satisfied? Do you feel better?" (81, italics in original)

Instead of hurting Amir or responding in a similar way, Hassan breaks the last pomegranate on his own forehead, and thus ends the violence. Hassan's pointed questions are quite unlike the ever-smiling, gentle, and polite Hassan; they seem more like Amir's words.

Prior to Hassan's rape something exceedingly odd occurs. When Amir goes out looking for Hassan and asks a dried fruit merchant whether he has seen him, the merchant, after inferring from Amir's American clothes that he is well-off, asks him: "What is he to you?" (61). The question implies that a Pashtun should not seek a Hazara boy. The man has seen Hassan being chased by boys like Amir without paying any attention. He knows that they are going to harm Hassan but such everyday violence against Hazaras seems to have been normalized in Afghan society. Sexual violence, such as the rape of either man or a woman, is considered a sign of masculinity, but being raped is framed as 'polluting.' Also, when the shopkeeper looks at Amir the first time, his gaze is 'queer' and can be read in several ways; but the moment Amir tells him his background, the man's gaze is homogenized, condensed, and transformed into a respectful gaze. Suddenly Amir becomes legible to the man.

Seen in the context of how bodies and behaviors are read in everyday life, Amir's attitude toward Hassan and his father's attitude toward him make sense. In such "extreme" cultures, life becomes substantially tough for queer people. Either queer people have to subdue their sexuality and embrace the dominant sexuality or leave society. This is why identities such as Hijras exist only in the Indian subcontinent, and the ways in which Hijra subcultures emerge are linked to the caste system. While Hijras are tolerated in the subcontinent, ordinary women and men are violently punished if they stray from compulsory heterosexual roles. Afghan society expects its men and women to be only heterosexuals. Moreover, it is not only a question of hetero/homosexualities; the very idea of sexuality is framed as a dangerous one. And, therefore, "sexuality" is guarded, mediated, and regulated—otherwise, the Pashtun-Hazara binary will dissolve. We see this in most explicit ways in Assef's behavior. His disgust toward Hazaras is related to Nazi ideology and to hypermasculinist Afghan culture. Also, it is the extreme culture of sexual repression that turns Assef and his friends into sexual predators. They act out their caste privilege and oppressed sexuality through acts of violence against the weak. Years later, when Amir saves Hassan's boy, Assef is abusing this boy sexually. Here, we see how the regulation of sexuality takes pathological forms that then spill over from one generation to the next.

The regulation, and suppression, of sexuality and the racial hygiene in Afghan society mirror the ways in which the caste system works. Usually when high-caste Muslims talk, they talk about themselves as being warriors, and they talk about their social inferiors as Untouchables, as if drawing from the cultural memory of caste. It is seen in the attitude of Assef toward Ali and Ali's supposed son Hassan. He considers himself of a pure race and would identify with those who call Hazaras an inferior "mice-eating" people (8). Also, he hates Amir because Amir "touches" Hassan, and this emphasis on "touch" is connected to the cultural practice of untouchability. The caste sense lurks in Afghan society, but it surfaces more in a sociological than in a religious way. Even after embracing Islam, people in Islamic societies in the subcontinent retain a sense of their upper-caste status. The Pashtun-Hazara issue that the novel engages with is, in its essence, a caste issue. The Brahmin and Untouchable binary, in its essence, is constituted in the same way Pashtuns seek to frame Hazaras in everyday life. In Afghan society, Untouchables exist but the practice of untouchability is articulated differently. The mechanisms through which certain bodies and behaviors are demonized and framed as defiling in Afghan society are the same as those that upper-caste people use to construct and control Untouchables in Brahminic cultures.

Regulation, intrusion, and domination over others not only impact the Hazaras, they create unrest and rage in upper-caste Pashtuns that go unexamined. We see these negative traits in Baba and, in a more convoluted way, in Amir's character; both exercise their hegemony, but they also suffer. Since the novel is told from Amir's perspective, we hardly know Baba: what has shaped him? What are the things that move or disturb him? However, we get to know Amir, and we see how his father inadvertently damages him, and how Amir continues "the damage" by unleashing cruelty on Hassan. There is one scene in the text where Amir tells Hassan a story and midway, just for pleasure, he tells another story to his unsuspecting listener. Although this creates in Amir a sense of power—as he says, "[w]ords were secret doorways and I held all the keys" (26)—such power also comes with responsibilities. One comes to inhabit multiple worlds because one has access to other cultures and other societies. Inhabiting such space also throws up challenges because then one has to contemplate, grapple with, and compare one's actions to a broader socio-cultural sphere that goes beyond Afghanistan and the Indian subcontinent, and that makes hiding in some kind of Pashtun privilege troubling and hypocritical. Also, in the context of the novel, Amir may feel superior to Hassan for the time being, but in the long run such a sense of power creates distance, leading to alienation from friends like Hassan and from oneself. In addition, Amir's reading ability through which he exerts his power over Hassan by default, reflects an "unequal" society in which it seems perfectly normal that one boy goes to school and the other makes breakfast for him. Instead of questioning such an unequal system, Amir and, more importantly, his father seem to accept it as a divinely ordained world-order. It is in this way that Afghan society keeps producing Hassans, Amirs, and Assefs; and enacting a kind of society in which inequality and violence seem natural.

Nowhere to be Seen: Women and Other Outcasts in the Afghan Household

> They made me invisible, shrouded and non-being.
> A shadow, no existence, made silent and unseeing
> Denied of freedom, confined to my cage
> Tell me how to handle my anger and my rage. (Shorish-Shamley)

Only men—Pashtuns, masculine, seemingly heterosexual—inhabit social space fully in *The Kite Runner*. Everything else such as transgressive women, effeminate men, non-normative bodies, or sexualities that can disrupt the dominance of Pashtun men in society are either discarded or severely subdued. So, the ways in which Afghan society engages with women, on the one hand, and queerness in its people on the other, differ only in degree, not in kind.

In *The Kite Runner's* all-male environment, a woman's presence is excluded even from home space. Women do not appear—we only hear about them. Either they are dead, or they have run away, and those who are fleetingly seen only appear to highlight some aspect of male life. We see women feeding their children, cooking for their men, following them, and largely confined to home space. Nowhere are they seen on their own; they appear as shadows of men. Women are seen as mothers, wives, daughters, and as women dependent on men. In such an imaginary, women have two options: either to defy and fight conventional roles, or to suffer and die silently. We see this in the case of Hassan's mother and Amir's mother—these two women speak eloquently through their absence in the novel, provided one pays attention.

In Baba's household, there are two motherless boys, Amir and Hassan—neither of them talks about his mother. For instance, every time Amir mentions his deceased mother, it is in connection with his father. All his energies are directed at winning the affection of his father. (In any given society, children learn quickly what to value and admire, and what to despise and shun.) At home, Amir subtly internalizes homophobia while in his school he gets a lesson in xenophobia; when he asks his teacher about Pashtun violence against the Hazaras, "'That's the one thing Shi'a people do well,' [the teacher] said, picking up his papers, 'passing themselves as martyrs.' He wrinkled his nose when he said the word Shi'a, like it was some kind of disease." (8) Strangely enough, the role of mother is played by Rahim Khan in Amir's life. Often when Baba ignores his son's writing talent, Rahim Khan encourages Amir by reading his stories. "'May I have it, Amir jan? I would very much like to read it.' Baba hardly ever used the term of endearment *jan* when he addressed me." (27, italics in original). Rahim Khan shows attributes—patience, sensitivity, empathy—frequently associated with women (and in some ways he emerges as the most "acceptable" version of Ali. Unlike Ali, shielded by his class and education, he does not invite society's hostility). When Amir's father "worries" about him, Rahim Khan defends Amir. The scene reminds one of many Bollywood films in which, when aggressive fathers voice similar concerns, their wives discreetly defend their sons and try to calm their men down. Rahim Khan's defense of Amir shows not only his concern for Amir but also his profound friendship with Baba. In a culture that is pro-men and family oriented, that expects its men and women to get married, and where polygamy is the norm, it is an achievement that Rahim Khan and Baba manage to follow single lifestyles.

Also, in this Pashtun household, Baba and Rahim Khan "talk" about (homo)sexuality without naming it. The nature of Baba and Rahim Khan's talk concerning Amir hinges on Amir's queerness. Also, at one point Rahim Khan tells Amir that he can always talk to him, as if encouraging Amir to come out. Although the text shows Amir's father as westernized, he is culturally an Afghan (this is reflected in his highly problematic attitude toward his son's behavior, which he considers undesirable because it is feminine and passive), and, therefore, cannot be open to queer sexualities. Unlike Baba, Rahim Khan—a motherly figure—seems to be more accepting, open, and generous like Ali and Ali's son, Hassan. We know Rahim Khan mainly as a friend of Baba, and how he surfaces in Amir's thoughts, but the private Rahim Khan remains hidden. There are moments in the text where it seems like Rahim Khan and Amir like Baba for the same reason. Rahim Khan talks about Baba's electric energy levels and refers to him as *"Toophan agha,* or 'Mr. Hurricane.'" (11). Amir sees his father in a similar register:

> My father was a force of nature, a towering Pashtun specimen with a thick beard, a wayward crop of curly brown hair as unruly as the man himself, hands that looked capable of uprooting a willow tree, and a black glare that would "drop the devil to his knees begging for mercy," as Rahim Khan used to say. At parties, when all six-foot-five of him thundered into the room, attention shifted to him like sunflowers turning to the sun. (11)

Clearly Amir as a young boy is completely infatuated with his father. Here, one can argue that these are just the sentiments of a boy who is proud of his father. On another occasion, however, after winning the kite tournament, he describes meeting his father in a very sensual and homoerotic way, "I walked into his thick hairy arms. I buried my face in the warmth of his chest and wept. Baba held me close to him, rocking me back and forth. In his arms, I forgot what I'd done. And that was good" (19).

Amidst all this, the only person who surfaces as a coherent character in the text is the one who is absent from it: Ali's wife, Sanaubar. She is assiduously framed as an Untouchable in the text whom Afghan society remembers as someone vicious although she has not committed any crime. She only runs away from a dysfunctional marriage. However, what is "questionable" is that, unlike men, women trapped in incompatible, violent, or loveless marriages have no recourse to divorce in Afghan society. Even if a woman gets a divorce, she faces stigma (Nader and Mashal). By running away, Sanaubar takes a pro-life, bold action, but since her action is transgressive, it continues to evoke disdain in society; she has disrupted the norms set by men. Instead of dying or embracing the norms, she defies them by leaving her husband.

Conversely, Baba's wife—Amir's mother— who also never appears in the text is both a proper wife and a proper mother. Unlike Ali's wife who survives in the novel, Baba's wife dies. One can argue that socio-cultural restrictions on upper-class and upper-caste Afghan women are higher because they belong to wealthy men. They are more thoroughly guarded and controlled. Also, in the text, Baba never seems to miss her; he seems to live a very fulfilling, active life in a hypermasculine environment. Once we hear from the narrator that Baba used to flaunt his wife's aristocratic status among his male friends, emphasizing her class, education, and genealogy. Baba's boasting about her amidst his friends, however, is less about her and more about him and his friends. She emerges as an exquisite artifact that he happens to possess. [4] Despite considerable class difference between Baba's and Ali's wife, they seem to share similar fates in

Afghan society, as we see from the way Hassan's mother and Amir's mother emerge in Amir's thoughts here:

> It was in that small shack that Hassan's mother, Sanaubar, gave birth to him one cold winter day in 1964. While my mother hemorrhaged to death during childbirth, Hassan lost his less than a week after he was born. Lost her to a fate most Afghans considered far worse than death. She ran off with a clan of traveling singers and dancers. (6)

Simply put, two women who appear in the text do so as phantoms: one is erased for her transgression, and the other is discarded by letting her die in childbirth[5] so that Baba can live in "his way." Also, since Sanaubar rejects societal rules, her fate is "considered far worse than death"; but Amir's mother has safely transcended the male-dominated Afghan society by dying.

In the novel, Baba does many things such as throwing parties, arranging surgery for Hassan, travelling, giving charity, and celebrating Amir's birthday, but makes no gesture to commemorate his wife in any register. She recedes into oblivion after giving him a son. Baba shows a similar indifference toward his son. For instance, although he celebrates Amir's birthday, his main focus is on socializing with his male friends and their families—Amir's birthday is merely an excuse to strengthen and display his own social position. In a way, the absence of women in Baba's life, his male friendships, his lack of genuine interest in his son or his deceased wife, and his contradictory take on queerness all point up Afghan society's norms that regulate "desire" in ways that create pathologies in its members.

Furthermore, at the birthday party, when Amir sits with Rahim Khan, he offers Amir emotional support (though it is not clear for what reason), fulfilling the role of an absent mother. Here, Amir thinks of him thus: "I'd always thought of him as Baba's quiet alter ego, my writing mentor, my pal, the one who never forgot to bring me a souvenir [. . .] But a husband? A father?" (85–86). Here, Amir's thoughts suggests two things: he values Rahim Khan as a close family member, and he cannot imagine him as "a husband" of someone, which suggests that Rahim Khan is more like Ali than like Baba, and that in Amir's eyes he is a mother-like figure. For this reason, he finds Rahim Khan's presence comforting and accessible. There is a point when Amir almost wants to tell him something significant, but he censors himself. "For a moment, I almost did tell him. Almost told him everything, but then what would he think of me? He'd hate me, and rightfully." (87). Although Amir knows that he trusts Rahim Khan, his "rightfully" indicates the grip of dominant norms upon him. While he is struggling with such inner thoughts, fireworks go off and in a flash of light he sees: "Hassan serving drinks to Assef and Wali from a silver platter. The light winked out, a hiss and a crackle, then another flicker of orange light: Assef grinning, kneading Hassan in the chest with a knuckle." (87). This sight makes Amir cringe. But this "unease" could be Amir's and have nothing to do with Hassan. In the company of his father and Assef and Assef's parents, Amir feels choked to death in his own home. Here, Amir knows the "real" Assef, yet he refrains from exposing him to his father, knowing that his already fragile relationship with Baba may deteriorate further, which not only emotionally exhausts Amir but also intensifies his unease. Here, like Ali, Amir seems helpless in front of Assef's masculinity and the overall hypermasculine environment on display that his father and mainstream Afghan society admire. Amir's heightened discomfort hints that he is reduced to the position of an outcast—of a woman, of a despised Hazara like Ali, of a raped Hassan. What traumatizes him is his inability to stand up for himself (and Hassan) against Assef, against his father, and against the cloying Afghan culture.

Being an overtly "sensitive" boy—not a virtue in Afghan society (Echavez et al.)—Amir is shielded by his class and caste privilege. Without his privilege, he would have declined into Ali's position. When even his own (educated) father resents his son's reading habits and judges him negatively, one can imagine how Amir would be judged if he were exposed to everyday Afghan society in the way Ali is. Also, it is interesting to see how viciously he plots the removal of Hassan from his house, and even his city. Simply put, he wishes Hassan (or himself) dead. This could be his own wish to remove himself from that society forever, and to start afresh elsewhere where he can live freely. In a somewhat mild but also very charged way, this emerges on his birthday. He feels like an outsider amidst 400 guests in his own home. (The only people he feels close to are Rahim Khan and Hassan. Rahim Khan is an acceptable version of Ali, and Hassan is Ali's version in the world of teenagers.) Except for those of Rahim Khan and Hassan, he rejects all other gifts, which suggests his rejection of society at large. He likes his father's expensive gift but a sense of fragility surrounds it that is also a defining feature of his relationship with his father, and by implication, with Afghan society.

Society's treatment of outcasts like Ali gives us clues to the queer dimensions of Afghan society. Ali is a lifelong "friend" (and servant) of Baba sahib, and Hassan (Ali's son) of Amir, yet these friendships are complex and culturally coded. Ali and Hassan live in "a modest little mud hut" (5) on the grounds of Baba's mansion, which some think "the prettiest house in all of Kabul" (34); but neither Baba, as Ali's friend, nor Amir as Hassan's friend, is troubled by such an arrangement. Also, while Baba pontificates about "virtues," he fathers Ali's supposed child, Hassan—something that Rahim Khan also knows. This complicated web of secrets surrounding relationships, which includes Ali, his wife, Baba sahib, and Rahim Khan, seems difficult to gauge. Issues of class, caste, homosexuality, and women-domination all seem to lurk underneath these "proper-looking" relationships. Even in the adolescent world of Hassan, Amir, and Assef, the same dynamics are seen at work minus the presence of a woman. Later, when we hear that Hassan is Amir's half-brother, it comes as an "unpleasant" surprise. In retrospect, Baba's generosity (and righteousness) toward Hassan is the generosity of a father for his illegitimate child; there is no genuine altruism involved. Rather, his secretive acts expose his hypocrisy because they are meant to maintain the status quo. Baba's lifelong but hidden secrecy is not any different from Ali's visible handicap that society despises. Although Baba can hide behind his wealth and position, it does not mitigate the "damage" that such maneuvering involves.

Not only do Pashtun men live privileged lives, they outsource their guilt to men they consider their social inferiors—such as the

Hazaras. One can argue that such widespread contempt for Ali among Pashtun men is, therefore, a contempt for oneself, both in caste and sexual sense. Several relationships that emerge in the novel shows how upper-caste Pashtuns transfer their own sense of "lack" onto those others they consider inferior in a sexual or caste sense—some examples are Assef/Hassan's, Amir/ his father's, and Amir/Assef's relationship. However, unlike these relationships, wherever masculinity is not at stake, and where there is no strain to prove or to hide something, relationships gather a different hue such as in Amir/Hassan's, Amir/Rahim Khan's, Hassan/Ali's bonding. Rahim Khan's affection for Amir may be the result of his lifelong relationship with his father; and Ali's affection for Hassan is just his fatherly attitude toward his son, but these relationships are not marked by sexual "repression." Instead of dominance and suppression, they are hinged on reciprocal relationality.

The text shows Amir's city's landscape as male dominated. Women are neither seen in public spaces such as bazaars nor in home spaces (see Bohn). Such regulation and even erasure of their presence demonstrate Afghan society's complicated relationship with sexuality. Assef and his friends are a striking example of how caste and sexual regulation affect not only minority groups but also the Pashtuns in Afghan society. Although they are sporty and virile teenagers, they grow up to be violent because they flock together in boys-only groups. A similar pathology among men is seen at another point in the novel—when one of a group of soldiers sees Hassan, he makes an unprovoked verbal attack on him by claiming to have had sex with his mother:

One of them saw us, elbowed the guy next to him, and called Hassan.
"Hey, you! " he said. "I know you." [. . .]
"You! The Hazara! Look at me when I'm talking to you!" the soldier barked. He handed his cigarette to the guy next to him, made a circle with the thumb and index finger of one hand. Poked the middle finger of his other hand through the circle. Poked it in and out. In and out. "I knew your mother, did you know that? I knew her real good. I took her from behind by that creek over there."
The soldiers laughed. One of them made a squealing sound. (6–7)

It is a telling scene because although they mention Hassan's mother's anatomy, there is no woman around—therefore their sexual gesture is meant for Hassan. The narrative uses Hassan's mother's sexuality, but the sexual performative takes place between men. The sexuality of a woman is invoked, but what happens stays within the male domain.

Through the world that *The Kite Runner* portrays, Hosseini, perhaps inadvertently, reveals far more problematic dimensions of Afghan society. In the world of children, we see how class conflict, misogyny, and the dominant norms of adult Afghan society make an appearance. Although Amir himself suffers in seeking his father's approval, he is very conscious of his class status and considers himself superior to Hassan. Once when Hassan criticizes his story, Amir's inner voice tells him: "*What does he know, that illiterate Hazara? He'll never be anything but a cook. How dare he criticize you?*" (30, italics in original). In a far more damaging way, the impact of societal norms is seen in Assef and his friends. They have already learned whom they can harass and mock—their attitude toward Ali and Hassan is no accident. For instance, more than Hassan, Assef hates Amir because he socializes with a Hazara. "How can you talk to him, play with him, let him touch you?" (36). The seemingly "benign-looking" (Amir and Hassan's) and toxic (Assef and his friends') world of these boys indicates the intricate reality of Afghan society. The overt and covert violence and erasure of outcasts such as women, Hazaras, and non-normative bodies and behaviors occur with such ferocity so that Pashtun men can remain Pashtuns, conveying power on the surface, but inside getting marred by the same power.

Notes

1. Ironically, Chughtai, a Muslim writer known for her progressive, feminist views, describes an untouchable woman sweeper with utmost disdain in the story.

2. In most matrimonial advertisements, men and women mention their caste preferences. Also, the incidents of violence that occur on a daily basis are predominantly connected with cross-caste marriages.

See Michael Safi. "India: Teenage Girl Murdered and Mutilated by Family for Eloping, Say Police." *The Guardian,* 11 Jan. 2019, www. theguardian.com/world/2019/jan/11/india-bihar-honour-killing-family-mutilated-teenage-daughter-eloping-say-police.

3. Sarukkai describes how a brahmin outsources his own sense of bodily 'pollution' and 'disgust' to the body of the untouchable. In Hosseini's novel, although Islam endorses equality and brotherhood, the novel's Pashtun characters act in similar ways to Hazaras.

4. As in Hindu religious and cultural practices, women are considered as 'objects' that can be bought and sold. Although the idea behind these practices is that they benefit women, they, in fact, very often harm them. In the Hindu Dowry system, it is the bride's family that gives money, gold, and household things to the groom's family, while in Afghan marriages the opposite happens, but with similar consequences for women. For instance, in most Afghan marriages the groom almost buys his bride by paying 'mahr' in order to "obtain sole rights to the bride for economic, sexual, and reproductive services." (See *Afghan Women*).

5. One hundred thousand pregnant women die every year in Afghanistan. Among many reasons, one reason is that women are not encouraged to visit doctors. (See *Afghan Women*).

Works Cited

Afghan Women. The University of Montana, 2012. www.umt.edu/mansfield/dclcp/Programs/afghanistan/afghan_women.php.

Ambedkar, B. R., and Vasant Moon. *Dr. Babasaheb Ambedkar: Writings and Speeches*. Education Department, Government of India: 2003, vol. 17, Part 1, pp. 369–75, www.mea.gov.in/Images/attach/amb/Volume_17_01.pdf.

Azarbaijani-Moghaddam, Sippi. "Manly Honor and the Gendered Male in Afghanistan." MEI (Middle Eastern Institute), 23 Apr. 2012, www. mei.edu/publications/manly-honor-and-gendered-male-afghanistan.

Bohn, Lauren. "'We're All Handcuffed in This Country.' Why Is Afghanistan Still the Worst Place in the World to Be a Woman." 8 Dec. 2018, time.com/5472411/afghanistan-women-justice-war/.

Chughtai, Ismat. "A Pair of Hands." Translated by Tahira Naqvi and Syeda S. Hameed. *A Chughtai Collection.* New Delhi: Women Unlimited, 2004. 162–75.

Echavez, Chona R., Sayed Mahdi Mosawi, and Leah Wilfreda RE Pilongo. "The Other Side of Gender Inequality: Men and Masculinities in Afghanistan," *Research for a Better Afghanistan*, Jan. 2016. pp. 44–94, www.refworld.org/pdfid/577b5ae04.pdf.

Hosseini, Khaled. *The Kite Runner.* 2003. Bloomsbury, 2011.

Nader, Zahra, and Mujib Mashal, "In Afghanistan, 'I Feel Like a Divorced Woman Is Up for Grabs,'" *The New York Times*, 17 Apr. 2017, www. nytimes.com/2017/04/17/world/asia/afghan-women-divorce.html.

Roy, Arundhati. "The Doctor and the Saint." In *Annihilation of Caste.* Verso, 2014, p. 24.

Sarukkai, Sundar. "Phenomenology of Untouchability," *Economic and Political Weekly*, vol. XLIV, no. 37, 12 Sept. 2009, pp. 39–48. *JSTOR*, www.jstor.org/stable/25663542.

Shorish-Shamley, Zieba. "Look into My World." 10 Dec.1998. *Angelfire*, www.angelfire.com/on/wapha/my_world.html.

The Kite Runner Two Decades Later: Three Things Every Reader Should Know _____

Alla Ivanchikova

When, in 1999, Khaled Hosseini first conceived the possibility of writing a story set in Afghanistan, there was no market for such stories. The country was in the grip of a theocratic rule, from which the eyes of the world had been withdrawn. The United States' moral publics, who, in the 1980s, were captivated by carefully curated scenes of Afghan suffering (exemplified by the Afghan Girl on the iconic cover of *National Geographic* in 1985) and, with the protagonists of *Rambo 3* (1988), admired the gallantry and nobility of the rugged Afghan men who fought against the imposition of Soviet-style modernity, by the early 1990s had lost their interest in this distant nation's fate. The reason for that was simple: the Soviet government had withdrawn its troops from Afghanistan and the Afghan socialist state was defeated. There was no more need for empathetic identifications with the distant other: moral outrage over the plight of Afghan children and fundraising efforts for the Afghan jihad fighters ended. In spite of the unimaginable humanitarian catastrophe brought about by the civil war that began in 1992, three years after the Soviet withdrawal, Afghanistan receded into media darkness. Khaled Hosseini's 25-page story, inspired by the news from the land of his childhood, where the Taliban, it was said, had banned kite flying, was rejected by the literary journals he submitted it to (Wilson).

In that, he was not alone. Eve Ensler—seeking to expand the scope of her famous *Vagina Monologues*—traveled to Afghanistan in 2000, in order to investigate, and report on, the oppression of women under Taliban rule. She collected interviews and smuggled back a video of stoning acquired by a feminist organization (the Revolutionary Association of Women in Afghanistan), which, upon her return, she could not get on air. "When I returned to the United States [in 2000]," she recalls, "I brought Freshta's videotape [depicting an execution of a woman at the stadium] and an article I had written about my experience in Afghanistan to several TV stations and major publications. With the exception of one magazine, *Marie Claire*, I could not engender any interest in the story. No one could understand what the terrible plight of Afghan women had to do with their own interest, their own comfort and security" (36). Photographer Lynsey Addario, who was one of the select few journalists who had received the Taliban's permission to travel to Afghanistan and, circa 2000, brought back pictures of the country in the grip of a humanitarian crisis, could not get her photographs published. "In 2000," she recalls in her book, "no one was interested in Afghanistan" (77). This changed overnight, however, in the aftermath of the 9/11 tragedy and the US administration's prompt decision to respond by sending troops to Afghanistan: Afghanistan became not only visible, but hypervisible in the mass media—reporters flocked to its major cities in thousands, to report on the swift successes of the NATO mission.

In this essay, I want to draw attention to three issues that anyone who reads, studies, or teaches *The Kite Runner* should be aware of. The fact that Khaled Hosseini's *The Kite Runner* became a runaway bestseller is not a coincidence. Having appeared at the right time in the right place, it fed into the political climate in which the US's political establishment sought support for the invasion of Afghanistan, and the reading publics were hungry for stories that explained not only the tragedy of Afghanistan but also the tragedy of 9/11. *The Kite Runner*, which held the spot of the number one *New York Times* bestseller for almost two years (2005–07, Hoby), did just that. In retrospect, one can say that Hosseini's debut novel holds significance as the first post-9/11 bestseller that reframed how Americans were to relate not only to Afghanistan, but also to the Muslim world in the twenty-first century—staging a "forgetting" of US prior involvement (as supporting terror) to a new mode of engagement (fighting terror). Therefore, *The Kite Runner*, as well as Hosseini's subsequent Afghanistan-based novels, should be understood both as a product of their historical moment and formative for this new relation. The distance of almost two decades gives us a vantage point from which to view the novel's literary success, its shortcomings, and its lasting legacy.

My second point is related to the first: *The Kite Runner* should not be taken as a window upon Afghanistan and its culture—no more so than, say, Ben Affleck's *Argo* (2012) should serve as a window on Iranian culture. Unfortunately, *The Kite Runner* often fills precisely this role. Film scholar Mark Graham writes: "It is not an exaggeration to say that *The Kite Runner* has become not only the single most important source of information on Afghanistan for American readers but also the most widely read American story ever written about the modern Islamic world" (147). Having been translated in 42 languages, *The Kite Runner* is a text frequently used by schoolteachers and college professors who seek to expand, globalize, or decolonize their curriculum by including novels about other cultures. Hosseini's identity as an Afghan American serves as a stamp of authenticity, an indicator of his privileged access to Afghan culture. The novel's widespread use as a didactic text is both astonishing and alarming. In the context of the War on Terror, anthropologist Jennifer Fluri observed that 98 percent of American personnel who arrived to Afghanistan were ill prepared for this work, lacking any prior knowledge of Afghan history or culture. The remaining two percent, who reported having some prior knowledge, referred mainly to having read *The Kite Runner*. In what follows, I will outline the main reasons why *The Kite Runner* fails as a didactic text and thus should not be used as a text from which to gain knowledge about Afghanistan's history and culture. *The Kite Runner*'s mixture of humanitarianism and anticommunism both indexes and reinforces the highly distorted way Afghanistan was represented in the NATO-centric, and particularly in US media. While *The Kite Runner* is a step up from *Rambo 3*, the novel's anticommunism not only erases the history of left-wing progressive movements in Afghanistan's twentieth-century history—movements that fought for economic equality, racial equality, and women's rights—but also hides the role the US administration played in canceling Afghanistan's alternative socialist modernity and bringing on a massive humanitarian crisis.

Finally, I will briefly contextualize *The Kite Runner* in the context of Hosseini's literary Afghanistan project as a whole. Following *The Kite Runner*'s success, Hosseini wrote two other Kabul-based novels—both of which reframe and revise *The Kite Runner*'s approach to narrating Afghanistan's tragic history. These stories become increasingly complex, reflecting both Hosseini's enduring struggle to explain the tragedy of Afghanistan to his readers in the West and exemplifying the disappointments regarding humanitarian wars that characterize the second decade of the 9/11 wars era. *The Kite Runner*'s virulent anticommunism also recedes somewhat, tempered by an appreciation of the successes of left-wing modernity. Hosseini's second novel, *A Thousand Splendid Suns,* has as its central character a woman born on the day of the socialist revolution in Afghanistan. As such, she embodies Afghanistan's interrupted socialist modernity; the book foregrounds the centrality of women's emancipation to that project thus interrupting the fantasy that the compass needle of women's liberation always points to the West. Hosseini's third novel, *And the Mountains Echoed,* no longer celebrates US interventionism and is deeply critical of NATO's alliances with the warlords—former mujahideen (jihad fighters) who fought the socialist state. Predictably, these two novels came nowhere near to the success of *The Kite Runner*. By positioning the first novel within this larger arc, we are able to see both *The Kite Runner*'s success and limitations in a different light. When reading Hosseini's novels, it is important to keep these three points in mind. These notes, I hope will be useful to students, teachers, and readers of Hosseini.

The 9/11 Wars and Military Humanitarianism

In his 2011 book, reporter Jason Burke coins the term "the 9/11 wars" to refer to the multiple, widely distributed conflicts that began as a direct or indirect consequence of the attacks on the Twin Towers in 2001, of which the war in Afghanistan was the first and the longest war. Hosseini's three Afghanistan-based novels reflect the changing political and cultural climate during the course of the two decades of these 9/11 wars: the initial excitement and self-certainty in regards to military interventions in NATO-centric media gave way to a sense of anxiety, and later, to widespread disillusionment and critique of this ruinous misadventure. The invasion of Afghanistan was supposed to be a war of retaliation (hunting down Osama bin Laden), but also a humanitarian intervention—an operation to depose the uncooperative theocratic Taliban and to install a decisively pro-American yet democratically elected government—not only to ensure American security but also to liberate the Afghan people. In the course of the following two decades, it became a deeply confusing war. "The Afghanistan Papers," publicized by *The Washington Post* in 2019, paint a picture of a mission without clear objectives, a widely expensive conflict without end. As Stephen M. Grenier reports, over 900 billion dollars were spent on security, aid, and reconstruction projects, dwarfing the Marshall Plan for Western Europe after World War II (about 12 billion)—with little to show for it (1). The Taliban, in 2020, once again controls the majority of the country's territory. Ghost schools and ghost hospitals, without students or patients and with caving roofs, now pepper the Afghan countryside as a testimony to the failures of America's neoliberal "reconstruction" model (Murphy, Rose). What began with a bang is slowly ending with a whimper[1]—a protracted, unpublicized withdrawal, which began in 2014 and has not yet ended for fear of the Taliban's likely return to power, which would simply annul any gains of US involvement over the last two decades.

A vast corpus of works—novels, films, and memoirs—now exists in the Anglophone world, reflecting on the NATO-led engagement in Afghanistan. In the early years of the War on Terror, however, that was not the case. Corinne Fowler, in 2008, observed that 2001–07 were marked by a shortage of narratives about Afghanistan; Rebecca Stuhr in 2009 attests to the same. *The Kite Runner* was the first bestseller that provided a quick, easily digestible explanation of what had happened in Afghanistan prior to 9/11. It presented Afghanistan as, in the 1970s, a peaceful albeit a provincial place; emphasized its links to the United States rather than to its northern neighbor, the USSR; and explained the subsequent crisis as the work of US–enemies, the Russians, and the Taliban.

The intervention from the West, dramatized as Amir's rescue of his nephew, Sohrab, was presented as a long-overdue, morally necessary effort. Hosseini's explicit endorsement of interventionism earned him praise by the political establishment, the novel eulogized by Barbara Bush and the film adaptation screened in the White House in 2007. As such, it reflected the political climate of the early years of the War of Terror—legitimizing the military invasion as a humanitarian effort—a rescue of the entire people—while presenting the intervening powers as moral agents. As a model, US military humanitarianism in Afghanistan linked aid provisions to military goals.[2] While the bulk of cultural legitimation work was done by journalists who produced articles about the success of US–led liberation, describing Afghan people dancing in the streets of Kabul and Afghan women throwing away their burqas, fiction writers had a major role to play as well. *The Kite Runner* not only reassured its US readers that, from the Afghan perspective, US–led intervention was a moral act, but also translated Afghan culture into American vernacular. Hosseini's Afghan American identity was, no doubt, a key ingredient in the novel's success. *The Kite Runner* forged an image of Afghanistan as a younger, more innocent, brother of the United States—a Sohrab we need to protect, and ultimately raise to be more like ourselves. Literary critics were quick to point this out. Joseph R. Slaughter, for instance, wrote:

> The novel ultimately elevates the invasion of Afghanistan to an act of humanitarian intervention not only by representing the Taliban as a vicious sect of homosexual pedophiles intent on repressing human personality; it also assures its American (and Allied) market readers that "we" are on the side of the people (and therefore that the aptly named "Operation Enduring Freedom" is a liberationist rather than imperialist venture) and, more pointedly, that these are people like us—people who "love . . . the *idea* of America" [italics in original], enjoy Coca-Colas, appreciate John Wayne and Charles Bronson films, read *Les Misérables* and Ian Fleming novels, pursue happiness, and desire upward mobility. (321)

The triumphalism that touted Afghanistan as a model rescue state reflected, to a degree, the reality on the ground: with the prompt retreat of Taliban forces into Pakistan in the fall of 2001, Afghanistan was in fact relatively free of resistance to NATO troops and did not yet face any significant security problems. Kim Barker—a journalist whose story became the inspiration for Tina Fey's film *Whiskey, Tango, Foxtrot*—wrote about the relaxed atmosphere in Kabul during these early years: "In Kabul that spring of 2005, the lack of war was as obvious as the bikinis at the pool of *L'Atmosphère*, the restaurant of wicker chairs, glass-topped tables, and absurdly priced wine that had become the equivalent of the sitcom *Cheers* in the Afghan capital" (47). The enthusiasm about the success of humanitarian invasions was short-lived, however: the security situation in Afghanistan began to deteriorate in 2006; the horrors of the Iraq war became more widely recognized around that time as well. By 2009, the situation became so dire that President Obama ordered a complete policy review and General David McKiernan, the commanding officer of US forces in Afghanistan, was relieved of his duties.[3] Hosseini's two subsequent novels reflect this change in policy and attitude.

Aside from legitimizing the intervention, *The Kite Runner* also reframed the US publics' orientation towards Afghanistan—away from supporting the global war *of* terror (against communism) towards fighting the global war *on* terror. This reorientation required forgetting the uncomfortable fact that it was precisely the extensive American support and training, in the 1980s, of the Afghan and Arab insurgent groups that has left in its wake al-Qaeda, responsible for the tragedy of 9/11, and the Taliban, responsible for the oppression the United States was determined to lift through its military intervention. Elsewhere, I called this maneuver "Hosseini's Faustian Bargain"—a way of making readers in the global North feel good about themselves through the story of Afghanistan, without feeling implicated in the scene of the crisis.[4] Despite the revelations of the 9/11 commission and major journalistic reports, such as Steve Coll's book *Ghost Wars,* most Americans, especially younger generations, remain oblivious of the role played by the United States in propping up the terror networks responsible for many twenty-first-century crises. Hosseini's runaway bestseller, I believe, played a nontrivial role in this forgetting.

To briefly remind the reader of this uncomfortable history: shortly after the victory of the socialist revolution in Afghanistan in 1978, the US government began to covertly fund, arm, and train the insurgent groups who sabotaged the Afghan socialist state. This support started prior to,[5] but grew significantly after the USSR decision to send troops to prop up the socialist government (between 1979–89) and lasted until the Afghan socialist government was defeated in 1992. These insurgents—"mujahideen" or jihad fighters—were a loose constellation of mostly deeply conservative, ultra-patriarchal groups who opposed the socialist government efforts to empower women and ethnic minorities, redistribute social wealth and land, and create a countrywide secular education system. The most radical Islamist groups received the most support from both the United States and Saudi Arabia. Political scientist Fred Halliday recalls, post-9/11:

> During the Soviet occupation of the 1980s, the most fanatical Islamist groups—funded by the CIA, Pakistan, and the Saudis to overthrow the communist government in Kabul—were killing women teachers, bombing schools, and forcing women back into the home in the areas they controlled. Such enemies led the first leader of communist Afghanistan, Nur Mohammad Taraki, to refer to the opposition as ikhwan ash-shayatin ("the satanic brotherhood," a play on "Muslim Brotherhood"). Bin Laden himself, in both his 1980s and post-1996 periods in Afghanistan, played a particularly active role not just in fighting Afghan communists, but also in killing Shi'a, who were, in the sectarian worldview of Saudi fundamentalism, seen as akin to communists. The consequences of this policy for the Arab and Muslim worlds, and for the world as a whole, were evident from the early 1990s onwards. It took the events of the clear morning of 11 September 2001 for them to penetrate the global consciousness. (82)

During the Reagan era, the term mujahid (singular of mujadhideen) was positively charged and held particular appeal for the US Christian

Right, serving as a "legitimizing concept" (Magnus and Naby 259).[6] Historian of the Soviet-Afghan War David Gibbs recalls that, "In 1985, a special program was set up at Boston University to train Mujahiddin [sic] journalists, funded by the US Information Agency and directed by openly right-wing faculty members." However, liberal and progressive Americans, hailed via stories of human rights abuses in a young socialist state (via media representations such as *National Geographic*'s "the Afghan Girl issue"), were also widely drawn into supporting the anti-Soviet jihad, which, by 1985 drew thousands of troops from the wider Arab world—creating the backbone of the terror network that would bear on the World Trade Center bombing of 1993 and the tragedy of 9/11. The image of the Afghan Girl on the 1985 *National Geographic* cover was designed to foment US publics' support for the Afghan anti-Soviet jihad at the moment when Reagan's administration made a controversial decision to arm them with Stinger missiles, state-of-the-art anti-aircraft weapons that could be used effectively against Soviet and Afghan governmental aircraft. The word "terrorist" was not used in US media back then, even though the fight against the socialist state more often than not included bombing civilian targets—schools, universities, airports, public markets, and general infrastructure. Historians Ralph Magnus and Eden Naby, sympathetic overall to the mujahideen cause, nevertheless note that "wholesale destruction of villages, irrigation works, and agriculture" were common (147). After the tragedy of 9/11, the Reagan-era "freedom fighter" became a "terrorist," and the extensive US role in helping set up and funding transnational terror networks during the Cold War became an uncomfortable topic. Gibbs observed, in 2002: "There has, in short, been a fairly dramatic and Orwellian shift in the tone of public discourse regarding Afghanistan. While Islamic extremism is now viewed with great hostility, in the 1980s U.S. policy strongly supported such extremism; there is scarcely any recognition that a little more than a decade ago, the U.S. press waxed eloquent about the Afghan 'freedom fighters.'"

An attentive reader should notice that *The Kite Runner* is very careful not to address any of that history. Instead, it simply skips the entire era of US covert involvement in Afghanistan's affairs, by having its protagonist leave the country shortly after the Soviet invasion. The entire era of socialism in Afghanistan (1978–92) thus disappears from view. Omitted also is the subsequent era, 1992–96, after the socialist state is defeated by the mujahideen and when the ultimate crisis arrives: as Afghan cities, one by one, fall into mujahideen hands, the urban population of Afghanistan is subjected to a patriarchal backlash against the freedoms they had enjoyed as citizens of a secular state. The scene of Amir's return takes place during the Taliban rule era (presumably around 1999–2000), some time before the NATO-led invasion of 2001. The Taliban were a disciplined group of fundamentalists trained in Pakistan who defeated the warring groups of the mujahideen and took power in Afghanistan in 1996. Like the mujahideen, they were religious conservatives; in contrast to them, however, they managed to reestablish the functioning state (Islamic State of Afghanistan) and the rule of law (sharia). The novel's depiction of Amir's reentry into Afghanistan communicates to the reader that, while the Soviets caused the disaster, the Taliban completed it. Observing the devastation everywhere around him, Amir asks his local guide what had happened—a question the audience also wants to know the answer to. "The *Shorawi* [communists] cut a lot of [the trees] down," the guide explains, along with "the killings, always the killings" of the Taliban, the "beard police," and the sexual abuse of children (246). The Taliban, presumably, complete what the Soviets started during Amir's childhood—the rapes, the devastation, and the neglect of infrastructure or beauty (as in chopping down the trees).

This framing of Afghanistan's history reorients American readers away from supporting terror (by forgetting that such support ever took place) towards fighting terror post-9/11. This story makes American readers feel good—because they are hailed as rescuers, as good people and not as creators of the dire crisis in Afghanistan. And yet, Afghanistan's tragedy—which Amir observes upon his return to Afghanistan circa 2000—is one in which US readers should feel implicated. *The Kite Runner* provides what Timothy Aubry calls a therapeutic narrative—a way to feel good (again). But what is the price we have to pay for such a feeling, predicated on forgetting? The price, as many have suggested (Mamdani, Bose), is that we fail to learn key lessons from our own history. We fail to keep our governments accountable for the crises created in distant lands. Most importantly, we fail as ethical human beings in a globalized world.

The Window on Afghanistan and the "Anticommunist Imaginary"

In some ways, it is easy to understand why *The Kite Runner* is so frequently taken as a window on the culture of Afghanistan. Its main achievement is presenting Afghanistan not as a desolate terrain, its culture in need of a civilizing mission, but as a country that is, to use Graham's words, "in dialogue with modernity" (148). In a cultural climate where both journalists and politicians trafficked in images of "medieval Afghanistan," Hosseini's novel was a breath of fresh air. Afghanistan's history emerged in his book as beautiful and complex, containing an intrigue to be curious about—as a nascent modernity, followed by a violent interruption, perhaps to be restored again.[7] The image of Afghanistan Hosseini conjures is both nostalgic and reparative—it resurrects a lost world. There is a longing in this novel by an exilic writer not only for a lost homeland, but also for a prior era—a longing many readers can relate to. This portrait of 1970s Afghanistan is, in many ways, historically accurate. From the 1950s into the 1970s, Afghanistan entered an era of rapid development. Its modernizing monarch, Zahir Shah, welcomed aid and experts from the USSR, the United States, Europe, and Iran; major infrastructure development projects were undertaken, and the state invested heavily in education. Literacy levels grew rapidly, and a thin layer of an educated class emerged. Afghanistan became a tourist destination on a so-called "hippie trail" and was frequented by foreigners. So why is the novel's depiction problematic?

Fredric Jameson, in his *Political Unconscious,* argued that an individual text should be understood as an utterance in a larger conversation—"a symbolic move in an essentially polemic and strategic ideological confrontations between the classes" (1297). Within this framework, he proposed that we pay attention to what he calls ideologemes—"the smallest intelligible unit[s] of the essentially antagonistic collective discourses of social classes" (1292). Ideologemes are essentially stock ideas, stock images, or tropes that promote the dominant sociopolitical stance reinforcing the status quo. Here I propose to view *The Kite Runner* as an utterance in a larger dialogue—about the meaning of the Cold War, of the idea of socialism, and of our collective future. As such, the novel is a part of what, for the purposes of this essay, I will call the anticommunist imaginary.

The anticommunist imaginary is an endlessly shifting yet internally consistent set of tropes, images, and shortcuts that is designed to provide justification for capitalism's dominance and to preemptively foreclose any questions about whether a better world is possible. It is a framework of representation that serves to justify political actions within and outside of the United States, against state or non-state actors that are associated with what is imagined as communism. The anticommunist imaginary did not vanish with the dissolution of the Soviet Union; in fact, we see it alive and well in the twenty-first century—indexing the fact that the ghost of communism still haunts the global capitalocene.[8] Its images and tropes serve to uphold and fortify the belief that socialist policies can only lead to disaster, civil strife, and loss of freedom; it seeks to convince us that socialism is therefore unnatural—a perversion, in fact, of human desire for individual liberty, of society based on innovation-breeding free competition, and of entrepreneurial instinct that is an integral part of human nature. Capitalist realism, as discussed by the late Mark Fisher, is part of that paradigm and one of its post-1989 variations.[9] In contrast to Orientalism, anticommunism as a moral, political, and representational framework remains undertheorized and goes largely unnoticed within NATO-centric academic contexts. It is notable, that, while literary and cultural critics were quick to point out *The Kite Runner*'s endorsement of US interventionism, imperialism, and neo-orientalism (Keshavarz, Miller, O'Rourke), they have not commented on the novel's anticommunism—a gap that evidences the pervasiveness of the anticommunist imperative.

As I have demonstrated elsewhere, in NATO-centric contexts, during the Cold War and beyond, Afghanistan figured as an argument against socialism and as a symbol of socialism's failure. The miscarriages of the Afghan revolution, the missteps of the nascent socialist government, and its subsequent reliance on Soviet military support were amplified in Western media to foment anti-Soviet sentiments and play into the anticommunist foreign policy of the Reagan administration—a policy that involved suppression of socialist revolutions not only in Afghanistan, but also in Latin America (Nicaragua and Guatemala).[10] US–based Cold War-era media mythologized the Afghan people as the people who embodied anticommunism, as the fighters against communism. Similar to how during McCarthy's era, American communists were presented as un-American, Afghan communists or progressives were viewed, in US media, as un-Afghan. Consider, for instance, the following assessment of left-wing Afghans by military historian Anthony Joes: "[Afghan communists] were a tiny minority—city-dwelling, peasant-despising, religion-hating, and teacher-killing" (175). "Winning hearts and minds was not their style, but rather wholesale destruction, the killing of civilians, or the driving them into exile" (202). Afghans who opposed communism are described by Joes simply as "the brave, sorrowful people of Afghanistan"—as *the people as such* (229). The reality was that Afghan society (like every society) was divided—between conservatives and progressives, nationalists and cosmopolitans, traditionalists and technocrats, monarchists and republicans. The communist revolution of 1978 had among its supporters diverse groups of Afghans. In contrast to Joes's description of the progressives as "city-dwelling," the revolution had the backing of the rapidly expanding mass of first-generation students who came from rural areas and knew first-hand the crippling poverty of their parents' lives in the countryside. In contrast to Joes's labeling of the revolution's supporters as "teacher-killing," many of them were in fact teachers who believed that eliminating illiteracy should be one of the revolution's most immediate goals. Supportive of the revolution were also many women who sought in the Marxist program the hope for dismantling gender-based oppression endemic in the Pashtun traditional culture. By contrast, insurgent groups objected to the education of women and within the first year of war destroyed about 1,400 schools, according to some reports (Braithwaite).

So, what marks *The Kite Runner* as a part of the larger anticommunist imaginary? In *The Kite Runner*, the Afghan communist revolution of 1978, although not discussed in detail, figures as the main cause of the country's ruin. It figures as a sexual assault, an inexplicable historical rupture, and an assault on nature. The rich history of indigenous Afghan leftist movements is invisibilized while socialism is presented as an outside imposition—reduced in its entirety to the Soviet intervention, "the Russians." Baba, a wealthy businessman, whose vision of social justice is predicated on charity and not redistribution, embodies the spirit of capitalism. Moreover, by endorsing it so wholeheartedly, first, as a successful Afghan businessman, and then as an immigrant entrepreneur in California, his character provides a sense of renewal for American readers, resuscitating both capitalist modernity and the idea of the entrepreneurial self. We are reassured that, even if we ourselves have grown wary of the endless competition for ever diminishing resources in the global North, this 300-year old mode of production still works well for those on the globe's periphery.

One of the well-worn Cold War-era ideologemes *The Kite Runner* deploys is the trope of socialism as an assault on nature. Consider the already-mentioned scene from *The Kite Runner*—one in which Amir, upon his return to the city of his childhood and witnessing, for the first time, the heart-wrenching devastation, asks his guide: "Where are the trees?" To which the guide responds: "The *Shorawi* [communists] cut a lot of them down" (246). In the 2007 cinematic version of *The Kite Runner*, the phrase morphs into an even starker charge: "The Russians chopped them down." Within NATO-centric contexts, this passes for an explanation as it builds on a pre-existing repertoire of images: Cold War imagery of the Soviet-Afghan war used, to great effect, the tropes of rape and the assault on nature when speaking about socialism.[11] But what does Amir's guide refer to and what, if anything, happened to the trees in Afghanistan?

Trees in Afghanistan were, in fact, a major nonhuman casualty of war (Rubin). The story of trees, however, is much more complex than *The Kite Runner* makes it out to be. Archival images of 1989 Afghanistan (available on Getty Images) show the following scene: on a bitterly cold winter day, residents on Kabul—among them older men, women, and children—are shown working hard on removing mature trees lining one of the boulevards in the nation's capital.[12] The scene takes place in the very last days of the Soviet withdrawal from Afghanistan, which began in 1988 and would be complete in early February—a few days after these photographs were taken. The novel (and film) might be referring to these archival images, to this memory. During the socialist era, residents of Afghan cities, who were either pro-government or simply did not want to join the ranks of the mountain-based insurgents, were often referred to, by the opposing side, as "the Russians." This usage was still common even in the early post-9/11 days, as evidenced, for instance, by Edward Girardet's article from the fall of 2001. In these archival images, Kabuli residents, or "the Russians," if we follow this usage, are in fact chopping down the trees in Kabul, but why, and why on such a bitterly cold day? When these photographs were taken, Kabul was surrounded by the mujahideen (Getty Images also has archival photos of their artillery pointing at the city) and the residents of Kabul were preparing for what was going to be a protracted siege and bombardment of the city—by preparing alternative air landing strips and by clearing wooded areas for greater visibility to protect the city from snipers. So while Hosseini uses the memorable image of chopped down trees as a metaphor for Soviet violence, here, in these pictures, they signify the coming civil war in the aftermath of Soviet withdrawal.

Eve Ensler, who is more invested in critiquing the Taliban, uses butchered trees as a figure of Taliban's violence against women: "When the Taliban took the garden, they had chopped down most of the ancient trees for kindling to keep themselves warm. They had tried to chop this tree, but it would not come down. So, one night, they put a bomb in the trunk and blew it up. Blew it up—the most beautiful, the grandest and greenest, the most luscious, the holderof-hope tree. They blew her up. Now there was a blackened-out hole in the ground" (44–45). The tree here becomes a beautiful woman disfigured, killed by religious fanatics. In reality, most of the trees were destroyed during the years of civil war in the aftermath of the mujahideen "victory" over the socialist state, when entire orchards and forests were chopped down for firewood due to the complete collapse of infrastructure or destroyed by four years of rocket shelling. A memoir by Qais Akbar Omar, an Afghan who was in Kabul during the horrific years of urban warfare, describes that era vividly and his text is of high didactic value.

To sum up, Hosseini's debut novel fails as a didactic text because of its extreme political investments (in anticommunism, in making US publics feel good by forgetting their government's role in fueling the flames of the Soviet-Afghan war). These investments are also responsible for its popularity and elite endorsements.

The Kite Runner and Subsequent Novels

In his second and third novels, Hosseini navigates away from the simplistic shortcuts employed in *The Kite Runner*. In his second novel,[13] *A Thousand Splendid Suns,* Hosseini revises his version of Afghanistan's history by explicitly addressing the horrors of the mujahideen rule in the aftermath of the defeat of the socialist government in 1992. He also brings into view the centrality of women's liberation for the Afghan socialist project and does not tout the "capitalist-rescue narrative."[14] By foregrounding the similarities between socialist and liberal-capitalist liberation projects, Hosseini mocks NATO-allied countries' belief in their exceptionality.

The novel is set in the same time period as its predecessor: prior to the communist revolution, which takes place halfway though the novel. The so-called golden age of Afghanistan now appears considerably less idyllic, when seen through the eyes of the main character, Mariam. Whereas *The Kite Runner*'s Amir is a privileged son of an upper-class man who has a personal servant, Mariam—one of the two novel's central characters—is a woman and herself a part of the servant class. Moreover, she is a *harami*: an illegitimate child fathered outside of wedlock. After her father's family arrange for her marriage to an older, religiously conservative and brutish man from Kabul, her life trajectory is predetermined. Her circumscribed life is contrasted to that of the novel's second main character Laila. Laila is born on the day of the communist revolution—her classmates give her a nickname, "Revolution's Girl." As such, she embodies the expectations of the new society— one that seeks to empower women in every possible way. Laila's father, a schoolteacher, wholeheartedly supports the socialists' feminist cause. "This is a good time to be a woman in Afghanistan," he tells his daughter. A generation apart, Laila and Mariam belong to different worlds as women: Laila is born into the world where gender equality becomes the official ideology promoted by the state. This is exemplified by scenes from Laila's school:

> [Laila's teacher] was a sharp-faced young woman with heavy eyebrows. On the first day of school, she had proudly told the class that she was the daughter of a poor peasant from Khost. She stood straight, and wore her jet-black hair pulled tightly back and tied in a bun so that, when Khala Rangmaal turned around, Laila could see the dark bristles on her neck. Khala Rangmaal did not wear makeup or jewelry. She did not cover and forbade the female students from doing it. She said women and men were equal in every way and there was no reason women should cover if men didn't. (111)

Hosseini still finds it necessary to criticize the communists: the teacher is not a particularly likeable character and Laila's father is fired, after the revolution, from his teaching position. And yet, when seen from the Afghan women's perspective, the socialist era is no longer portrayed as unnatural or associated with sexual violence; on the contrary, it is portrayed as a unique period in Afghanistan's history during which women gained relief from the oppressive gender customs. When seen through Afghan women's eyes, the socialist era is elevated above the "golden age" that preceded it, bringing into view the multiple oppressions endured by Mariam but not Laila. In spite of the occasional jab at the communists, the symmetry or symbolic equivalence of the socialist era and the NATO era in this novel is a radical departure from the virulent anticommunism of *The*

Kite Runner. It is still optimistic, like *The Kite Runner*, about the future of Afghanistan following the US intervention.

Hosseini's third novel, *And the Mountains Echoed*, published in 2013, however, has none of these sentiments. It portrays the West as hypocritical and double-dealing, while critiquing the humanitarian mode of representing distant suffering as pornographic. Taken together, these three novels illustrate a trajectory where Hosseini wrestles with the limitations of his first novel, revises the story of Afghanistan he was destined to bring to the global community of readers, and writes his way out of what elsewhere I called "the Faustian bargain (*Imagining Afghanistan*)." These revisions and changes mark Hosseini as a serious writer who is faithful to his life project: bringing the story of Afghan suffering to the world's reading publics. Despite their smaller readership, his subsequent two novels have significant didactic value and should be considered first by anyone who seeks, in fiction, a window upon Afghanistan.

Notes

1. I borrow this characterization of the West's involvement in Afghanistan from Christina Lamb.

2. For instance, as Stephen M. Grenier reports, "US PRTs (Provincial Reconstruction Teams) often linked humanitarian assistance to the willingness of local residents to provide information on insurgent activity" (8).

3. Some argue this was unfair: see, for instance, Stephen M. Grenier, "America's Longest War."

4. See the chapter on Hosseini in my *Imagining Afghanistan: Global Fiction and Film of the 9/11 Wars*.

5. See Gibbs's "Reassessing Soviet Motives."

6. See, for instance, Reagan's statement of 1983.

7. *The Kite Runner* was not the first text in the Anglophone context to depict Afghanistan during what is sometimes referred to as the Golden Age of Afghanistan (the rapid modernization era of 1933–73); in 1986, M.E. Hirsh published a novel titled *Kabul* that focused on the very same era. *The Kite Runner* was the first text, however, to popularize this image.

8. Capitalocene is a play on the term Antropocene (a new geological era following Neocene). Introduced by historian Jason Moore, capitalocene is meant to capture the idea of capitalist economy's dependence on exploiting the environment for profit—a phenomenon that became apparent during the debates on the issue of climate change.

9. Fisher defines capitalist realism as "widespread sense that not only is capitalism the only viable economic and political system, but also that it is now impossible even to *imagine* a coherent alternative to it" (2).

10. For more information of US suppression of socialist revolutions worldwide during the 1980s, see Mamdani.

11. The famous *National Geographic* issue featuring the Afghan Girl on the cover also proffers a camel allegedly killed by the Soviets. See my "Imagining Afghanistan in the Aftermath of 9/11: Conflicting Literary Chronographies of One Invasion" for my analysis of sexual violence in *The Kite Runner*.

12. See, for instance, image # 057455 49 at www.gettyimages.com/detail/news-photo/workers-chop-down-trees-for-a-landing-strip-january-14-1989-news-photo/741057?adppopup=true.

13. For an in-depth discussion of how Hosseini's work evolves in these two novels, see chapter 2 in my *Imagining Afghanistan: Global Fiction and Film of the 9/11 Wars*.

14. A term introduced by Bose to describe the genre in which Afghan women are rescued by Western entrepreneurs or through entrepreneurship, such as *Kabul Beauty School*, among many others.

Works Cited

Addario, Lyndsay. *It's What I Do: A Photographer's Life of Love and War.* Penguin, 2015.

Argo. (film) Directed by Ben Affleck. Screenplay by Tony Mendez, Chris Terrio, and Joshuah Bearman, 2012.

Aubry, Timothy. "Afghanistan Meets the *Amazon*: Reading *The Kite Runner* in America." *PMLA,* vol. 124, no. 1, 2009, pp. 25–43.

Barker, Kim. *The Taliban Shuffle: Strange Days in Afghanistan and Pakistan.* Doubleday, 2011. Aka as *Whiskey, Tango, Foxtrot: Strange*

Days in Afghanistan and Pakistan. Anchor, 2016. Filmed as *Whiskey, Tango, Foxtrot* (see below).

Bose, Purnima. *Intervention Narratives: Afghanistan, the United States, and the Global War on Terror.* Rutgers UP, 2019.

Braithwaite, Rodric. *Afgantsy: The Russians in Afghanistan 1979–1989.* Oxford UP, 2011.

Burke, Jason. *The 9/11 Wars.* Penguin, 2011.

Coll, Steven. *Ghost Wars: The Secret History of the CIA, Afghanistan, and bin Laden, from the Soviet Invasion to September 10, 2001.* Penguin, 2004.

Denker, Debra. "Along Afghanistan's War-torn Frontier." *National Geographic*, vol. 167, no. 6, June 1985, pp. 772–97.

Ensler, Eve. *Insecure at Last.* Villard, 2006.

Fisher, Mark. *Capitalist Realism: Is There No Alternative?* Zero Books, 2009.

Fluri, Jennifer. "'Foreign Passports Only': Geographies of (Post)Conflict Work in Kabul, Afghanistan." *Annals of the Association of American Geographers*, vol. 99, no. 5, Dec. 2009, pp. 986–94.

Fowler, Corinne. *Chasing Tales: Travel Writing, Journalism, and the History of British Ideas about Afghanistan.* Rodopi, 2007.

Gibbs, David. "Forgotten Coverage of Afghan 'Freedom Fighters.'" *Fair,* 1 Jan. 2002.

_____. "Reassessing Soviet Motives for Invading Afghanistan: A Declassified History." *Critical Asian Studies*, vol. 38, no. 2, 2006.

Girardet, Edward. "A New Day in Kabul: After 24 Years of War, Afghanistan's Capital Is Breathing Free. Can Its Fledgling Recovery Last?" *National Geographic*, Dec. 2001.

Graham, Mark. *Afghanistan in the Cinema.* U of Illinois P, 2010.

Grenier, Stephen M. "Framing the War in Afghanistan." In *Coalition Challenges in Afghanistan: The Politics of Alliance,* edited by Stephen M. Grenier and Gale A. Mattox. Stanford UP, 2017.

Halliday, Fred. *Political Journeys: The Open Democracy Essays.* Yale UP, 2012.

Hirsh, M.E. *Kabul.* Thomas Dunne Books, 1986.

Hosseini, Khaled. *The Kite Runner*. Riverhead Books, 2003.

_____. *A Thousand Splendid Suns*. Riverhead Books, 2008.

_____. *And the Mountains Echoed.* 2013. Bloomsbury, 2014.

_____. "If I Could Go Back Now, I'd Take *The Kite Runner* Apart." Interview with Hermione Hoby. *The Guardian,* 1 June 2013. www. theguardian.com/books/2013/jun/01/khaled-hosseini-kite-runner-interview.

Ivanchikova, Alla. "Imagining Afghanistan in the Aftermath of 9/11: Conflicting Literary Chronographies of One Invasion." *Journal of Textual Practice*, vol. 31, no.1, 2017, pp. 197–216.

_____. *Imagining Afghanistan: Global Fiction and Film of the 9/11 Wars.* Purdue UP, 2019.

Jameson, Fredric. From *The Political Unconscious. The Critical Tradition: Classic Texts and Contemporary Trends*, edited by David H. Richter. Third ed. Bedford/St. Martin's, 2007, pp. 1290–306.

Joes, Anthony James. *Victorious Insurgencies: Four Rebellions that Shaped Our World.* UP of Kentucky, 2010.

Keshavarz, Fatemeh. *Jasmine and Stars: Reading More than* Lolita *in Tehran.* U of North Carolina P, 2007.

The Kite Runner (film). Directed by Mark Forster. Perf. Khalid Abdalla. Distributed by Dream Works Pictures, 2007.

Magnus Ralph H., and Eden Naby. *Afghanistan: Mullah, Marx, and Mujahid.* Westview Press, 1998.

Mamdani, Mahmood. *Good Muslim, Bad Muslim: America, Cold War and the Roots of Terror.* Doubleday, 2005.

Miller, Matthew T. "'The Kite Runner' Critiqued: New Orientalism Goes to the Big Screen." *Common Dreams,* 5 Jan. 2008.

Moore, Jason M. "Anthropocene or Capitalocene? Nature, History, and the Crisis of Capitalism." In *Anthropocene or Capitalocene? Nature, History, and the Crisis of Capitalism*, edited by Jason M. Moore. PM Press, 2016.

Murphy, William S. "Review of School and Health Clinic Buildings Completed Under the Schools and Clinics Construction and Refurbishment Program" (Report No. 5-306-10-002-O). 24 June 2010. https://pdf.usaid.gov/pdf_docs/PDACS008.pdf.

National Geographic. June 1985.

Omar, Qais Akbar. *A Fort of Nine Towers.* Farrar, Straus and Giroux, 2014.

O'Rourke, Meghan. "Do I Really Have to Read 'The Kite Runner'?" *Slate Magazine,* 25 July 2005.

Rambo 3. (film) Directed by Peter MacDonald. Carolco Pictures, 1988.

Reagan, Ronald. "Proclamation 5033—Afghanistan Day, 1983." March 21, 1983. www.presidency.ucsb.edu/ws/index.php?pid=41077.

Rodriguez, Deborah. *Kabul Beauty School: An American Woman Goes Behind the Veil.* Random House, 2007.

Rose, Megan. "Afghanistan Waste Exhibit A: Kajaki Dam, More Than $300M Spent and Still Not Done." *ProPublica,* 19 Jan. 2016.

Rubin, Alissa J. "Severed Trees in Orchards Mirror Afghan History." *The New York Times*, 10 July 2010.

Slaughter, Joseph R. *Human Rights, Inc: The World Novel, Narrative Form, and International Law.* Fordham UP, 2007.

Stuhr, Rebecca. *Reading Khaled Hosseini.* The Pop Lit Book Club. Greenwood Press, 2009.

Whiskey Tango Foxtrot (film of Kim Barker's *The Taliban Shuffle*). Directed by Glen Ficarra and John Requa. Perf. Tina Fey. Screenplay Robert Carlock, 2016.

Whitlock, Craig. "The Afghanistan Papers." *The Washington Post*, 9 Dec. 2019.

Wilson, Craig."'Kite Runner' Catches the Wind". *USA Today*, 18 Apr. 2005.

"I always felt like Baba hated me a little": Fathers and Sons in *The Kite Runner*_____

Calum Kerr

Despite its straightforward prose style, *The Kite Runner* is a complex book, with a twisted timeline, and many different plot and subplot strands. Thematically it deals with power and powerlessness, with the history of a nation, with attacks and their aftermath, and many other subjects. Arguably, however, one of the clearest themes in the book, which is examined in several different ways, is that of the relationships between fathers and sons. We are presented with many different fathers—biological, adoptive, chosen—and many different sons–legitimate, illegitimate, lost and found—and the relationships between them are shown in many different ways, and they change as the text—and narrative time—progresses. An examination of this web of relationships is one way to understand *The Kite Runner* and unpick meaning from the text. In particular, the following will show how the various relationships impinge on the protagonist, Amir, and his hero's journey.

Baba and Amir

One of the clearest and most central father/son relationships in the novel, is that between Baba and the narrator/protagonist, Amir. Baba is mentioned briefly in the first chapter (2), which is little more than a framing device for the story that follows. In the second and third chapters, however, Amir starts to talk in much more detail about his father and his exploits—building the "best" house, wrestling a bear, building an orphanage, his good marriage—and also a physical description of him that shows him as vibrant and dominating (3–20). Amir's reporting of his father's nickname, "Mr. Hurricane," (11) only serves to reinforce the impression he gives us of his father as literally a force of nature. This focus on his father so early in the book shows the importance of the character.

These tales of Baba's prowess, and the others that emerge as the novel progresses—particularly the scene in which Baba stands up to the Russian soldier as they escape from Afghanistan (99–102)—paint a picture of a strong man in control of his environment. However, it must be remembered that this is Amir's perspective of his father—and to a large extent the perspective of Amir as a young boy—which is untempered by a deeper understanding of human nature and what often lies beneath such shows of strength. Although Amir does not always acknowledge them in the earlier sections of the text, we see other aspects to Baba that give us, the reader, a more rounded understanding of his father. The good treatment of Ali and the doctor hired to fix Hassan's harelip speak of a softer side to the man. And, while later events may cast a more self-serving light on these actions, Baba's rushing home to be with his family on the night of the coup shows a deep level of caring (32).

Amir is often so caught up in himself—especially when young—that he fails to recognize the different sides to his father. However, he is clear in his ambivalence towards his father, and Baba's possible ambivalence towards him. In the line "I always felt like Baba hated me a little" (17), Amir is suggesting that his father blames him for the death of his mother, Baba's wife, during childbirth. This emotion is certainly possible, and the fact that Amir takes after her, rather than after his bearlike father, would only serve to amplify this feeling. However, it is also clear that Amir sometimes "hates" his father, despite his descriptions of Baba acting as protestations of hero-worship. In the scene where Amir presents his short story to his father, only to have it ignored, he says he wants to drain his father's blood from his own body (27). This shows his own burst of hatred toward his father, but it is interesting in that it is turned inwards, towards himself, with a desire to self-harm, rather than outward towards his father. This is symptomatic of the relationship between the two throughout the book and forms a large part of Amir's character. It becomes clear that he is afraid of being unable to live up to his father, and his father's wishes, but at the same time desires to be his own person and not trapped by expectations that may or not exist outside of his own mind.

Later in the text, once the narrative moves to America, we start to see a different relationship between the two men. As Amir has reached adulthood and started his own life, and Baba has reached an older age with some infirmity, so Amir takes on more of the role of parent and Baba that of child. This is reflective of many parent/child relationships where, over time, the burden of care switches from one to the other; however, it is notable that this is accompanied by a change of location. In Afghanistan, Baba was in his element, able to command the people around him. In America, Amir discovers his ability to control his own life, and is forced to take care of his father. Thus, the two different cultures are reflected through the men and their relationship, with Baba being the representative of the old, pre-coup Afghanistan, and Amir being more a part of a Western liberal democracy. As such, Baba's death, shortly after Amir's wedding, (151) can be seen as the passing of a torch from Baba's liberal, secular Afghanistan, to Amir's diasporic Afghan America.

In this light, Baba's involvement in Amir's wedding can be seen as a last flicker from that old Afghanistan. We are told that Baba pays for much of it, with most of the balance of his life savings, and that he is able to call in old favors from people he knew back in Kabul (148). As such, after watching the decline of Baba, and his increasing frailty, we see a final burst of the man who could wrestle a bear, win the best wife, and command orphanages to be built. The lifting of his pain, just before his death, suggests a shifting of his burden, and we see this being taken up by Amir in the following chapters, with his own burdens and his increasing desire for redemption, which he eventually finds in a form of fatherhood.

Amir's relationship with his father is also colored by his jealousy of the fatherly affection that Baba shows to Hassan—a jealousy that culminates in Amir taking action against both Hassan and Ali. The later revelation that Hassan was also Baba's son, and so Amir's brother, again changes the relationship, bringing in a feeling of betrayal at being lied to, even if only by omission. This revelation brings Amir a realization that his father was not the monument from his childhood, nor the frail old man from before his death, but a real human being with the same flaws as himself; flaws that needed repair. As Amir says:

> As it turned out, Baba and I were more alike than I'd ever known. We had both betrayed the people who would have given their lives for us. And with that came this realization: that Rahim Khan had summoned me here to atone not just for my sins, but for Baba's too. (197–98)

And with this statement Amir makes clear that the fathers and sons in the book share a common theme with many fathers and sons throughout literature, including Shakespeare's *Hamlet*: that of the sins of the fathers being passed to the sons for atonement and redemption.

Ali and Hassan

Ali and Hassan's relationship is not as well documented as Baba and Amir's—largely because the story is told from Amir's limited perspective—and yet it is at least as complex. The fact that Hassan is not actually Ali's son, but rather Baba's, allows for a re-reading of the relationship. In the sections before the revelation, Ali would seem to be a model father devoted to his son, and willing to sacrifice his home, his happiness, and ultimately himself for his son. Once we learn of Hassan's true parentage, this devotion takes on a new dimension, as we see Ali as guardian to not only a child from an unfaithful wife, but also from his best friend who had betrayed him. This widens Ali's sacrifice to include many more aspects of his life, and highlights the relationship between Ali and Baba, a relationship that is then reflected in the ones between Amir and Hassan, and eventually between Amir and Sohrab.

To a large extent, Baba acts as a parent towards Ali. This is not due to any great disparity in their ages, but more because of the difference in their class, wealth, and ethnicity. Baba is in a position of power over Ali, which he sees as a responsibility rather than an advantage. While still employing him as a servant, as he would have been culturally trained to do, he still ensures his well-being and is hugely distressed when Amir's actions cause him to leave. Amir comments that his father never referred to Ali as his "friend," (22) and this can be seen as both another example of the cultural pressure that would make it unthinkable for a Pashtun to class a Hazara as a friend and as an indication that the responsibility he feels for Ali makes the relationship more unbalanced than the term would suggest. He is responsible for providing food, shelter, protection, and a living for Ali, which presents him in a more paternal role.

This, of course, is a relationship duplicated between Amir and Hassan, though we see that the young Amir is ill-equipped to manage this dynamic, with the conflicting presence of Ali and Baba's individual devotions to Hassan providing complications. Amir's failure to accept his responsibility for Hassan—the paternal responsibility of the ruling class—and the confusion caused by Baba's love for the boy, cause Amir's jealousy, something he does not truly realize until the revelation of Hassan's true parentage. At that point, he becomes aware of the role he should have played towards the boy, and, therefore, his quest to find Sohrab—a boy to whom he can become a true father—serves as his attempt at redemption for this mistake.

Rahim Khan

Rahim Khan's role in Amir's life also confuses the issue of fatherhood in the novel. When Amir is a child we see Khan playing the role of a surrogate father, something to which he returns when he makes contact again many years later. Although unrelated to Amir—described as Baba's 'best friend and business partner' (5)—Rahim Khan is a constant presence in the boy's life, and one that outlasts his real family to act as the agent of Amir's redemption. Upon his introduction, Amir describes a photo taken when he was just a baby (5). It features Baba, Rahim Khan, and Amir—the boy alone with his two fathers, the women absent as they so often are in the text. Amir notes that while he is in Baba's arms, with his father looking "tired and grim" (5), his small baby hand is curled around Rahim Khan's little finger. In this way the photo represents the relationship that extends through the book between Amir and the two men: his father providing the material support, but with a lack of emotional connection, while Rahim Khan provides the guiding hand that leads Amir through his life.

This guidance is most prominent in the scene where Amir presents his first completed short story to his father, as mentioned above. In this scene, Baba rejects Amir. He acknowledges the story's existence, barely, but shows no enthusiasm for it and does not offer to read it. This is just one of many such awkward moments between Baba and Amir, repeated along Amir's journey to become a writer and a man. However, Rahim Khan takes up the role of mentor at this point. He takes the story from Amir and reads it (27–28). He then goes on to encourage and support Amir's desire to write. This serves as a clear example of the difference between Baba and Rahim Khan. As Khan says to Baba in the earlier conversation overheard by Amir, when Baba is expressing concerns about his son, '[. . .] sometimes you are the most self-centered man I know.' (19) This is in response to Baba voicing the realization that Amir is not like him, and he cannot relate to a child who does not take an interest, or act, in the same ways he would. However, ironically, this attitude itself is reflected in Amir and emerges in his own self-obsession and the jealousy and selfishness he shows towards Hassan.

Rahim Kahn, in contrast, is outward looking, and shows clear concern for the others around him. When Baba is unable to relate to his son, Rahim Khan fills the role, allowing the two men between them to act as one ideal father—as we saw from the photo in the opening pages. Khan continues his support of Amir as the boy grows, an influence that does not end with their parting upon Baba and Amir's flight from Afghanistan. He returns to Amir's life once the boy has become an adult, and reassumes his role as mentor, providing a chance for Amir to undo the damage he did as a child. This is just another example of how Rahim Kahn's focus is outward to other people, and yet, as we hear his story, we start to realize that it is not just people in general, but Amir in particular, whom he chooses to guide, just as any father would.

In Amir's absence, Khan takes on the role of managing the boy's responsibilities to his one-time friend, Hassan. However, as any good mentor should, he does not solve the problems for Amir,

---

but instead calls him back to attend to them himself. He is the cause of Amir's return to Afghanistan and is also the source of revelation to Amir about both Hassan's death and the two boys' shared parentage. In the scene in Peshawar where Rahim Khan reveals these truths to Amir (194–95) he is also performing the key function of the mentor figure within the hero's journey as described in Joseph Campbell's *The Hero with a Thousand Faces*: he is ushering Amir across the threshold of adventure. (Campbell 77–89)

In a mythological narrative, this is usually a moment that occurs earlier, with most of the story taking place as part of the adventure; but in *The Kite Runner*, this moment does not come until the middle of the book. The preceding half features foreshadowing of this adventure, and also provides several smaller adventures; however, the return to Afghanistan, and Amir's rescuing of Sohrab can be seen as the main hero's journey in the text. When Rahim Khan reveals what he must do, Amir—keeping true to Campbell's schema—rejects the "call to adventure," quite literally, by refusing the journey, cursing at Khan, and storming out of the apartment (Campbell 59–68). However, a wider look at the novel, in general, shows that most of Amir's life up until that point has been a rejection of calls to adventures of one kind or another. This is what Rahim Khan seeks to change, and what his fatherly role allows him to do: he finally forces Amir to face up to his life, the legacy of Baba, his failed responsibilities to both Ali and Hassan, and finally his need to become a father himself. To follow the idea of the hero's journey to its logical conclusion, the "elixir" that Amir attains from his adventure, is becoming a father to Hassan's son, and thereby achieving redemption.

Having set Amir off on his "adventure," Rahim Khan leaves the story, as the mentor figure needs to do. Their job is to set the hero onward, but it is the hero's job to complete the adventure (Campbell 69–77). This removal of Khan is accomplished twofold in that he physically leaves Amir's life, and refuses to reveal where he has gone, but also he tells Amir, in his final letter (262–64), that his illness is catching up with him, and he does not have long to live. In this, we see Rahim Khan passing the mantle of "father" on to

Amir, at exactly the moment that Amir takes charge of Sohrab. This mirrors Baba's death coming so soon after Amir's marriage—the other main milestone on his path. Thus, at the end, we can see again how Baba and Rahim Khan act as one father, ushering Amir, through their actions in life, but also in death, to adulthood, marriage, and fatherhood.

General Taheri

Amir's eventual father-in-law, General Iqbal Taheri is another example of a father in the text, one who provides a useful contrast and context for understanding the fatherly roles of Baba, Rahim Khan, and Amir. As father to Soraya, Amir's wife, and therefore Amir's father-in-law, he appears in the book at the same time as Baba is declining, and to some extent fills the gap in Amir's life up to the point where Rahim Khan calls Amir back to Afghanistan. Then, as a result of his time there, Amir is finally able to swap the role of son for that of father.

Baba is portrayed as quite a liberal father, who has strong opinions about life, politics, and culture but is willing to allow his son to find his own path—even if that may be a path he does not necessarily agree with or even understand. In contrast General Taheri is a stricter and more traditional father. Part of this can be seen in the consistent use of his military title. Although we learn that this was his title when he was in Afghanistan, at the time of the story this no longer has meaning. His first name is revealed as Iqbal, but this name is only used three times in the whole book, and never by Amir who continues to refer to him as "the general," "General Taheri," or the more honorific "General Sahib." This is a level of respect that might be expected from a man to his father-in-law, especially coming from a more traditional culture. However, it also fits with the personality of the General and shows him to stand apart from the names of Amir's other father figures: the more familiar Baba—which is the Afghan word for "father," and the only name we are ever given for him—and also Rahim Khan, who allows Amir to use his full name.

The stricter approach that the General takes, both with his own daughter and with Amir, serves a useful function in the book. Unlike Baba's more laissez-faire attitude—where his lack of understanding of his son manifests in a resignation and a refusal to engage—and Rahim Khan's greater understanding and guidance, the General's more forthright opinions and refusal to back down give Amir something to push against. This is particularly true in the scene towards the end of the book where the General expresses concern about what people will say about the appearance of Sohrab in their family. Amir's response is curt and more forceful than much of what we have seen of him throughout the book up to this point:

> "[. . .] People will ask. They will want to know why there is a Hazara boy living with our daughter. What do I tell them?"
> [. . .]
> "You see, General Sahib, my father slept with his servant's wife. She bore him a son named Hassan. Hassan is dead now. That boy sleeping on the couch is Hassan's son. He's my nephew. That's what you tell people when they ask."
> They were all staring at me.
> "And one more thing, General Sahib," I said. "You will never again refer to him as 'Hazara boy' in my presence. He has a name and it's Sohrab."
> No one said anything for the remainder of the meal. (315)

In this short scene we can see the more traditional and more authoritarian side of General Taheri come to the fore. We have seen it before in his early attitudes to Amir at the market and in his general treatment of his daughter after she ran away with a man. However, here we see it manifest itself in a less caring manner, with some racist overtones. His desire to keep up appearances with regard to his community and the suggestion that there should be some "excuse," some lie, to explain the presence of Sohrab indicates a level of uneasiness and embarrassment that is undoubtedly due to his cultural background. The added problem of Sohrab being from the group perceived—back in Afghanistan, at least—as ethnically inferior to the General's Pashtun people, just adds to his unwillingness to be open and honest about the boy. Amir's response—where he advocates using not just the truth, but the whole truth—not only silences Taheri himself, but also shows a maturity in Amir that has been lacking previously. In finally taking a stand against the General's prejudices and adherence to the "old ways" of Afghanistan, Amir is taking a stand against the larger divisions that he was exposed to in childhood. These divisions came between him and Baba, as well as between him and Hassan, and caused much of the trouble that required him to, in Rahim Khan's words, find *"a way to be good again"* (2). In this way, General Taheri represents not just an individual father figure, but also the patriarchal nature of both pre- and post-Taliban Afghanistan. This gives Amir something more tangible to react and rebel against, as he had found that being one man against the might of the Taliban was too hard and almost killed him. In this concrete form he finally finds a way to push himself from a delayed adolescence—almost an arrested development that could be seen from him being a simple "storyteller," a dweller in make-believe—and finally into both adulthood and fatherhood.

Of course, there is another fatherly aspect to General Taheri's role in the novel, that of father to Soraya, rather than just father-in-law to Amir, and the differences in gender relationships between cultures that this reveals are worth investigating on their own. However, that would expand to an entirely different essay encompassing the sometime presence, but much larger absence, of female characters in the novel, and the influence that these presences and absences have on the male characters, and on the narrative as a whole. As such, I will leave that thought here and move on.

Amir and Hassan

After the relationship between Baba and Amir, perhaps the most crucial father/son relationship in the novel—representing as it does, the climax, culmination, and reward of Amir's journey—is that between Amir and Sohrab. However, an understanding of this needs an examination of the childhood relationship between Amir and Hassan, where Amir takes on a role for his friend which, as mentioned above, is at times akin to that of a father and son.

The relationship between Amir and Hassan is a complicated one. They are separated by just one year in age—with Amir the elder—making them more like contemporaries, or the brothers they really are, than any more hierarchical dynamic. However, Amir's position as a Pashtun and Hassan's as an Hazara has a bearing, as do their roles, with Amir being the son of the family for whom Ali and Hassan are servants. One result of this is that Amir is educated while Hassan is not. This creates a power imbalance between the two, which places Amir in a superior position which, in his childishness, he takes advantage of. He thus places himself over the slightly younger boy and takes it upon himself to teach and guide Hassan, even if this is not always in the best of directions.

There would seem to be three key moments in this relationship: the conversation the boys have while watching kite fighting in which Amir asks Hassan if he would eat dirt if he, Amir, told him to (47–48); the events that transpire around Hassan's rape in the alley (62–69); and, the events that lead to Ali and Hassan leaving Baba's employ (90–95).

In the first of these, when Amir asks Hassan if he would eat dirt, we see his first realization of the power he has over the younger boy. Just as he has been leading Hassan in various games and activities, now he realizes that he can command him in other things, and the power of this responsibility daunts him. It is the first intimation for Amir of what it entails to have responsibility for another life, and he immediately shies away from it when Hassan challenges him by asking if he would ever actually ask him to eat dirt. This shying away from responsibility is a recurring motif for Amir, only resolved when he takes on the care of Sohrab and exemplified in the above exchange with General Taheri.

The second key moment, the attack on Hassan in the alley, reinforces for Amir the burden of responsibility and, in a way, is a repeat of the "dirt-eating" scene, but on a much larger scale. Amir witnesses the attack and does nothing to stop it. However, the position of responsibility he has for Hassan means he feels he should have done something to help. The complicated absence and presence of Baba, who is both protective of Amir but also often distant from a son he does not understand, can be seen as having an influence here, as can Amir's jealousy of Hassan caused by the latter's secret parentage. In not helping and, after the events, failing to address them in any useful way, Amir abrogates his responsibility, and compounds the failings of his father in his own actions. This can, of course, be excused by his age—as Rahim Khan comments later in the book—as he has a responsibility he is unable to shoulder. However, it is an event that leads us to both the next key moment and the final adoption of Sohrab.

The third key moment between Amir and Hassan is a direct outgrowth of the second. Unable to cope with his failure to take on the burden of responsibility that Amir now realizes he has for Hassan, he decides instead to rid himself of the problem by ridding himself of Hassan entirely. It is crucial that the particular instrument that he uses to attempt to have Ali and Hassan dismissed from the house is a watch he has been given by Baba. Using his father's gift to undermine his own responsibilities shows just how poorly Amir is living up to what he knows he should do and allows us to see two fatherly relationships—one positive and one negative—side by side. During the scene in which Baba confronts Ali and Hassan, Amir realizes that Hassan is protecting him by not revealing the truth to Baba, and in this moment we see a switch of the fatherly role, with Hassan taking care of Amir rather than the other way around. This provides Amir with an example that stays with him and allows him to make the change of character that enables him to fight for Sohrab in the way he should have fought for Hassan.

Amir and Sohrab

The final father/son relationship is, in concert with the Baba/Amir relationship, one of the most important in the book. As Amir finally completes his *Bildungsroman* journey of maturation, he assumes fatherhood over Sohrab, who is a clear analogue for Hassan, and a chance for Amir to try once again to assume responsibility for another, and this time get it right.

Sohrab, as Hassan's son, and therefore Amir's nephew, is another Hazara in a position subordinate to the Pashtuns around him and is also in a very vulnerable position, much as Hassan was. His plight, identified by Rahim Khan, is what allows Amir to finish the adventure that began when he first failed Hassan at the point of his attack in the alleyway. Sohrab's life has been no less difficult, and he has suffered many traumas in the course of his short life. That these are, at least in part, at the hands of his father's childhood bully, Assef, allows a strong parallel to be drawn between the historic treatment of the Hazara by the leading Pashtuns and the escalation in persecution seen under the Taliban. In this way, the story, as it approaches its close, become less of a personal narrative and more a political commentary on issues of race in Afghanistan—both contemporaneous with the novel but also historical. As such, at times, Sohrab can be seen as a symbol of the ethnic problems in the country, rather than just a character; a foil for a country that is now run by Assefs rather than Babas. However, in terms of Amir's journey, his role as an individual is the most crucial. As is common to the hero's journey, Amir must undergo a series of final tests in order to achieve his goal. In this case, it comes in two ways: the beating from Assef (250–55) and Sohrab's suicide attempt (296–99).

During Assef's attack on his childhood rival, Amir starts to laugh, as he finally feels the relief from the burden of guilt he has carried since Hassan's rape in the alley—this is the beating he should have taken back then. However, this is also the moment at which he finally puts someone else's life and needs above his own, as the transition to adulthood and fatherhood requires. It is the moment at which the arrested development mentioned above is finally set in motion once more, as he takes on the responsibility he has been avoiding for most of his life, and puts himself front and center, instead of relying on others to protect him. This is a moment of sacrifice; however, it would serve nothing for Amir to die at this moment, so he cannot give himself fully. Sohrab, like his father before him, steps forward to protect Amir, and effects their escape with the aid of a catapult, reflecting Hassan's earlier defeat of Assef.

So, it is with Sohrab's attempted suicide, rather than the beating, that Amir finally faces his ultimate test and realizes his potential as a father. The suicide attempt is caused by Amir suggesting that Sohrab go back into an orphanage while he attempts to arrange for adoption of the child in the United States (297). This obviously reminds Sohrab of the various beatings, humiliations, and sexual assaults he suffered in the Kabul orphanage—a series of terrible events analogous to Hassan's attack in the alleyway, but scaled up because it represents an attack by the whole Taliban, rather than just individual bullying. Amir's failure to do whatever it might take to protect Sohrab from this eventuality is therefore also analogous to his failure to protect Hassan. As he falls back on various officials and bureaucrats, it is symbolic of him slipping back into his previous comfortable, protected state. Putting his own physical form at risk for Sohrab was a big step, but seeing this potentially ruined by his own inability to sustain his responsibilities is the final push he needs to assume his proper role as father and protector. That this transformation has taken effect can be seen in the exchange with General Taheri above. Amir is back in his normal life, able to resume his previous roles, and yet, we see from his new forthright attitude that he has changed and has no desire to return to his former state. He has finally adopted his responsibilities, and both his own sins from childhood and also the sins of his father, Baba, have been resolved, as the joining of Amir and Hassan's son bring together the two sides of his life.

Conclusion

The web of father/son relationships in *The Kite Runner* is a complex one and is intimately tied up with concepts of power, class, politics, and ethnicity. As such, it serves as both an interesting examination of Amir's life and a critique of Afghan society, albeit from the westernized perspective of a diasporic Afghan. However, this complex web works with one goal: to provide examples of father figures, present and absent, encouraging and dismissive, supportive and failing, and to show how they can work against each other, or in combination, to nurture or neglect their "sons." That the roles of father sometimes fall to brothers or friends just adds to this complexity, but the extra cultural insight this affords adds extra depth to the narrative. In the end, the various father/son relationships serve the purpose of moving Amir from a privileged and self-centered child, into a selfless and open adult. Thus he completes the hero's journey, bringing self-knowledge back to his ordinary world, and completes his extended process of maturation. As such, there is a hope in the text that Afghanistan itself can achieve similar goals and become a more open, tolerant, and stable society.

Note

1. Amir and Soraya's failure to conceive a child of their own even with medical assistance can be seen as another refusal of the call. The fact that both of them are nominally capable of creating a child, and that the diagnosis is one of "'Unexplained Infertility'" (162), allows for an interpretation of it being caused by Amir's body also refusing to aid in his journey to fatherhood.

Works Cited

Campbell, Joseph. *The Hero with a Thousand Faces.* 1949. Fontana, 1993.

Hosseini, Khaled. *The Kite Runner.* 2003. Bloomsbury, 2004.

"You have been in Afghanistan, I perceive": Perception, Sensation, and Cognition in *The Kite Runner*

Nicolas Tredell

In Sir Arthur Conan Doyle's *A Study in Scarlet* (1887), Sherlock Holmes, on first being introduced to John H. Watson M.D., says "You have been in Afghanistan, I perceive." Astonished by this first example of Holmes's apparently preternatural percipience, Watson asks: "How on earth did you know that"? (13). Holmes does not immediately explain but, in the next chapter, he outlines his reasoning and conclusion to Watson: "Where in the tropics could an English army doctor have seen much hardship and got his arm wounded? Clearly in Afghanistan." (25). The encounter is set at the time of the Second Anglo-Afghan War (1878–80), at the height of Britain's imperial power, and Watson, as first-person narrator, has already summarized his sufferings and injuries in that war, which brought him "misfortune and disaster" (9), leading him, like Amir in *Kite*, to a hospital in Peshawar in what is now Pakistan, and leaving him with his "health irretrievably ruined" (10). Conan Doyle, through Watson and Holmes, thus offers an image of Khaled Hosseini's native land that has become familiar once again to Western eyes in the twenty-first century: Afghanistan as a place of trauma, of pain and death, for at least some of those Westerners who venture there and implicitly for the indigenous population, though Watson makes no mention of their suffering.

Kite, in contrast to *A Study in Scarlet*, does focus upon the sufferings of figures who are, or were, part of the indigenous population of Afghanistan: Amir, the narrator; his part-Hazara half-brother Hassan; their father Baba; Hassan's supposed father, Ali; Rahim Khan, his father's close friend and Amir's own mentor; General Iqbal Taheri, living in exile in California with his wife Khanum, and their daughter Soraya, who becomes Amir's wife. Moreover, the novel portrays the much more widespread sufferings of Afghans, both in their native land and in the diaspora that takes some of them to the United States. This focus on suffering might appear to reinforce an all-too-familiar image of Afghanistan, which does not lack some valid empirical and existential basis (no familiar image does), but which arguably omits a balancing awareness of other modes of living and being in a complex country.

Without denying the cogency of this form of criticism, this essay approaches *Kite* from the perspective of cognitive literary theory, which assumes a continuity between the ways human sensory and cognitive processes operate in everyday life and the ways they operate in the reading of imaginative literature. Perception involves both sensation, as experienced in the interactions between the external world and the senses of sight, hearing, smell, taste and touch, and cognition, knowing and understanding things, often through inferences from, and verbal and conceptual constructions of, sensations. Imaginative literature offers readers a simulation, a kind of virtual reality experience, which they do not confuse with actuality but which they inhabit and respond to, during and sometimes after the reading experience, as if it were real.

A key reason for the success of *Kite* is its evocation of both sensation and cognition, which the reader experiences imaginatively on the body and in the mind. This essay analyzes *Kite*'s evocation of seeing, hearing, smelling, and touching—the visual, the aural, the olfactory and the tactile—and also of the sensations and cognitions of pain, particularly of the kind of physical and psychological distress caused by respiratory difficulty, a recurrent motif in the narrative. Each of these sensory responses also arouses cognitive activity as those who experience them seek to identify and assess the nature of what is seen, heard, smelled, touched, and felt as physical pain. It is important to bear in mind, however, that in many passages in *Kite* these perceptions and understandings often function as an ensemble, as they do in actual life. For example, the scene in which Amir first sees the Taliban in the flesh involves sight, taste, the shrinking of his own flesh, the thudding of his heart, and the inhibition of his respiration. By separating out these elements in our investigation, however, we can gain a more precise sense of how the narrative achieves its often visceral effects on readers who open themselves to what it has to offer.

Seeing

Perception of a visual kind is central to the crucial event of *Kite* that recurs in the narrator's memory at key points throughout the narrative and that helps to drive the plot and, in the narrator's view, to determine his identity —"I became what I am today" (1) are the first words of Chapter 1, and the last four of those words are reiterated at the end of that short chapter: "And made me what I am today" (2). The event that proved so formative is largely (not wholly, as we shall later discuss) an act of seeing, of pained, impotent witnessing; but rather than using the verb "to see," the narrator uses the verb "to peek," meaning to look quickly or furtively: "I remember the precise moment, crouching behind a crumbling mud wall, peeking into the alley near the frozen creek" (1). By using the present participle form of "to peek" he suggests, in some sense, an act that is still ongoing, endlessly repeated in remembering, in retrospect: "Looking back now, I realize I have been peeking into that deserted alley for the last twenty-six years" (1). The adjective "deserted" is inaccurate as a literal description of the alley, but we might interpret such inaccuracy as an index of the narrator's evasion of the full complexity of the event: the alley did have people in it at the time: even if it was, in a sense, deserted by hope and, indeed, by the narrator himself.

Jean-Paul Sartre's play *Huis clos* [*In Camera*] (first performed 1944) shows three characters trapped in an existential version of Hell in which the chief torment is subjection to the judgment of other people; as one of them, Joseph Garcin, asks "Can one judge a life on the basis of a single act?" ["*Peut-on juger une vie sur un seul acte*"? (88)]. Certainly Amir, in his own personal hell for much of *Kite*, feels this is both possible and inevitable and that his own life is judged by that act of nonintervention in Hassan's rape, not because other people are aware of it (though his literary and ethical mentor Rahim Khan is, as he realizes in due course) but because he himself is (even if one assumes that part of that self-awareness is due to the internalized imagined judgment of other people, what Freud called the superego). But the act by which Amir feels his own life is judged is one of omission rather than commission, a failure to intervene for which he bitterly reproaches himself and which he knows was due, not only to cowardice, but also, and more profoundly, to his complicity in the racist attitudes of the rapist Assef, to his secret sharing, partially and on some level, of Assef's conviction that the rape mattered less because the victim was a Hazara rather than a Pashtun (Amir does not know at this stage that Baba is Hassan's father and that Hassan is, therefore, a Hazara-Pashtun hybrid).

In Chapter 7 òf *Kite*, in the build-up to Assef's assault on Hassan, Amir sees two objects that function as metonymies—parts standing for wholes—of the situation: one stands for Hassan's triumph as kite runner (and thus for Amir's kite-fighting triumph that briefly wins him his father's approval); the other stands for his violation as rape victim: "the blue kite" and "Hassan's brown corduroy pants thrown on a heap of eroded bricks" (66). At two points as the rape unfolds, Amir stops watching and another sense takes over from sight, that of hearing; then he runs away. When he sees Hassan again soon afterwards, Hassan is holding the blue kite but there is a "dark stain in the seat of his pants" and "tiny drops" fall "from between his legs" and stain "the snow black" (69). But although Amir perceives the two latter phenomena visually, he refuses to grasp their full significance cognitively, at the time pretending to himself that he has not seen them; a gap opens up between perception and conscious cognition. Even so, those metonymies of Hassan's violation will not go away: in Chapter 8, he finds that "always, my mind returned to the alley. To Hassan's brown corduroy pants lying on the bricks. To the droplets of blood staining the snow dark red, almost black" (79).

Earlier in the novel, in Chapter 2, visual perception features vividly in the narrator's evocation of Hassan's appearance as a boy; his face is "almost perfectly round," "like a Chinese doll chiseled from hardwood: his flat, broad nose and slanting, narrow eyes like bamboo leaves, eyes that looked, depending on the light, gold, green, even sapphire" (3). On one level, there is visual beauty here, in the similes of the Chinese doll and of bamboo leaves, in the play of light across Hassan's eyes with its fleeting resemblances to the hues of precious metals and gems; but it also turns Hassan into an aesthetic object that is racially marked, constructed as an example of Orientalism in the simile of the "Chinese doll" and the description of the "slanting narrow eyes." These mark Hassan visually as different, as looking more like a Hazara rather than a Pashtun like Amir, despite their common paternity. Amir's perception is partly structured by a racist framework, and this will be crucial to his ill-treatment of Hassan and his passive complicity in his rape by Assef.

Over and above the outward signs of his ethnic difference Hassan is also further marked visually as "disfigured" in the last sentence of the paragraph, and again the narrator offers, as a perception surviving in memory, the final element in a face the narrator "can still see": "the cleft lip, just left of mid-line, where the Chinese doll maker's instrument may have slipped, or perhaps he had simply grown tired and careless" (3). Here again, continuing the Orientalist aesthetic image, Hassan is seen as a crafted object, a Chinese doll, but an imperfect one, whose supposed flaws are the result of slippage or fatigue and carelessness. Later, in Chapter 4, this perception takes on a representative significance, with Hassan's physiognomy standing for his own and Amir's country of origin: "to me, the face of Afghanistan is that of a boy with a thin-boned frame, a shaved head, and low-set ears, a boy with a Chinese doll face perpetually lit by a harelipped smile" (22). If, on the one hand, this may seem to reinforce an image of Afghanistan as a disfigured country, it serves, on the other hand, to challenge the idea of Afghanistan, cherished by the racist Assef, as exclusively a Pashtun nation, even if Hassan, as Baba's illegitimate and publicly unacknowledged son, is part Pashtun (as the narrator knows by the time he is retrospectively recounting his story).

An important aspect of Amir's visual experience in Afghanistan as a boy, evoked in Chapter 4, is vicarious: his sightings of America, or of a quasi-mythical image of America, by means of his visits, with Hassan, to the Cinema Park in Kabul where they watch Westerns (23). Afghanistan is a landlocked country, and Amir never travels beyond its borders until he and Baba flee to Pakistan, so it is through cinema that he sees the image of, gets to know, the sea; in Chapter 11, he recalls this in his account of his initial sighting of an actual ocean, in California: "The first time I saw the Pacific, I almost cried. It was as vast and blue as the oceans on the movie screens of my childhood" (118). The narrator does not spell out here the elements of his emotion, but readers can infer them from the narrative that has gone before (and, on rereading, what they recall of the narrative that comes after). Amir's imminent tears well up from memories of those many cinema visits in Kabul he shared with Hassan; from his guilt at what he did to Hassan; from a sense of exile from his landlocked native country; and from the joy of seeing in reality, in three dimensions and with a full sensorium, what he has only previously seen on the screen.

That emotional experience of seeing, in reality, a phenomenon previously seen only on screens occurs again in Chapter 20 on his return to Afghanistan—but the mix of emotions is very different this time. In Kabul, Farid, Amir's driver and later friend, identifies, in a discreet murmur, an approaching truck as "Beard Patrol" (216): "That was the first time I saw the Taliban. I'd seen them on TV, on the Internet, on the cover of magazines, and in newspapers. But here I was now, less than fifty feet from them" (216). That physical proximity triggers the sensations of fear—and the verb "triggers" is all too appropriate given that the men in the truck all have "Kalashnikovs slung on their shoulders" (216–17) and seem trigger-happy, ready to use their weapons at the slightest provocation. When the "roaming eyes" (217) of a Talib with a whip fall on Amir and hold his gaze, he feels more naked than he has done in his entire life.

The Sartre play we mentioned earlier, *Huis clos*, is in some sense a dramatic demonstration of the Sartrean philosophy and psychology expressed in his book *L'Être et le néant* [*Being and Nothingness*], published the previous year, 1943. One crucial aspect of Sartre's analysis is the idea of the Other whose gaze always threatens to fix and define you—this is the meaning of the famous line that comes near the end of *Huis clos*: "*l'enfer, c'est les Autres*" ["Hell is other people"] (92). One of Sartre's memorable examples is being caught looking through a keyhole; the keyhole-viewer enjoys the power of the gaze over whatever they observe through that aperture but if someone else catches them at it the positions are reversed and the voyeur becomes voyeurized, the object rather than the agent of the gaze, fixed as a Peeping Tom.

In *Kite*, the control of the gaze is crucial to the power the Taliban exert upon the civilian population; in effect, they make everyone else feel as if they had been caught looking through a keyhole: it is the Taliban who are entitled to look and for others to return their look is dangerous, potentially fatal, as Farid warns Amir in Chapter 20 immediately after his first encounter with the men in the truck: "Don't ever stare at them! Do you understand me? Never!" (217). The Taliban constantly scrutinize the populace for visual signs of deviance, and one flagrant sign for men is the absence of a beard (for which Amir tries to compensate with an ultimately unconvincing false one).

Given the Taliban's control of the gaze, the particular way in which Assef's hold over Sohrab and Amir is broken has powerful significance in the overall thematic and symbolic pattern of *Kite*. The organ of the gaze, the eye, and its vulnerability are crucial to the stand Hassan, and later his son Sohrab, make against Assef's brutality. In Chapter 5, when Assef and his cronies corner Hassan and Amir, Hassan aims his slingshot, loaded with a walnut-sized rock, at Assef and, despite his own fear, warns him that "[i]f you make a move, they'll have to change your nickname from Assef 'the Ear Eater' to 'One-Eyed Assef,' because I have this rock pointed at your left eye" (37). Assef backs down, though doubtless his humiliation helps to fuel the revenge he takes soon afterwards when he rapes Hassan.

In Chapter 22, Assef, now a powerful Talib official who Amir, without then recognizing him, has recently seen casting the first stone (though not for the first time) at the public execution of an adulterous couple, challenges Amir, who has come to rescue Sohrab, to a fight and starts to beat him mercilessly. Hassan's son Sohrab lifts his slingshot, loaded this time with a brass ball from a table support, and pleads with Assef in vain to stop beating Amir. Amir sees the scene with his own eyes, which are themselves damaged, bleeding from the battering Assef has given him. He sees Assef, infuriated by Sohrab's pleas, lunge at the boy, who then fires the slingshot:

[Assef] put his hand where his left eye had been just a moment ago. Blood oozed between his fingers. Blood and something else, something white and gel-like. *That's called vitreous fluid,* I thought with clarity. *I've read that somewhere. Vitreous fluid.* (254, italics in original)

That Assef should lose an eye and be struck half-blind is a physical trauma that symbolizes his moral blindness but also the moral blindness of Amir himself when, long ago, he did nothing to defend Hassan against Assef.

Amir's guilt over his failure to defend Hassan has already resulted, in Chapter 19, in that peculiar but familiar form of visual experience called dreaming, in which the sleeper seems to see things that are not before their eyes and that they may never have witnessed. In this dream, which occurs after he has learned that the Taliban murdered Hassan, he sees the executioner: a *"tall"* man *"dressed in a herringbone vest and a black turban"* who places the barrel of his rifle *"on the back of the kneeling man's head"* and fires: Amir says: *"I see the face behind the plume of smoke swirling from the muzzle. I am the man in the herringbone vest."* (210, italics in original). In the special sight granted by dreams, Amir himself is Hassan's executioner.

While visual perception and sensation are especially important in *Kite*, because they are crucial in Amir's agonized impotent witnessing and recollection of Hassan's rape by Assef, other sensations, felt through, on and in the body, are also of key significance at crucial moments in the novel. We shall next consider hearing; smelling; tactile sensations; and respiratory sensations, those involved in one of the most fundamental activities of sentient mammals that also takes on, in humans, considerable emotional and symbolic significance: breathing.

Hearing

Like seeing, hearing is a form of perception that involves cognition, a process of understanding what is being heard and its significance. In Chapter 5, on 17 July 1973, the first signs of civil violence in later twentieth-century Afghanistan impact more on the ear than the eye: a roaring "like thunder"; "the *rat-a-tat-tat* of gunfire," an onomatopoeic evocation, and its "rapid staccato;" a siren; shattering glass; shouting (31, italics in original). They seriously scare everyone in Baba's house, including the formidable father himself, "because none of us had ever heard gunshots in the streets" (31). The shots signal the overnight overthrow of King Zahir Shah, who has reigned for forty years; his cousin Daoud Khan takes control in "a bloodless coup" (32) but those martial sounds herald the bloodshed to come.

In Chapter 8, while staying at Kaka Homayoun's house, Amir says aloud, in the middle of the night when everyone else is asleep (but partly hoping someone will wake and hear him): "I watched Hassan get raped" (75). But this is not strictly true. Amir does not witness the whole sequence of events that make up the rape of Hassan because he twice turns away at the worst moments; there may be an element of narrative tact here on the part of the author, since to describe such a scene would be to risk accusations of voyeuristic complicity in sexual violence; but if Amir had witnessed the whole thing, it would still be possible to indicate this without graphic description. Instead, the narrative shows, in Chapter 7, how visual perception gives way to an aural perception that makes Hassan's violator sound bestial: "I could hear Assef's quick, rhythmic grunts" (67). Near the end of that chapter, Amir's re-encounter with Hassan soon after the rape involves a further significant moment of aural perception when Hassan starts to speak but his voice cracks and he falls silent (and hearing the sound of silence is an essential form of aural perception). As Amir pretended not to see the visual signs of Hassan's violation, the stained pants and tiny drops falling from between his legs, so he pretends he "hadn't heard the crack in [Hassan's] voice" (69).

Hearing also features in the dream we discussed above, in which Amir sees himself as Hassan's executioner. When the man in the herring-bone vest fires, *"The rifle roars with a deafening crack"* but Amir himself emits no sound: he wakes "with a scream trapped in [his] throat" (210, italics in original). As on the occasion of Hassan's rape as a boy, Amir stays silent. In Chapter 22, in the scene discussed above in which Sohrab fires a brass ball from his slingshot that puts out Assef's left eye, the moment of firing impacts first on Amir's hearing, and the narrator employs onomatopoeia: "The slingshot made a *thwiiiiit* sound when Sohrab released the cup" (254, italics in original). The sounds that follow are those of human anguish, but this time the tables are turned (by means of the ball from the table support) and the anguished sounds come from Assef, not his victims: Assef shrieks, screams, "OUT! GET IT OUT!" and continues to scream "OUT!" (254, block capitals in original), driving home the brute fact that the brass ball is still stuck in his eye socket, and his screams persist as Amir and Sohrab escape.

As well as the many significant aural moments of sound and silence in *Kite*, we also find a range of olfactory evocations, appealing, if not always appealingly, to the sense of smell.

Smelling

Kite has a considerable olfactory repertoire ranging from agreeable aromas to sickening stenches. Early in the novel, in Chapter 2, Amir's father Baba is linked with the odor of his study, also called "'the smoking room,'" "which perpetually smelled of tobacco and cinnamon" (4). At this stage of the twenty-first-century, many people have learned to experience the odor of tobacco as repellent but here it is mingled with the aroma of cinnamon and together these are redolent of the father to whom Amir longs to be close but who, for the most part, keeps him at a distance. Inhaling the mingled scents of tobacco and cinnamon offers Amir a proxy intimacy with Baba.

In Chapter 11, Amir, now with Baba in California, recalls the six months they spent in Peshawar waiting for visas in a "grimy one-bedroom apartment" that "smelled like dirty socks and cat droppings" (113). In their new country, he registers "the smells of the gas station" where Baba now works—"dust, sweat, and gasoline—on his clothes" (112). In a bar in Hayward, in Alameda County,

California, to which Baba takes him to celebrate his graduation from high school at the late age of twenty, "the acrid smell of beer I'd always disliked permeated the walls" (115) and, as Amir drives a dozing Baba home, he smells "tobacco on him and alcohol, sweet and pungent" (116) —the tobacco recalling one of the smells of Baba's study, in his house back in Kabul, evoked in Chapter 2.

During the kite contest in Chapter 7, Amir, though strongly focused on cutting the last remaining kite, a blue one, with his own red, yellow-bordered kite in order to win, is also aware of "[t]he smell of steamed *mantu* and fried *pakora*" that "drifted from rooftops and open doors" (57, italics in original). But three sentences later, actual aromas turn into a metaphor of an abstract idea on which he is focusing: "All I smelled was victory" (57). "Smelling victory" is a familiar enough image but one that demonstrates how sensory experience can serve as a basis for cognitive concepts.

Other smells stay at the sensory level but contribute to an overall cognition of a constricting situation. In Chapter 10, for example, Amir, Baba, Kamal and his father, and other escapees from Kabul are stranded in Jalalabad, and Amir tells us that the moment the door to the basement where they must hide opens, the "THE STENCH OF SOMETHING DAMP, like mildew, bludgeoned my nostrils" (104, block capitals in original). Here, "mildew" evokes sensations of dampness and softness that are complicated and partly contradicted by the hard-hitting verb "bludgeoned," which conjures up a sensation of being struck aggressively by a thick, heavy stick. In Chapter 20, when an old beggar in Kabul leans forward to take the money Amir hands to him, "his stench—like sour milk and feet that hadn't been washed in weeks—flooded my nostrils and made my gorge rise" (217). This nauseating aroma adds an extra dimension of degradation to the plight of a man who, as Amir soon discovers, once taught Farsi literature at the University of Kabul and knew Amir's mother.

In the last three examples we have just considered, the evocation of an olfactory sensation leads into the evocation of other sensations: "the stench of something dank, like mildew" invokes the sense of touch; the verb "bludgeoned" arouses the memory and imagination of pain; the "rising gorge" indicates imminent vomiting. We shall turn now to the sense of touch and to the perception of pain, which are closely connected in the novel.

Touch and pain

Painful tactile sensations linked to abrasive materials and the drawing of blood are particularly evident in the descriptions, in Chapter 6 of *Kite*, of the physical effects of holding "the glass-coated cutting line" of the kite (44), made up of string and "a mixture of ground glass and glue" (44). By the time spring comes, "every boy in Kabul bore telltale horizontal gashes on his fingers from a whole winter of fighting kites" and they would "compare [their] battle scars on the first day of school" (44). These wounds are painful but willingly borne: "The cuts stung and didn't heal for a couple of weeks, but I didn't mind" (44).

In Chapter 7, in the kite contest itself, Hassan's hands are quickly "bloodied by the string" (55). When Amir "slice[s] a bright yellow kite with a coiled white tail," he sustains "another gash on the index finger and blood trickle[s] down into [his] palm" so that he has to let "Hassan hold the string" and suck the blood dry, then blot his finger against his jeans (56). The same scene contains further references to Amir's "bloody hands" (57) and "bloodied hands" (59). These last two phrases conjure up the familiar image of "blood on your hands" to indicate complicity in crime; as a result of his kite fighting, Amir literally has blood on his hands; but he will soon have metaphorical blood on his hands when he fails to intervene to try to save Hassan from being raped by Assef, a violation that also draws physical blood.

In a dream Amir later has in Chapter 7, a *"familiar shape,"* who we infer is Hassan, reaches out a hand on which he sees *"deep, parallel gashes across the palm, blood dripping, staining the snow"* (65, italics in original). This is part of a crucial strand of *Kite* in which physical trauma from the mild to the acute is bound up with emotional experiences that are also a form of learning as well as a source of psychological pain. In the kite fighting, Amir engages in communal combat that does not separate but brings together those pursuing a common objective, even if only one of them will attain that objective; but soon afterwards, he shirks the individual combat that might have saved Hassan from rape and his own self from moral obloquy.

Kite links not only touch with pain but also breathing, or its inhibition, in a further powerful strand of sensory evocation in the novel.

Breathing

In Chapter 4, Amir, then ten years old–it is July 1973–writes his first short story, sparked off by Hassan's admiration of a tale he has started to make up while pretending to read it from a book. While he is telling that tale, Hassan's approval, and perhaps his awareness that he is tricking Hassan, affect him physically, making him "a little breathless" (26). But when Amir announces to his father that he has "written a story" (27), Baba's response is to say, "that's very good" —and "nothing more" (27). The silence that follows lasts perhaps less than a minute but seems painfully prolonged, and, once again, affects Amir's respiration and his perception of the physical atmosphere around him: "Air grew heavy, damp, almost solid. I was breathing bricks" (27).

In Chapter 8, when Amir pelts Hassan with pomegranates, vainly trying to provoke him to retaliate and thus to ease his own guilt for not intervening to try to stop the rape, he ends up "exhausted and panting" (81), from both the physical effort and the emotional intensity of his aggression. In the following chapter, as he anticipates getting rid of Hassan and Ali by his plot to brand Hassan as a thief, his motivation is expressed partly in a metaphor drawn from respiration: "I wanted to be able to breathe again" (92).

The most powerful moment in the novel in which respiratory sensations come to the fore occurs in Chapter 10 when Amir, Baba, Kamal, and his father and others get into the tank of a fuel truck to make the journey from Jalalabad in Afghanistan to Peshawar in Pakistan:

PANIC.

You open your mouth. Open it so wide your jaws creak. You order your lungs to draw air, NOW, you need air, need it NOW. But your airways ignore you. They collapse, tighten, squeeze, and suddenly you're breathing through a drinking straw. Your mouth closes and your lips purse and all you can manage is a strangled croak. Your hands wriggle and shake. Somewhere a dam has cracked open and a flood of cold sweat spills, drenches your body. You want to scream. You would if you could. But you have to breathe to scream.

Panic. (105–06)

Here, the shift into the present tense gives a sense of painful immediacy, the use of capital letters heightens the sense of urgency, and the deployment of the second person "you" draws in the reader. The deprivations of air here press close to the ultimate respiratory distress of death, where respiration stops altogether. The respiratory distress generates other bodily symptoms–the hands wriggling and shaking, the cold sweat not merely oozing but spilling in a flood– as well as psychological panic and the unarticulated but acute awareness that one—you—is coming to the very edge of death. In a way that recalls and intensifies Amir's earlier image, in Chapter 4, of "breathing bricks" (27) when his father ignores his boyhood writing, the air thickens and nearly solidifies. This interchange, in which the most insubstantial of the four elements, air, seems almost to alchemize into the thickest, earth, reinforces the enormity of what is happening: "The air wasn't right, it was too thick, almost solid. Air wasn't supposed to be solid. I wanted to reach out with my hands, crush the air into little pieces, stuff them down my windpipe" (106). Amir and almost all the others in the fuel tank survive to reach Pakistan; but when they climb out into the air, they find Kamal dead and his father crying, three times, that he "won't breathe," and making a desperate last appeal: "Allah, help him breathe!" (108) before grabbing the gun of Karim, the people trafficker, and shooting, not Karim, but himself, shoving the barrel into his mouth and stopping his own breath forever.

The fundamental distress of inhibited breathing returns in Chapter 11, which is set in California. We mentioned above how

Amir drove Baba home after his father had taken him out to celebrate his high school graduation. When they arrive, Baba reveals the surprise present he has bought Amir for the occasion: an "old model Ford," "a Grand Torino," a car of his own for his journeys to and from college (116). They take it for a drive round the block and when he parks it in the lot of their apartment building and turns off the engine, he thanks his father and feels warmly grateful to him; but then, after a short silence, his father says, "I wish Hassan had been with us today" (116). Amir has an instant and intense respiratory response: "A pair of steel hands closed around my windpipe at the sound of Hassan's name" (116). Amir rolls down the window and waits "for the steel hands to loosen their grip" (116). This moment of acute sensation is also a moment of cognition, even if Amir does not, perhaps cannot, put into words what he knows at this point: it is the knowledge of the enormity of Hassan's absence, of his own responsibility for this, and of the way it grieves Baba as well.

Conclusion: To Breathe More Freely

In Chapter 20 of *Kite*, in his first fear-filled encounter with the Taliban in Kabul, it is only when the Talib, who has been holding Amir's gaze, looks away that "I found I could breathe again" (217). Here fear produces an incapacity to breathe properly that also anticipates the very real possibility, in this situation, that the Taliban may turn against him, and he may never breathe again. Instead, it eventually works out in the novel that Amir is able to breathe more freely, in a psychological and ethical sense, because he is able to start to atone partly for his desertion and entrapping of Hassan by helping, with his wife Soraya, to rear Hassan's orphaned son. If this is a partial redemption for Amir as an individual, it also provides an intimation of a possible partial remedy for Afghanistan in its treatment of the Hazaras and indeed for any country with a racist past: in order to breathe more freely in the present it is necessary to acknowledge that past and to start to try to compensate for it.

Works Cited

Doyle, Sir Arthur Conan. *A Study in Scarlet*. 1887. Penguin, 1981.

Hosseini, Khaled. *The Kite Runner*. 2003. Bloomsbury, 2011.

Sartre, Jean-Paul. *Huis clos* suivi de *Les mouches*. 1947. Gallimard, 1976.

"Avoid them like the plague": Clichés, Style, and Situations in *The Kite Runner*_____

Nicolas Tredell

"Avoid them like the plague" (172). This is the attitude to clichés, consciously and comically encapsulated in a cliché, which a creative writing teacher at San José State University in California, in Chapter 15 of *The Kite Runner*, advocates to a class that includes Amir, the first-person narrator of the novel and, at that time, a novice writer. But Amir inwardly dissents, employing two more clichés to do so; he has "always thought clichés got a bum rap" since they are often "dead-on"—absolutely accurate. Regrettably, he feels, "the aptness of the clichéd saying is overshadowed by the nature of the saying as a cliché" (172). This might look like a preemptive strike against the kind of criticism of *Kite* epitomized by the well-known critic Harold Bloom who dismissed Hosseini's first novel as "composed in clichés" (7). It seems rather odd that Bloom does this in his introduction to a collection of short essays and articles on *Kite* in the Bloom's Guides series for students—it is rather like a tourist guide in Washington DC rubbishing the Capitol building because it incorporates architectural features used in earlier edifices rather than highlighting the distinctive uses to which it puts those features; but besides Bloom's lack of decorum, in the classical sense of failing to fit his tone and language to the occasion, there are at least four serious objections to his indictment.

Four Objections

Firstly, his indictment does not consider, as Amir does, the possible positive uses of clichés, which may be, as Amir suggests, a precise verbal shorthand for common experiences. Secondly, it does not allow for the fact that the strenuous attempt to write a supposedly cliché-free text, encouraged by, among other things, creative writing classes, may result in a prose that is forced and mannered, moving too far from the energies of everyday speech. Thirdly, it does not take into account the possibility that the charge that a work of fiction is composed in clichés is itself a critical cliché, an easily available, even lazy way of categorizing and dismissing a work one dislikes for what may be other unacknowledged and unexplored reasons. Fourthly—and this is the most important for the purpose of this essay—Bloom's indictment, insofar as it is offered as an overall judgement on *Kite*, is inaccurate and cannot survive a close reading of the novel that attends not only to individual phrases but also to their place in the whole narrative.

Clichés both of expression and situation do of course, occur in *Kite*, as in any text (Bloom's introduction, even though it runs to only four paragraphs across one-and-a-quarter pages, is packed with them). Hosseini's first novel eschews stylistic exhibitionism, but it does not lack felicity and originality in its language, as this essay aims to demonstrate. In our case for the defense, we shall first consider, and challenge, Bloom's specific examples. We shall then explore how, more generally in *Kite*, alleged clichés are reanimated in three main ways: by drawing attention to them, effectively saying "I know these are clichés," but affirming their appropriateness and thus prompting us to look at them afresh; by putting them into different contexts that reawaken and extend their possibilities of meaning; and by developing them in ways that give new emphases to their original phrasing and meaning. Finally, we shall discuss clichés not only of expression but also of situation, those "stock situations" that recur in narrative fiction and in drama.

Clichés and Contexts

To support his case, Bloom offers only four examples, chosen, he tells us, by opening the novel "at random" (7) and selecting, from a mere two pages, three words and one phrase that he abstracts from their narrative contexts: "smiles that 'wilt,' lines 'etched' into aging faces, 'things . . . cooling off again' between former friends, 'gnawing' of nails" (7, Bloom's ellipsis in quote). The first two phrases Bloom selects, "wilt" and "etched," occur in Chapter 8, in a paragraph that makes a vital contribution to a scene that dramatizes a key phase in the most important relationship in *Kite*, the one between Amir and

Hassan. It is worth quoting the paragraph in full and bearing in mind its context in the whole novel:

> Hassan's smile wilted. He looked older than I'd remembered. No, not older, *old*. Was that possible? Lines had etched into his tanned face and creases framed his eyes, his mouth. I might as well have taken a knife and carved those lines myself. (80, italics in original)

Even if we accept that "wilt[ed]" is cliché, "Hassan's smile wilted" is a concise expression that quickly conveys, in the context, the impact of Amir's question as he tosses the overripe pomegranate up and down: "'What would you do if I hit you with this?'" (80). It also relates to a whole body of imagery in *Kite* that, going back to Shakespeare and earlier, employs images of natural growth as a measure of shortfalls in human fruition: Hassan is unable fully to flourish because of general racism and Amir's refusal to nurture him because he shares that general prejudice. "He looked older than I'd remembered" is a familiar expression, summing up a common experience of seeing someone again after an interval who seems to have aged more than one had anticipated, but the narrator does not leave it there, going on to qualify, amplify, and modify the adjective in a way that extends and defamiliarizes it: "No, not older, *old*"; and the enormity of the italicized adjective in this context is due to the fact that readers know that Hassan here is still a young boy. In the next sentence, "etched" may be a cliché—or perhaps simply a familiar usage—but the narrator almost immediately extends it, in the next sentence, and he once more does so in a defamiliarizing way that also turns what might in other circumstances be a mere observation (this person looks older than I recalled) into an awareness of culpability tantamount to a violent physical assault: "I might as well have taken a knife and carved those lines myself" (80).

This paragraph is a vital stage in the build-up to the core of this scene, a key element of the symbolic and existential patterns in the novel, in which Amir pelts Hassan with pomegranates, vainly trying to provoke his devoted friend into retaliation, until "Hassan was smeared in red like he'd been shot by a firing squad" (81)—a powerful simile in itself and one that echoes the bodily violation

Hassan has already suffered in the previous chapter in his rape by Assef and anticipates the swift and brutal death that, in Chapter 17, the Taliban will mete out to him as an adult with a bullet in the back of the head (192). To carp about supposed clichés in this scene is to affect or display an inability for imaginative engagement with the total experience the text offers.

The neglect of context is especially evident in Bloom's erroneous observation that the "cooling off" the narrator mentions is "between former friends"; it is in fact between Amir and his father, Baba, and indicates a significant phase in one of the key relationships in the novel; and again the familiar phrase "cooling off" serves well enough because of the way the novel elsewhere evokes those moments of warm intimacy between father and son, which the latter values so highly but which are so rare. The present participle "gnawing" takes on greater force through its connection, in its context, with reading and writing: "I'd gone back to thumbing through Hãfez and Khayyám, gnawing my nails down to the cuticles, writing stories" (81). Both "thumbing" and "gnawing" suggest how, for Amir, literature is a hands-on, bodily business. The anxiety signaled by the nail-gnawing relates both to the cooling of his relationship with his father and to his literary development as a reader and, above all, as a writer, and the depth of this anxiety is indicated by the phrase "down to the cuticles," the particularly sensitive part of the nails; this relates to a whole network of evocations of physical trauma in a novel that is a *Bildungsroman*, a novel about its protagonist's education by life, a *Künstlerroman*, a novel about the development of an artist, and a document, fictional but all-too-plausible, of pain suffered and only partly transcended.

This close examination of Bloom's rather exiguous evidence has argued that it does not support his general charge that *Kite* is "composed in clichés" (7). We can now pursue this argument in relation to other parts of the novel.

Reanimating Clichés

Clichés are usually "dead" metaphors and similes that have become so familiar they have lost their evocative power, like reliefs and inscriptions on coins worn smooth through frequent use; but the adjective "dead," applied to metaphors and similes, is itself a metaphor and, unlike animate creatures, metaphors and similes pronounced dead can be reanimated in the three main ways we outlined at the end of the third paragraph of this essay: by drawing attention to their familiarity while also implicitly or explicitly affirming their effectiveness; by placing them in different contexts; and by verbally extending them in new ways. An example of the first technique of reanimation occurs at the end of the passage in Chapter 15 with which this essay began, where the narrator contends that clichés get "a bum rap" (172); he concludes his defense by giving, as an example of a cliché, "the 'elephant in the room'" but affirming its absolute accuracy in certain situations: "Nothing could more correctly describe the initial moments of my reunion with Rahim Khan" (172).

Much earlier in the novel, in Chapter 2, we have an example of a passage that combines an implicit acknowledgment of employing a familiar usage with a recontextualization that gives it added weight. "People say that eyes are windows to the soul. Never was that more true than with Ali, who could only reveal himself through his eyes" (7). The opening of the first sentence, "People say" implicitly acknowledges that the phrase that will follow will be a familiar one, an example of common wisdom, and this duly follows: "eyes are the windows of the soul." The narrator has signaled, by the words "People say," that he is using the phrase not because he cannot think of anything better or fresher but because it seems to be a common expression that fits the situation. The next sentence takes it further, reminding us of what we have read a little earlier: that Ali has "a congenital paralysis of his lower facial muscles" that means he cannot smile and is "perpetually grim-faced" (7). This creates a different context for the familiar phrase: for Ali, the eyes are his only means of conveying emotion through facial expressions.

As a further example of the second form of reanimation, which works by recontextualization, consider the moment in Chapter 3 when Baba, in an unusual gesture of apparent affection, takes Amir on his lap as a prelude to challenging what the mullah at school has told his son: that drinking is a terrible sin. "I felt as if I were sitting on a pair of tree trunks" (14). The comparison of thick limbs to tree trunks is not new; but it works in the context to exemplify and to give particularity and solidity to what we have already been told, and will later be told, of Baba's bodily stature and strength and also serves as a preparatory physical reinforcement of the verbal challenge to the mullah's ideas that he will offer his son as the latter sits in his lap. It contributes to the total impression of the force of Baba's physique and personality that is so potent in *Kite* and makes his increasing bodily weakness and emaciation later on in the novel, when he is dying from cancer, more poignant by contrast. The arboreal image of "tree trunks" also suggests close contact with the natural world, which includes here the "natural" relationship of intimacy and affection between father and son for which Amir yearns but that he only occasionally enjoys.

An example of an image, in this case a simile, which is not wholly unusual, but which fits the context and is developed in significant ways, occurs in Chapter 8, at the lavish party Baba has thrown for Amir's thirteenth birthday. Amir, when he refuses Assef's invitation to join in a game of volleyball the following day, sees "the light wink out of Baba's eyes" (84)—Baba does not, of course, know that Assef has raped Hassan. The general image of the light fast-fading from the eyes is not new; but the phrasal verb "wink out" vividly conveys the quick change in Baba's expression and signals at once to Amir and to the reader the father's instant withdrawal of sympathy from his legitimate but disappointing son.

In Chapter 9, after the party, a moment from it recurs in Amir's mind, and, in his role as narrator, he uses a simile drawn from the predigital projection technology of the time to convey the insistent repetition of that moment upon his inward eye: "Like the times Kaka Homayoun's projector got stuck on the same slide, the same image kept flashing in my mind over and over: Hassan, his head downcast, serving drinks to Assef and Wali" (89). It is this recurrent image that will help to prompt him to drive Hassan from Baba's house.

The use of the technological projection of still images as a metaphor for mental processes is not new in fiction—Marcel Proust, in *À La Recherche du Temps Perdu* [*In Search of Lost Time*] (1913–27), famously describes a magic lantern that becomes, in the novel as a whole, a metaphor of how the imagination can transfigure solid reality, albeit in a fragile and fleeting way: "it substituted for the opaqueness of my walls an impalpable iridescence, supernatural phenomena of many colors, in which legends were depicted as on a shifting and transitory window" (1992, 8) ["*elle substituait à l'opacité des murs d'impalpables irisations, de surnaturelles apparitions multicolores, òu des legendes étaient dépeintes comme dans un vitrail vacillant et momentané*" (1988, 9)]. Proust's lantern is magical but not supernatural, producing its effects through a combination of optical physics and psychology; Hosseini's slide projector also produces its effects through a combination of optical physics and psychology, but its magic here signifies a malign mental process; it becomes an image of obsessive, recurrent memory ("over and over").

If we pursue the simile a little further, as the text permits and encourages us to do at this point, we can say projectors throw images on to a screen (or a flat white surface such as a wall that functions as an equivalent of a screen), and we can link this with the psychoanalytic idea of a "screen memory" that serves to mask another, more painful recollection; here the memory of Hassan with downcast head, serving drinks to his rapist and the latter's father who are, in Baba's view, welcome guests at Amir's birthday party, both masks and references the more painful memory of witnessing the rape itself.

Near the end of Chapter 9, when Hassan and Ali do finally leave Baba's house as a result of Amir's machinations, Baba drives them to the bus station on a rainy day and Amir watches them through the window as they depart. The text evokes the wet weather that complements Amir's sense of mingled relief, guilt, and mourning. In the sentence "Slithering beads of rain sluiced down my window" (94), the alliteration of "*Sl*ithering" and "*sl*uiced" and the noun "beads" combine to give a sense of the weight and movement of the rain, which resembles heavy tears. Although the phrase itself is not a cliché, it might seem that the situation is, in coming close to what

John Ruskin, in *Modern Painters* (152–67), called "the pathetic fallacy," in which meteorological conditions act in quasi-human ways that seem to reflect particular states of mind: thus, "slithering" might suggest a snake and link with the serpentine cunning that Amir has employed to ensure Hassan's eviction, while "sluiced down" might relate to the free flow of tears that Amir does not, in fact, shed but might do if he fully acknowledged the enormity of his treachery and the extremity of his loss.

This simple mirroring of emotions by the weather, however, is complicated by the last clause of the chapter, which reads: "all I saw was rain through windowpanes that looked like melting silver" (95), where there is a strange contradiction between the aesthetic beauty conjured up by the simile—"melting silver"—and the sadness of the situation. This, again, might seem a familiar trope, in a sense the ironic reverse of "the pathetic fallacy," in which the weather seems to contradict, rather than confirm, an emotion; and it is part of a wider familiar trope in which perception of beauty occurs at the same time as the awareness of pain and opens up the sense of a disjunction between the aesthetic and the experiential and of the incapacity of beauty, even or especially when one is aware of it, to allay emotional or physical suffering; but it effectively amplifies the pain and poignancy of the situation here.

We shall return to the issue of clichés of situation later in this essay; now we will consider key examples of phrases and images that draw on a familiar repertoire but develop them in distinctively different, defamiliarizing ways

Familiar But Strange

Consider the passage early in *Kite*, in Chapter 4, when Amir pretends to read to Hassan from a book but, in fact, makes up his own story, knowing that Hassan cannot read and check that story against the text. "To him, the words on the page were a scramble of codes, indecipherable, mysterious. Words were secret doorways and I held all the keys" (26). There are three metaphors here: codes and locked doors and keys (which we can treat, in this instance, as one metaphor, though it might not always be so). These metaphors give specific form to the adjective "mysterious" that immediately precedes it, and the sentence that includes them is especially evocative and rhythmically phrased. Later, Hassan will learn to read and write and will be able to unlock those doorways himself with the keys of literacy, but for the moment Amir holds power over him, and by concealing his own spontaneous authorship of the story, he deceives Hassan—one of a chain of deceits and evasions. The "secret doorways" image both fits the immediate situation being described and relates to extended themes in the novel: the power of words, individually and in narratives; the relationship between Amir and Hassan in which Amir's racism, mendacity, and manipulation come up against Hassan's undying loyalty.

Later in the novel, a word, in Chapter 17, this time a proper name, sparks off a process for which the novel offers another striking image. This is Amir's response to Rahim Khan's use of the name of Ali, whom Amir once thought was Hassan's biological father: "Hearing Rahim Khan speak Ali's name was like finding an old dusty music box that hadn't been opened in years; the melody began to play immediately" (188). The "music box"—and, more generally, the closed or locked box—is a familiar motif but again it is given new force by its context and the way it is extended. The simile of "an old dusty music box" that nonetheless starts "to play immediately" is a striking one, conveying the sense of a memory that seems neglected, obscured by time and dust, but at once returns when it is triggered. That return is imaged in an aural metaphor, as a melody heard by the inward ear, but a failure of visualization follows it, an inability inwardly to see Ali's face and—particularly important given the "congenital paralysis of his lower facial muscles" (7) mentioned back in Chapter 2 of the novel—his eyes; this failure generates a metaphor: "time can be a greedy thing—sometimes it steals all the details for itself" (188).

Metaphors of time are common enough in literature but often aim to convey its slowness or swiftness or inexorability: for example, "the world-without-end hour" in Shakespeare's Sonnet 57 (57; 5); "Times wingèd Charriot hurrying near" in Andrew Marvell's poem "To His Coy Mistress" (26; 22); "Time like an ever-rolling stream /

Bears all its sons away" in Isaac Watts' hymn "Our God, Our Help in Ages Past" (8; 8.1). There is a phrase from Ovid's *Metamorphoses*, "*tempus edax rerum*" (380; 15, 234), most commonly translated as "time, the devourer of things" but also, in Arthur Golding's 1565 translation, as "Time, the eater up of things" (442; 15, 258), which is an ancient and enduring example of an image of time as greedy, but *Kite* turns and develops this ancient trope here by making time greedy, not for the youth and life of human beings, but for the details that give vivacity and specificity to human memories, and this is significant in a novel in which memory figures so strongly, usually as a guilt-generating burden; Amir, for the most part, remembers all too well that which he would rather forget; but here he cannot recall visually what he would like to remember. Of course, making time take the rap may seem a form of displacement; it may be that it is not time that eats up the details but the censor in Amir's own troubled psyche that blocks him from fully recalling a figure woven into his earlier life whose son (as he then believed him to be) he betrayed; but, whatever the motivation for the image, it remains an intriguing one.

There is a range of other examples of phrases and images that the text of *Kite* defamiliarizes and develops. Read closely, the language of Hosseini's first novel cannot be dismissed as a composition in cliché. There is, however, another kind of cliché—situational cliché—which the novel might seem to exhibit, and we shall now consider this possible charge.

Clichés of Situation

As well as clichés of expression, which usually take the form of dead metaphors and similes that may be reanimated in the ways we have described above, there are also clichés of situation that can occur in narrative texts and are perhaps particularly evident in novels and plays—and in real life. Philip Larkin's poem "Fiction and the Reading Public" gives examples of these, envisaging a venal, vulgar reader who wants the kind of excitement from a novel that fictional versions of real-life situations like the following can provide: "Your

---

childhood, your Dad pegging out, / How you sleep with your wife"
(109; 1.7–8).

The title of Larkin's poem comes from a once influential book
by the mid-twentieth century Cambridge literary critic Q. D. Leavis.
Her *Fiction and the Reading Public* (1932) argued that there had
been a cultural decline that had resulted in canny authors who
produced bestsellers made up of stock situations that catered to a
debased reading public—of which the reader in Larkin's poem is
representative—who wanted sensation and consolation rather than
the bracing challenge of real literature. This argument was linked
with an almost automatic suspicion of bestselling authors who, it
was felt, must be bad to sell so well. This disdain for bestsellers,
not necessarily arising directly from Q. D. or F. R. Leavis, became
widespread in the mid-twentieth century and lingered into the
twenty-first; it underlies Bloom's attack on *Kite* and some other
assaults on Hosseini's first novel; there is still an assumption in
some quarters that a novel that sells millions of copies, as *Kite* has
done, must be bad—or at least, to use a mid-twentieth century term,
"middlebrow," denoting a mediocre piece of fiction that was not
utterly base and that even purported to tackle serious themes but fell
well below the highest literary standards.

Kite is vulnerable to this charge insofar as it includes all the
elements Larkin's poem gives as examples of stock situations—
childhood, a dying father, matrimonial sex (even if the last is
discreetly handled)— and adds more that figure strongly in our
twenty-first-century sense of what constitutes "real life": child
rape, war, public execution on the dark side and, on the brighter
side, the possibility of matrimonial and familial happiness and the
ambivalent but alluring trajectory of success and fame (in Amir's
rise to prominence as a novelist). Childhood, death, and sex (not
necessarily matrimonial and perhaps conspicuous by its absence)
are, of course, universal elements of life as well as common aspects
of fiction, and rape, child abuse, war and execution, and success
and fame are fairly recurrent features of human history; fictional
and factual narratives characteristically deploy several of these in
explicit or indirect ways.

In *Kite*, however, these elements are given particular prominence by the parallels, repetitions, and substitutions in the structure and plot of the novel: for instance, Hassan's threat in Chapter 5 to shoot a walnut-sized rock from his slingshot into Assef's left eye in order to protect Amir (36–37) is paralleled and then actualized in Chapter 22 by Hassan's son, Sohrab, who turns the threat into reality by shooting a brass ball from a table base into Assef's left eye (253–54), and thus not only duplicates but also extends and intensifies his father's rescue of Amir into a punishment for Assef's rape of his father. Baba fails to encourage, indeed barely acknowledges, Amir's literary endeavors, but Amir finds a substitute, a surrogate father in this respect at least, in Rahim Khan, who acts as a kind of mentor (e.g. 87). In Chapter 13, Amir and Soraya confirm they cannot have children, but Sohrab becomes their substitute son and at the end of the novel it seems possible that Amir might be the kind of father to Sohrab that his own father never was to Hassan or to Amir himself; Amir fails to help Hassan as a boy but risks his life to rescue Hassan's son, his own half-nephew.

These parallels and substitutions give the novel a quality that makes it less like "real life" as usually conceived but takes it into the realm of fable, fairy-tale, and allegory—and this too risks entering into a climate of cliché because fables, fairy tales, folk tales and allegories, in their generic components if not their specific details, are familiar or accessible to us all in one way or another. Such apparently non-realistic elements of the plot and structure of *Kite* help to make the novel highly readable but might also, as one steps back from immersion in the story, seem to invite Fabian's remark in Shakespeare's *Twelfth Night*: "If this were played upon a stage now, I could condemn it as an improbable fiction" (59; 3.4.126–27).

The narrator, however, defends what might seem unlikely coincidences in his story, as he defends clichés, with another proverbial saying that might itself sound like a cliché. In Chapter 22, he recognizes the true identity of the senior Talib whose "dark round sunglasses" (236) had, in the previous chapter, make him look, ironically, like John Lennon, the ex-Beatle and popstar preacher of peace and love. The Lennon lookalike is, in fact, Assef: "What was the old saying about the bad penny? My past was like that, always turning up" (246). The implicit claim, reinforced by the proverbial expression, is that coincidences and recurrences do happen not only in fiction but also in real life, and the familiar quality of the proverb, in this context, sounds an ironic counterpoint to the extreme, life-threatening situation Amir is in while also signaling the possibility, if he survives, of returning to the security of everyday commonplaces.

The narrator of *Kite* also offers a more explicit defense of coincidence, which, as with his defense of clichés of expression, might seem a preemptive strike against the charge that his tale is an improbable fiction, one that relies on what we have called clichés of situation. This occurs after his encounter with the old beggar on the streets of Kabul who turns out to be a former university lecturer in Farsi literature who knew his mother and who, in just over a page, teaches him "more about [his] mother" than Baba, his father, "ever did" (219). Afterwards, the narrator remarks that "most non-Afghans would have seen [this] as an improbable coincidence, that a beggar on the street would happen to know my mother" (219). But "in Afghanistan, and particularly in Kabul, such absurdity was commonplace" (220). Here, improbable coincidences are seen as a peculiarly Afghan phenomenon and thus spring from the setting of this part of the novel and the provenance of its narrator and other key characters; but it could be argued that such coincidences are a necessary staple of all narrative and possibly of life. Most people have experienced, even if only occasionally, coincidences that seem improbable, and they are even more likely to occur in narratives, particularly in narratives not wholly wedded to realism.

Larkin's poem "Fiction and the Reading Public" envisages a final demand from the imagined reader of novels: a feel-good ending that gives a vague sense that a benign providence has guided events towards an optimistic outcome—that things have, in a notable catchphrase used by the English entertainer George Formby, "turned out nice again." It may appear at the end of *Kite* that things "turn out nice again," even if only in a provisional way. Sohrab becomes the child Amir and Soraya never had and caring for him at last enables the couple to start to fulfil their thwarted parental aspirations and helps

Amir to make at least some atonement for his cruel, cowardly, and racist rejection, in his boyhood, of Hassan. As the novel concludes, it seems possible that Sohrab is starting to emerge from his silence and relate to Amir as a surrogate father, opening up the possibility of a father-son relationship that Baba, for different reasons, never enjoyed with his own sons, Amir and Hassan, and of a mother-son relationship Amir never had because his mother died giving birth to him. This may seem too easy a resolution of the agonies of Amir's own life and, in a more general way, of the conflicts between Hazara and Pashtun. It may seem, as with the deployment of such elements as your childhood, your father dying, and your sexual life with your spouse, to provide the oversweet cloying icing on the cake of a book that now seems both destined and designed to become a global bestseller.

That partly depends, however, on how we define the genre of *Kite*: it is neither tragedy nor comedy but occupies the kind of territory explored most famously in those late Shakespeare plays we now call "romances"—*Cymbeline, Pericles, The Winter's Tale,* and *The Tempest*—in which characters create through their own folly seemingly intractable situations that the play eventually resolves in a partly magical and improbable way so that, things "turn out nice again"; this is also the case with *Kite*, where the kinds of parallels and substitutions we have mentioned contribute to the novel's magical and improbable progress and resolution. We need not see these as clichés or evasions but as drawing on common aspiration and experience; we want things to turn out nice again and sometimes—not always–they do. In *Kite*, however—and this is part of its strength—that kind of resolution is not enough to erase the mark, embodied in Amir, of immitigable loss. There may, indeed, be in Rahim Khan's phrase that recurs in the novel, "*a way to be good again*" (2, 168, 198, 270); but there is no way to wipe off wholly what the Romantic poet and visual artist William Blake called "the tears of woe" (179).

Works Cited

Blake, William. "If you trap the moment." In "Poems from the Note-Book 1793," no. 42. *Complete Writings with Variant Readings*, edited by Geoffrey Keynes. Oxford UP, 1974, p. 179. https://www.poetrynook. com/poem/if-you-trap-moment-its-ripe.

Bloom, Harold. Introduction. Khaled Hosseini's *The Kite Runner*, edited by Harold Bloom. Bloom's Guides series. Infobase Publishing, 2009, pp. 7–8.

Golding, Arthur. *The.xv.* [15] *Books of P. Ouidius Nafo, entytuled Metamorphosis, tranflated oute of Latin into Englifh meeter by Arthur Golding Gentleman, A worke very pleafaunt and delectable.* 1567. Quotation above from *Ovid's* Metamorphoses, edited with an Introduction and Notes by Madeleine Forey. Penguin, 2002. archive.org/stream/shakespearesovid00oviduoft/ shakespearesovid00oviduoft_djvu.txt.

Hosseini, Khaled. *The Kite Runner*. 2003; Bloomsbury, 2011.

Larkin, Philip. "Fiction and the Reading Public." In *The Complete Poems*, edited and with an introduction and commentary by Archie Burnett. Faber & Faber, 2014, pp. 108–09.

Marvell, Andrew. "To His Coy Mistress." In *The Poems & Letters of Andrew Marvell in Two Volumes: Vol. I: Poems*, edited by H. M. Margoliouth. Clarendon P, 1927, pp. 26–27. www.poetryfoundation. org/poems/44688/to-his-coy-mistress.

Ovid [Publius Ovidius Naso]. *Metamorphoses Books IX–XV* [9–15]. With an English translation by Frank Justus Miller, revised by G. P. Goold. Harvard UP, 1994. https://www.thelatinlibrary.com/ovid/ovid.met15. shtml.

Proust, Marcel. *Du côté de chez Swann. A la recherche du temps perdu I* [1913]. Édition présentée et annotée par d'Antoine Compagnon. Gallimard, 1992.

_____. *In Search of Lost Time I: Swann's Way*. Translated by C. K. Scott Moncrieff & Terence Kilmartin. Revised by D. J. Enright. Chatto & Windus, 1992.

Ruskin, John. "Of the Pathetic Fallacy." *Modern Painters*. Vol. 3, Part 4, *Of Many Things*, Chapter XII [12]. [1856] Library Edition: The Complete Works of John Ruskin, National Library Association, ebook 2012, pp. 152–67. www.gutenberg.org/files/38923/38923-h/38923-h.htm#CHAPTER_XII.

Shakespeare, William. *The Sonnets*, edited by Katharine Duncan-Jones. Arden Shakespeare Third Series. Thomson Learning, 2007.

_____. *Twelfth Night*, edited with a commentary by M. M. Mahood. Introduction by Michael Dobson. Penguin, 2005.

Watts, Isaac. "Hymn [Our God, Our Help in Ages Past]." In *The Centuries' Poetry: Pope to Keats*, compiled by Denys Kilham Roberts. Centuries' Poetry series. Penguin, 1944, pp. 7–8. www.poetryfoundation.org/poems/50583/our-god-our-help.

The Kite Runner on Film: A Survey of Responses

Robert C. Evans

Khaled Hosseini's 2003 novel *The Kite Runner*, about two boyhood friends in Afghanistan named Amir and Hassan, sold extremely well. In fact, the book remained at the top of the *New York Times* best-seller list for two straight years. However, the 2007 film based on the book—directed by Marc Forster from a screenplay by David Benioff—was much less well received. In fact, the movie even helped generate some second thoughts about the book: some reviewers suggested that the film highlighted flaws already evident in the general structure, individual characterizations, and specific plot developments of the novel. The purpose of this essay, then, is to survey critical responses to the film. Bringing all this information together in one place may assist readers of the novel, viewers of the film, and especially students and teachers who view the film when studying the novel. Reviews of *all* films, unfortunately, often disappear from the Internet when particular links no longer work, when particular publications shut down, and when (as is increasingly the case), various publications move their content behind expensive pay walls.

Negative Reviews

Some negative reviews of Forster's film were particularly harsh. Joe Morgenstern of the *Wall Street Journal* said the filmmakers had "discharged their debt" to the novel "dutifully, but without daring or passion." He called the depiction of the boys' friendship "touching at the outset" but thought that ultimately the story "never catches fire" because the actors playing the boys were "nonprofessional youngsters who act as if they'd been directed to concentrate on one emotional state at a time—happiness, willfulness, devotion, submissiveness—and had done their work all too earnestly." Overall, Morgenstern thought the pace alternated between deliberate and sluggish. Even the crucial scene, an instant of betrayal that leads to the hero's decades-long quest for expiation and redemption, proves perfunctory, though it's tasteful enough, if that's what you want from a depiction of ghastly predation.

Morgenstern asserted that "the only reliable source of energy is Homayoun Ershadi, a powerful actor who plays Baba," Amir's father, and in fact many other critics also hailed Ershadi's performance. Indeed, Morgenstern implied that the movie would have succeeded better if it had concentrated more on Baba's tale.

Ken Fox, writing in *TV Guide*, was also disappointed by much of the characterization and/or acting, especially by Khalid Abdalla as the adult Amir, whom many critics found altogether too subdued. Fox called Abdalla "dull" but also criticized the allegedly "skimp[y]" adaptation, with its "bland melodrama and absurd dramatics." After faulting contrivances in the novel's own plot, Fox found the film even worse: "Stripped of Hosseini's smooth prose, the tale looks and sounds even clunkier, and the endless coincidences that somehow manage to make things 'good again' simply seem preposterous." Similarly, Mick LaSalle, at *SFGate. com* (affiliated with the San Francisco *Chronicle*), wrote that although the movie was in "many ways . . . worthy," the "terseness of Hosseini's prose has been replaced by . . . sentimentality," resulting in "a film that's longer and lusher and gushier than it should have been." LaSalle gave the movie only two-and-a-half stars out of a possible five.

Similarly unimpressed was Manohla Dargis, writing in the *New York Times*. Dargis argued that "David Benioff's clumsy screenplay doesn't broadcast its political naïveté as openly" as the book did, "but only because the filmmakers seem to assume that . . . the movie audience doesn't care about such matters." Dargis thought Benioff had "gesture[d] in the direction of Communists and mullahs, the Soviet invaders and the Taliban insurgents," but she maintained that "none of these players figure into the story in any meaningful fashion." In fact, Dargis claimed that "Forster, following the script's lead, scrupulously avoids politics and history—there are no causes or positions, just villains and horrors." Dargis thought Forster had offered only "a succession of atmospheric, realistic landscapes, colorful sights and smiling boys. And kites. Lots and lots of bobbing, darting, high-flying kites." Dargis also complained that despite "the film's far-flung locations (it was shot primarily in China), there is remarkably little of visual interest here; the setups are banal, and the scenes lack tension, which no amount of editing can provide." Like most other critics, she praised Homayoun Ershadi but thought the film lacked many other "credible performances." She found the "two lead child actors, both nonprofessionals, . . . predictably appealing, but only because they're children."

William Arnold, in the Seattle *Post-Intelligencer*, began with praise, calling *The Kite Runner* "sensitive" and "touching." But he ultimately judged it only "a qualified success" because of a flawed adaptation that "misses the mark by more than a few inches." Arnold thought the kite-flying was "a splendid visual metaphor" and that "the movie grabs us with its striking visuals and poignant, Oscar-worthy performances by Ershadi (as Amir's father) and Ahmad Khan Mahmoodzada (as the young Hassan)." But he wrote that "unlike the novel, the script can't get inside Amir's head, so what he's thinking and feeling during and after that crucial childhood rape of his best friend is never clear. His cowardly actions," Arnold said, "are not just unsympathetic, they're unfathomable." As his review progressed, his reactions became increasingly negative. He contended that "halfway through the movie . . . we lose all empathy and connection with [Amir] as a compelling protagonist." Arnold believed that a "gifted actor or even a strong star presence might have been able to bridge this gap, but Khalid Abdalla . . . walks through the role of the adult Amir with so little hint of a tortured soul that he seems to have no tragic dimension whatsoever." Arnold's review, then, evolved from initial praise to strong criticism.

Michael Phillips, in the *Chicago Tribune*, was also generally unimpressed. He considered the film, "with its handily reappearing and easily avenged villain," insufficiently convincing and argued that the movie compressed the book's "Dickens-but-worse hardship very tightly, so that the characters are perpetually shadowed by menace" and also so that "there's never any breathing room or offhanded behavioral surprise." He called Forster "all business here, his directorial eye seeing everything in straightforward, earnest, head-on and rather flat terms. Similarly," he complained, "Benioff reduces 'The Kite Runner' to its key plot points." Forster, Phillips argued, "clearly saw great computer-generated possibilities in the film's kite-flying sequences. Too many, in fact: The kite dogfights grow wearisome and fussy, and you're made grindingly aware of the digital trickery involved." He faulted the film for omitting much sense of "cultural dislocation," but he did praise "the lovely performance of Iranian native Ershadi, who suggests worlds of weary feeling in the role of Amir's father, a lion in his pre-Taliban homeland, a gas station attendant in his adopted country. The film," he wrote, "seems to breathe easier when he's on screen." But he thought Ershadi appeared too infrequently. Phillips gave the movie only two out of a possible four stars.

A slightly more generous grader was Matt Prigge, of the *Philadelphia Weekly*, who gave the film a "C." Prigge thought the movie displayed a "certain recklessness," saying that it "shoots first and thinks later." He did praise the movie "for being filmed largely in its native tongues (though China wound up standing in for Kabul for obvious reasons)." But he also thought it lost "most of its credibility," partly because the unskillful Forster had "pump[ed] the film full of slick crane shots and shameless music cues" and had "dumb[ed] down Hosseini's tale with plenty of for-the-ignorant-Westerners factoids." Prigge argued that no matter how one viewed the movie–as "faux-neorealist kiddie pic, immigrant saga, [or] actioneer" —it failed "to convince or coalesce" but instead " rest[ed] on the laurels of its source," hoping fans would "fill in the numerous gaps in the adaptation." Prigge found "something distasteful about a film that skips over the misery of one [character] to highlight the minor growth of another. Whether thanks to the muddled script or the blandness of Abdalla," Prigge concluded, "Amir's grief over his inaction remains strictly figurative, never visceral."

Ella Taylor, in the *Village Voice*, began by proclaiming that besides kites, "not much else soars" in a film she condemned as a "flaccid" potboiler and as "a drama as bland and beige as its tasteful palette," with sluggish "pacing" besides. "It doesn't help," she continued, that the adult Amir "is played with dour lack of expression" by Abdalla. She thought *"The Kite Runner* only wakes up, and then just a little, on its trips back to Kabul." Taylor could not "fault Forster's efforts to honor his subject—the dialogue is in Dari, an Afghan dialect, and the boys, both played by kids found in Kabul, make a soulfully appealing pair." But she thought the director's effort "to respect local culture drains even the final act . . . of the novel's propulsive momentum." She found the film, "like Hosseini's novel, . . . all too circumspect about America's role in making Afghanistan the mess it is today."

Another negative assessment—this one by Keith Phipps—began by stating that it would take "a special kind of heartlessness not to be moved by moments in *The Kite Runner*," but he quickly added that "it also takes an unusual amount of guilelessness not to be a little suspicious of it as well." Although praising the film's message, he thought "the means of delivery . . . gets in the way." According to Phipps, although the movie shifts gear from a film about the delicate relationships between children of different backgrounds to an immigrants-in-America story to finally an awkward action film, each part of *The Kite Runner* confirms Marc Forster as the Michael Bay of movie dramas.

Bay was a director known for slick, fast-paced, action-packed films, and Phipps thought that although in Forster's movie every detail had been "designed for maximum impact, . . . the effect grows deadening after a while." He considered it "okay to be manipulated, so long as you don't feel the strings being pulled. Here the tug is constant, and constantly distracting." He awarded *The Kite Runner* a "C."

Yet another negative review—but mixed with a bit of praise—came from Steve Davis of the Austin, Texas *Chronicle*. Davis considered the movie "faithful to the novel to a fault, retaining a level of narrative detail that bogs down the principal storyline." He thought that as "the simple and loyal Hassan, young [Ahmad Khan] Mahm[oo]dzada is perfectly cast—his eyes are expressive beyond their years, and he projects the inherent goodness essential to the role. But as the film progresses," Davis felt, "the narrative focus gets diluted and never really recovers." Davis thought some "of the improbabilities in the third act of Hosseini's book seem even more unlikely on the screen" than in the text: "the villain is a sadistic pedophile," and "the thematic essence" is "marred by the heightened melodramatics that undermined" the novel's conclusion. Nevertheless, Davis called the "kite-fighting sequences . . . magnificent," saying they had been "staged and shot by Forster like aerial dogfights." He added that "Alberto Iglesias' beautiful score adds much to these poetic skirmishes." Davis contended that "during these scenes . . . *The Kite Runner* soars, only to be inevitably brought down to earth by the remainder of the movie." He awarded the film only two-and-a-half stars.

Like Davis, Kenneth Turan of the *Los Angeles Times* offered a generally negative assessment that included some genuine praise. Turan called the movie "a house divided against itself," saying it ironically depicted one part of the novel "so well that its success underlines what's lacking in what remains." Turan, commending Forster's "gifted" work "with child actors," therefore felt "disappointment and regret" when the movie shifted from Kabul to "the flatter, less-nuanced sphere of Afghans exiled in California." He admired the filmmakers' efforts to "help the young actors capture the real camaraderie between the boys." But he felt that one reason the movie got

> into trouble despite being faithful to the book is that things play differently on screen than they do on the page. Even though Amir's actions are identical in both places, on the page, because he is the narrator, we have an instinctive sympathy with him. On screen, he is presented as one of many characters, and though we understand why he feels so glum so much of the time, it is not as involving to be with him as an adult as it is as a child.

Ultimately, Turan found the film "acceptable enough in a discreetly sentimental way" but thought that it generally lacked "the life that animates the flashback sections. 'The Kite Runner,'" he concluded "may fly, but it never soars."

Mixed Responses

David Denby, writing for the *New Yorker*, made the interesting point that shame–the film's main theme—"is rarely an active emotion." He felt that this might help account "for the movie's slight stiffness and hesitancy" but added that "the dangers of staging a rape scene with children may have been inhibiting as well." Denby kept wanting "the actors to cut loose" but thought "Khalid Abdalla is [mostly] forced to stand around looking stricken." He reported that Forster "worked with some of the actors through translators, which slowed the tempo and killed colloquial ease." Although Denby considered "the dialogue . . . well written," he sensed a "dead air around the lines." The "best things in 'The Kite Runner,'" he wrote, "are the portrait of Kabul's flourishing upper-class life before the Soviets and then the Taliban took over, and the depiction of the bleak hypocrisies of the Taliban period." He concluded that although the "movie's heart is certainly in the right place—it's a quietly outraged work," he wished it contained "more excitement."

In the New York *Daily News*, Jack Matthews also had mixed responses, calling *The Kite Runner* an "eye-opening story that doesn't quite hold together as a movie" but praising it for dealing with the subject of honor "in ways rare to mainstream film." Its "three sections," he observed, "are geographic—Afghanistan to California and back again," adding that if "that sounds confusing, it's just the opposite. The movie, like the novel, is as symmetrical as an equilateral triangle; you can be sure that hints dropped in part one will return before the end of part three. That symmetry," Matthews continued, "creates the film's one false note, which nearly destroys the entire third act. You'll know it when you trip over it, as I did. Still," the reviewer maintained, "this story is so different from anything else and so topical that it fascinates." Matthews said both the novel and the movie are crammed with literary devices that begin to build to a tinny sound. And I'm not sure Amir ever makes up for the harm he did to Hassan; despite Khalid Abdalla's genial performance, I didn't like Amir either as a child or an adult.

Nevertheless, Matthews thought "the movie has two extraordinary characters and performances. Non-pro Ahmad Khan Mahmoodzada breaks your heart as the innocent, wide-eyed child Hassan, and Homayoun Ershadi makes Amir's father a model of intuitive decency."

One especially substantial mixed review came from Ty Burr in the Boston *Globe*. Burr began by mocking Hosseini's book, reassuring readers that no "literature was harmed in the making of 'The Kite Runner,'" because, to be brutally frank, the beloved best-selling novel . . . doesn't qualify." Burr called Hosseini's work "a gripping fictional memory play that devolves into a human rights potboiler, with enough melodrama, coincidence, and guilt to make D.W. Griffith blush and Oprah swoon." But Burr quickly added, "That's all right—the movies run on melodrama and they always have. Even at its most tortuously plotted, the book has the sentimental sweep of cinema; it opens up like a film as you read it. An actual big-screen adaptation seems a little redundant."

Burr praised Forster for having "handsomely directed" the movie and even said the director's "way with a narrative is more skilled" than Hosseini's, even if "just as earnest. 'Kite Runner,'" Burr continued, "is an honorable, middlebrow affair . . . that replicates the strengths and shamelessness of the book. The first half" incisively portrays "a Kabul boyhood, the second a spiraling series of convenient events. Perhaps the nerviest aspect," Burr wrote, "is that it asks mainstream American audiences to attend to a tale lacking Hollywood stars and English-language dialogue, one that takes place in a country known to many only from misunderstood headlines."

Burr called the film "mostly a universal tale of youth—an Afghan 'To Kill a Mockingbird,'" and wrote that, "like that classic, 'Kite Runner' has an all-knowing father figure: Homayoun Ershadi as Amir's Baba, gruff and Westernized, spitting contempt at the Islamic priests. It also has a combination magic child/sacred martyr in Hassan." He praised the film's "soaring digital camerawork" but felt that the "delicate play of betrayal, guilt, and projection" was handled in the film "more clumsily than in the book," since "a camera can only photograph the outside of repression." Burr said, "our sympathy with [the adult] Amir is tested further by the blank-faced coldness of the young actor playing him." He felt, however, that the American scenes had "a mawkish but satisfying comic ordinariness to them" since they deal with "the drama of learning to fit in."

Once more comparing the novel and the film, Burr suggested that where "the book turned overwrought to the point of masochism, . . . Forster pulls back, easing up on most of the coincidences except the big one involving the return of a bully from Amir's youth." Burr found himself feeling

> of two minds about this. A movie that held on to all the breathless tearjerkery of the novel would probably have to star Bette Davis as Amir, but as amended by Forster the story is now touching and somewhat dull. The movie glances at the real horrors of a theocratic dictatorship—the public stonings, the private power-mongering—but only on the way to soothing a fictional dilemma.
>
> That's a loss. The symbolic self-flagellation Hosseini puts his hero through could make a great, crazy movie about guilt and homeland, assimilation and ethnic authenticity, but you'd need a less cautious cook to make it—one willing to break some eggs.

The Kite Runner, Burr predicted, would "be loved by many moviegoers for its taste and humanity," but he felt that despite "all the places Forster takes us he doesn't show us anything we haven't seen." Altogether, Burr offered one of the most considerable, if ambivalent, analyses the film received from any critic.

Also offering both praise and criticism was Rick Groen of the Toronto *Globe and Mail*. Groen called the film "a safe adaptation" that "lifts from the novel the sturdy bones of the plot, fleshes them out with a talented international cast, travels to China" for credible location shots, and "then mounts the whole tale on the screen with workmanlike aplomb." The result, Groen said, "is very easy to like and even, on occasion, to thoroughly enjoy. What it's hard to be is moved, emotionally affected." He thought the "movie faithfully transposes the well-oiled, melodramatic machinery of the book, but, in so doing, exposes it too, taking Hosseini's hidden mechanics and making them overt. And that exposure," Groen asserted, "leads to the principal problem—machines inspire more admiration than love." He found, in Forster's project, both "abiding strengths" and "smaller but disconcerting flaws." He thought the "aerial shots of the multicolored kites soaring above the city's winter sky, pale blue circled by snow-capped peaks, should be lyrical." On the other hand, "Hassan's grievous wound, suffered in a lonely back alley, should be appalling. Instead, both are credibly rendered, yet neither is deeply affecting." Referring to the rapidly paced conclusion, Groen wrote that "you may be excused if, amid the many emotional highs and lows, all you truly feel is rushed." He ended, however, on an ambiguously positive note, commenting that *The Kite Runner* "gains more than it loses from [its] strict fidelity to the source material. Sure, the movie doesn't have the heart of the book, but it does have a solid mechanical pump, strong enough at least to keep a robust story on two-hour life support."

A similarly mixed-to-positive take was offered by Lou Lumenick of the New York *Post*, who thought the film "often rises to the occasion" but "never quite soars." He called it "not quite edgy or artistic enough to satisfy the art-house crowd, but a tough sell for family audiences because of its extensive subtitles, two-hour-plus running time, and a (tastefully rendered) male rape scene." Limerick gave Forster "major props for terrific performances by genuine Afghan youngsters" and also "for shooting in Western China, which stands in quite convincingly for 1978 Kabul." He said the film was "at its best during scenes showing an exciting kite-fighting competition." Interestingly, concerning the film's emotional impact, he reported that there "was no shortage of sobbing at the screening I attended," but he felt that ultimately "this is more an entertaining than a profound film that somehow seems rushed and overlong at the same time." He called its "depiction of contemporary Kabul . . . sobering" but said the movie "tiptoes around politics as cautiously as it does that ambiguously-filmed rape scene." Lumenick called the film a "worthy enterprise" and a "respectable tear-jerker."

Another mixed-to-positive assessment came from Michael Sragow of the Baltimore *Sun*, who praised Forster and Benioff for their "sensitive, potent job" in depicting the boys' "asymmetrical friendship" and who particularly commended an instance involving a pomegranate as an especially "stunning moment, one of the most wrenching in movies this year." Sragow called Ahmad

> heart-shriveling as Hassan, a rare contemporary character who surprises you with the depth of his goodness. [Ahmad] gives a preternatural performance, with all the exuberance of childhood and the underlying resignation of a saint. Yet it wouldn't work without Zekeria's startling embodiment of psychological agony and reflexive treachery.

Sragow felt, however, that most of the film did not approach this "level of accomplishment." Like various other critics, he thought the "story of the grown Amir (Khalid Abdalla) constricts the narrative instead of merely framing it" and argued that although the boy playing Amir was quite effective, "Abdalla never develops a similar magnetism as the adult Amir," who was turned "into a vehicle for point-making and score-settling rather than a full-bodied character." Again, like other critics, he thought the film's failings actually exposed weaknesses in the book: "Staying faithful to a 371-page novel, the filmmakers inadvertently highlight its melodramatic underpinnings while pruning Hosseini's superb descriptions of Afghan and immigrant life." Sragow considered "Amir's road to salvation . . . too neatly paved" and argued that "the pivotal action contains a central coincidence that's terrible in more ways than one."

Sragow ended, however, by emphasizing the film's strengths, saying that "Ari's performance as Sohrab lifts the movie up even when the plot offers cheapjack catharses. His keen, subtle portrait of sexual mortification brings home the infuriating sadness of the worst child exploitation—and persuades you that a child can use his own innate outrage to surmount it, given the chance." Sragow felt that "Forster always works wonders with children" and that this skill "redeems the intermittent obviousness and flatness of this film about escaping an unforgiving fatherland."

David Ansen, in *Newsweek*, had mixed views that tended toward the positive. He praised the filmmakers for remaining "true to the book—to both its heart-tugging, sentimental power and its sturdy, symmetrical 19th-century storytelling, as well as its sometimes clumsy melodrama." Like many critics, he especially commended "Ershadi's soulful, morally complex Baba [as] the film's standout performance" but felt that the "two memorable Afghan child actors are the heart of the movie. We miss them when they vanish from the story. The grown-up Amir seems rather bland and mopey in comparison." In fact, Ansen argued that the "American scenes, which is where the book has been most severely condensed, don't seem to engage Forster as deeply" as the scenes set in Afghanistan. Ansen considered "Forster's re-creation of the war-ravaged city . . . vivid" and even felt that in its final third the film "momentarily transforms itself into a cliffhanging action movie." All in all, he argued that although the film was not "subtle," it still allowed viewers

> to see a country and a culture from the inside: it puts a human face on a tragedy most of us know only from headlines and glimpses on the nightly news. It helps that the Afghan scenes are played in Dari, not English. Forster's solid, unpretentious movie hits its marks squarely, and isn't afraid to wear its heart on its sleeve. Only a mighty tough viewer could fail to be moved.

Finally, one more mixed-to-positive assessment was offered by Shawn Levy of *The Oregonian*. He praised the filmmakers for having "taken pains to keep things [on a] human scale" and for having "largely avoided the temptation to turn a hard story colorful and pleasing. As a result," he felt, "their film balances heart and brain, wonder and revulsion, sadness and hope." He thought the film was "best in the 1970s section, when Forster has the spectacle of the kites and two strong child actors to play with them. Once we switch to America," he believed, "the strength is chiefly found in Ershadi's impressive portrait of a man bent but not broken." In contrast, he thought the "return to Afghanistan slips into clumsiness and sensationalism a bit too often." Generally, however, Levy praised the "powerful and comely filmmaking" and considered "the decision to shoot [the movie] with virtually unknown actors and a variety of unfamiliar tongues . . . commendable. And, too, now and again it really does soar like a kite, and for those moments it's well worth seeing." He awarded it a grade of B+.

Positive Responses

Although positive responses were less numerous than negative and mixed reactions, the film did receive some very enthusiastic praise. Peter Rainer, in the *Christian Science Monitor*, briefly commended the movie for offering a story "that, on some primal level, goes straight to the heart." Peter Travers, in *Rolling Stone*, although calling the film "sometimes rushed, oversimplified and skimpy on the details of Afghan culture that informed the book," felt that "the tale still takes hold." Commenting specifically on the rape scene, he wrote that Forster, "working from a truncated script by David Benioff, doesn't sensationalize the attack, but its brutality comes through strongly," and he particularly commended the two boys for "heart-rending performances." He predicted that this was a film audiences would "take to heart." Finally, in another very brief positive reaction, Lisa Schwarzbaum of *Entertainment Weekly* awarded it a B and called it a "pretty good adaptation of Khaled Hosseini's pretty good 2003 best-seller," saying that Forster seems to have been "invigorate[d]" by the challenge of making the film.

Unlike the three reviewers just quoted, Carrie Rickey, in the *Philadelphia Inquirer*, extolled the film at length. She called it "wrenching and exhilarating" and praised it as an "excellent literary adaptation." She commended Forster for having elicited "natural performances from both young actors" and for "subtly" depicting their relationship. And, like practically every other critic, she especially admired Ershadi as Baba, calling him "magnificent," although (again like others) she felt less enthusiasm for "Abdalla as the grown Amir, very handsome and very uncomfortable as the film's mournful-eyed narrator." Rickey did find the "final act, with Western China doubling for Afghanistan, . . . rushed and incomplete," but she ultimately praised the film's "redemptive spirit" as "undeniably moving." She awarded *The Kite Runner* three and a half stars out of a possible four.

Similarly enthusiastic was Dan Jolin of *Empire Online*, who gave the movie four stars out of five. He praised "scripter" David Benioff for having "proven largely faithful to Hosseini's work" but did regret that both

> the source and its adaptation are frustratingly heavy-handed at points. The story feels too contingent on coincidence, too tidy for something which presents such a complex, messed-up situation as the ethnic divisions in pre- and post-Soviet Afghanistan. For the sake of neat parallels and clear dramatic echoes, what could be a big, sprawling story is boiled down to the interplay of just a handful of characters, all loose ends neatly tucked away.

Nevertheless, Jolin called Forster "a master of finding the strong, warm pulse of humanity in any script through the performances he teases from his cast." He particularly praised the boy playing the young Amir for displaying "an intelligence and sensitivity that belies his age, transforming what could be inexplicable actions into somehow understandable responses to horrific events." Jolin also thought the actor playing Hassan would be "guaranteed to get tears welling. Bold and loyal to the point of self-sacrifice," Hassan "could easily have come across as an unrealistic ideal, but due to Mahm[oo]dzada he's heart-achingly convincing." Jolin called the "adult cast . . . just as good," even the often-criticized Khalid Abdalla, who, in Jolin's opinion, portrayed "the grown-up Amir as a quiet, contemplative soul who's forced to confront both the phantoms of his past and, at one point, a very immediate, physical menace. But most memorable," Jolin said (agreeing with practically every other critic), was Ershadi as Baba. All in all, Jolin extolled the film as an "engaging melodrama whose less convincing plot points are superseded by some astonishingly affecting performances from the mostly unknown cast."

Writing in the *Washington Post*, Robin Givhan seemed less interested in the film itself than in its use of, and implications for, American popular culture. But she also asserted that it was "impossible not to be charmed" by the two boy actors, arguing that "Ahmad Khan Mahm[oo]dzada and Zekeria Ebrahimi have faces far more expressive and eloquent than any of the dialogue they recite. In particular," she said, "Ahmad Khan, who plays Hassan, has a face of such exquisite soulfulness that it's almost too much to bear. It takes approximately five seconds to fall in love with him." Givhan argued that the boys' interest in American pop culture made them even more appealing to US moviegoers: "Audiences don't need these touchstones to ease them into the lives of those who speak different languages and live in unfamiliar places, but they help. Images of an old American western [film] giving children who speak Dari as much pleasure as some child in Iowa closes a gap. It makes the distance between those lives a little less daunting." This was a point that Givhan then explored for the rest of her lengthy review.

The producers of *The Kite Runner*, however, must have been especially gratified by Richard Schickel's glowing review in the widely influential *Time* magazine. Under the headline *"The Kite Runner* Flies," Schickel wrote that the movie "doesn't feel like it has been, as people used to say, 'ripped from headlines.' It instead has about it something of the air of a big, rich, very old-fashioned novel." Although suggesting that that novel might be considered "second-rate popular fiction" that had nonetheless inspired a piece of "first-rate" filmmaking, Schickel anticipated criticism of his enthusiastic review:

> Yes, [the film] is full of contrivance and coincidence. Yes, it comes to an uplifting ending that is not entirely plausible. And yes, we somehow never doubt that the good people of this tale are somehow going to triumph, even when they lose everything and are immersed in historical darkness. That's because they have the only qualities that count in stories of this kind—pluck, decency and resilient spirits.

Schickel argued that

> the film works as well as it does because Forster does not particularly force our feelings for his characters; bad things keep happening to them (loss of fortune and status, exile and illness, above all the way great historical events keep impinging on their little lives), but they keep gamely forging ahead, recouping their dreams. Or revising them. Or replacing them with new ones.

According to Schickel, Forster was "fortunate that Hosseini has provided him with a lovely, appropriately cinematic novel and [the] controlling metaphor . . . of kite flying." Schickel particularly admired the kite-flying competitions: "It is a pretty game, but one that also hints at the ferocities that will follow." Schickel concluded by listing aspects of the movie he especially admired: "I like the balance Forster and screenwriter David Benioff achieve between large historical events and purely personal ones, I like the easy, but never slack, pace of their storytelling, and, above all, I like the way sympathetic portraits do not shade into sentimental ones. This is," he asserted, "a confident and honorable movie—and a gripping one." Surely Forster and Benioff must have enjoyed such praise from such an important critic.

Even more gratifying, however, must have been the unstinting praise from Roger Ebert, who was, at the time, perhaps the most widely read and widely admired film critic in the United States. Ebert's opinions would often determine whether audiences did or did not go to see new movies, and he awarded *The Kite Runner* his highest possible score: four very solid stars. His opening sentences already foreshadowed the tone of his entire review: "How long has it been since you saw a movie that succeeds as pure story? That doesn't depend on stars, effects or genres, but simply fascinates you with how it will turn out? Marc Forster's 'The Kite Runner,' based on a much-loved novel, is a movie like that." After summarizing the plot, Ebert wrote that "Forster and his screenwriter David Benioff have made a film that sidesteps the emotional disconnects we often feel when a story moves between past and present." He commended the film, despite its flashbacks, varied locations, and diverse plot developments, for never losing sight of the main narrative: "This is all the same story, interlaced with the fabric of [the chief characters'] lives." According to Ebert, the "film works so deeply on us because we have been so absorbed by its story, by its destinies, by the way these individuals become so important that we are forced to stop thinking of 'Afghans' as simply a category of body counts on the news." He called the boys' performances "natural, convincing and powerful," predicting that adult actors would "envy" them for the "conviction and strength" of their role-playing. Ebert thought that "Ahmad Khan Mahmoodzada, as young Hassan," was "particularly striking, with his serious, sometimes almost mournful face."

But Ebert also praised practically every other aspect of the film. He wrote, for instance, that one area "in which the movie succeeds is in its depiction of kite flying. Yes, it uses special effects, but they function to represent what freedom and exhilaration the kites represent to their owners." He ended by saying that this was "a magnificent film," a conclusion that would have led many filmgoers, who deeply trusted the much-loved Ebert, to walk out their doors and head for the cinema.

Conclusion

The widely divergent reactions to Forster's film version of *The Kite Runner* raise many intriguing questions about the film, the novel, and the nature of criticism itself. Comparing and contrasting responses to the movie and the book can help us see each more clearly. Comparing and contrasting the often very negative assessments of the film with the sometimes very positive assessments can, in turn, lead us to wonder whether criticism can ever be wholly objective. Which critics, if any, make the most persuasive arguments? Which, if any, make the least persuasive arguments? Is openness to persuasion a worthwhile attitude? Is persuasion even possible in cases such as this? These are just a few of the many questions that arise when surveying varied reactions not only to *The Kite Runner* but to any other work of art.

Works Cited

Ansen, David. "Review of *The Kite Runner.*" Review of *The Kite Runner*. Directed by Marc Forster. Screenplay by David Benioff. *Newsweek*, 8 Dec. 2007, n.p., www.newsweek.com/review-kite-runner-94841.

Arnold, William. "'The Kite Runner' Comes to the Screen as a Mixed Blessing." Review of *The Kite Runner*. Directed by Marc Forster. Screenplay by David Benioff. Seattle *Post-Intelligencer*, 13 Dec. 2007, n.p., www.seattlepi.com/ae/movies/article/The-Kite-Runner-comes-to-the-screen-as-a-mixed-1258688.php.

Burr, Ty. "Returning to Afghanistan, With a Heavy Heart." Review of *The Kite Runner*. Directed by Marc Forster. Screenplay by David Benioff. The Boston *Globe*, 14 Dec. 2007, n.p. archive.boston.com/ae/movies/articles/2007/12/14/returning_to_afghanistan_with_a_heavy_heart/.

Dargin, Manohla. "From Memories, There's No Escape." Review of *The Kite Runner*. Directed by Marc Forster. Screenplay by David Benioff. *New York Times*, 14 Dec. 2007, n.p., www.nytimes.com/2007/12/14/movies/14kite.html.

Davis, Steve. Review of *The Kite Runner*. Review of *The Kite Runner*. Directed by Marc Forster. Screenplay by David Benioff. The Austin, Texas *Chronicle*, 21 Dec. 2007, n.p., www.austinchronicle.com/events/film/2007-12-21/573379/.

Denby, David. "The Kite Runner." Review of *The Kite Runner*. Directed by Marc Forster. Screenplay by David Benioff. *The New Yorker*, 10 Dec. 2007, n.p., www.newyorker.com/magazine/2007/12/17/hard-life-2-2.

Ebert, Roger. "You Should Come Home. There Is a Way to Be Good Again." Review of *The Kite Runner*. Directed by Marc Forster. Screenplay by David Benioff. RogerEbert.com, 13 Dec. 2007, n.p., https://www.rogerebert.com/reviews/the-kite-runner-2007.

Fox, Ken. "*The Kite Runner.*" Review of *The Kite Runner*. Directed by Marc Forster. Screenplay by David Benioff. *TV Guide*, 13 Dec., 2007, n.p., www.tvguide.com/movies/kite-runner/review/290786/.

Givhan, Robin. "In 'Kite Runner,' A Culture Swoops into View: Our Own." Review of *The Kite Runner*. Directed by Marc Forster. Screenplay by David Benioff. *Washington* Post, 16 Dec. 2007, n.p., www.washingtonpost.com/wp-dyn/content/article/2007/12/14/AR2007121400543.html. [Paywall].

Groen, Rick. "Takes Flight But Can't Quite Soar." Review of *The Kite Runner*. Directed by Marc Forster. Screenplay by David Benioff. Toronto *The Globe and Mail*, 14 Dec. 2007, n.p., web.archive.org/web/20071216132549/https://www.theglobeandmail.com/servlet/story/RTGAM.20071213.wkite14/BNStory/Entertainment/home.

Jolin, Dan. "*The Kite Runner* Review." Review of *The Kite Runner*. Directed by Marc Forster. Screenplay by David Benioff. EmpireOnline.com, 30 Nov. 2007, n.p., web.archive.org/web/20171207134540/http://www.empireonline.com/movies/kite-runner/review/.

LaSalle, Mick. "Hosseini's Dry-Eyed 'Kite Runner' Yields Mushy Movie." Review of *The Kite Runner*. Directed by Marc Forster. Screenplay by David Benioff. San Francisco *Chronicle*, 14 Dec. 2007, n.p., www.sfgate.com/movies/article/Review-Hosseini-s-dry-eyed-Kite-Runner-yields-3299560.php#photo-2446712.

Levy, Shawn. *The Kite Runner*. Review of *The Kite Runner*. Directed by Marc Forster. Screenplay by David Benioff. *The Oregonian*, 21 Dec. 2007, n.p., www.oregonlive.com/madaboutmovies/2007/12/review_the_kite_runner.html.

Lumenick, Lou. "Lofty Effort to Soar." Review of *The Kite Runner*. Directed by Marc Forster. Screenplay by David Benioff. *New York Post*, 14 Dec. 2007, n.p., nypost.com/2007/12/14/lofty-effort-to-soar/.

Matthews, Jack. "'Kite Runner' Doesn't Quite Fly." Review of *The Kite Runner*. Directed by Marc Forster. Screenplay by David Benioff. New York *Daily News*, 3 June 2008, n.p., www.nydailynews.com/entertainment/tv-movies/kite-runner-doesn-fly-article-1.272084.

Morgenstern, Joe. "Sluggish 'Kite Runner.'" Review of *The Kite Runner*. Directed by Marc Forster. Screenplay by David Benioff. *The Wall Street Journal*, 14 Dec. 2007, n.p., web.archive.org/web/20160101231816/https://www.wsj.com/articles/SB119759112354128281.

Phillips, Michael. "Stilted 'Kite Runner' Fails to Soar." Review of *The Kite Runner*. Directed by Marc Forster. Screenplay by David Benioff. *Chicago Tribune*, 3 Oct. 2007, n.p., web.archive.org/web/20071110190325/http://www.chicagotribune.com/entertainment/movies/chi-071003kite-story,1,2594112.story?ctrack=5&cset=true.

Phipps, Keith. *The Kite Runner*. Review of *The Kite Runner*. Directed by Marc Forster. Screenplay by David Benioff. *A.V. Club*, 12 Dec. 2007, n.p., web.archive.org/web/20071216004614/https://www.avclub. com/content/cinema/the_kite_runner.

Prigge, Matt. *The Kite Runner*. Review of *The Kite Runner*. Directed by Marc Forster. Screenplay by David Benioff. *Philadelphia Weekly*, 19–25 Dec. 2007, n.p., https://web.archive.org/web/20071222080539/ http://www.philadelphiaweekly.com/articles/16069.

Rainer, Peter. "New in Theatres: *The Kite Runner*." Review of *The Kite Runner*. Directed by Marc Forster. Screenplay by David Benioff. *Christian Science Monitor*, 21 Dec. 2007, n.p., https://www. csmonitor.com/2007/1221/p15s01-almo.html.

Rickey, Carrie. "A Chance to Redeem a Mistake." Review of *The Kite Runner*. Directed by Marc Forster. Screenplay by David Benioff. *The Philadelphia Inquirer*, 13 Dec. 2007, n.p., www.inquirer.com/philly/ entertainment/movies/20071214_A_chance_to_redeem_a_mistake. html.

Schickel, Richard. "*The Kite Runner* Flies." Review of *The Kite Runner*. Directed by Marc Forster. Screenplay by David Benioff. *Time*, 14 Dec. 2007, n.p., content.time.com/time/arts/article/0,8599,1694685,00.html.

Schwarzbaum, Lisa. "The Kite Runner." Review of *The Kite Runner*. Directed by Marc Forster. Screenplay by David Benioff. *Entertainment Weekly*, 9 Jan. 2008, n.p., ew.com/article/2008/01/09/kite-runner-3/.

Sragow, Michael. "Young Actors Give 'Kite Runner' Its Altitude." Review of *The Kite Runner*. Directed by Marc Forster. Screenplay by David Benioff. *The Baltimore Sun*, 21 Dec. 2007, n.p., https://web. archive.org/web/20080725172701/https://www.baltimoresun.com/ entertainment/movies/reviews/bal-to.kite21dec21,0,3784190.story.

Taylor, Ella. *The Kite Runner*. Review by Ella Taylor. Review of *The Kite Runner*. Directed by Marc Forster. Screenplay by David Benioff. Westword, 20 Dec. 2007, n.p., www.westword.com/film/the-kite-runner-5096800.

Travers, Peter. "The Kite Runner." Review of *The Kite Runner*. Directed by Marc Forster. Screenplay by David Benioff. *Rolling Stone*. 13 Dec. 2007, n.p., www.rollingstone.com/movies/movie-reviews/the-kite-runner-251948/.

Turan, Kenneth. "'Kite's' Tale Can't Get Off Ground." Review of *The Kite Runner*. Directed by Marc Forster. Screenplay by David Benioff. *Los Angeles Times*. 14 Dec. 2007, n.p., www.latimes.com/archives/la-xpm-2007-dec-14-et-kite14-story.html.

Staging *The Kite Runner*

Nicolas Tredell

The Kite Runner, with its vivid scenes and compelling narrative, is a novel rich in theatrical possibilities. But adapting it for the stage presents a range of challenges. Some of these are challenges that any substantial novel would present, but others are more specific to *Kite*. It is crammed with events and incidents that arouse excitement and emotion. Its geographical reach is wide, encompassing Kabul, Peshawar, and California. It engages with a variety of cultures and languages. It covers nearly forty years of historical upheaval in Afghanistan and the United States. It encompasses traumas and rites of passage in the lives of its chief characters that include birth, childhood, adolescence, young adulthood, middle age, old age, and death. It contains violent and disturbing scenes, difficult to represent adequately in the theater, particularly the event on which the narrative and plot of the novel turn—the rape of a boy by a teenager—which raises the issue of whether and, if so, how, such an act should be portrayed on stage. The novel has a first-person narrator who not only evokes but also analyzes and assesses his experiences from an older vantage-point, posing the questions of whether a dramatic adaptation should ignore this or find some way of incorporating it— and if so, what way.

As well as these questions that, as it were, the novel itself poses, there are also questions that relate to its main readership. Still largely ignored and sometimes explicitly disdained by academic critics, *Kite*, as a novel, has a vast popular readership, and online feedback, via Amazon and other digital platforms, suggests it has the power to arouse intense emotional engagements—affective responses for which academic criticism has no adequate appreciative vocabulary, reaching easily for dismissive terms such as "melodramatic" and "sentimental." Any stage adaptation, however, needs, in some sense, to produce similar emotional engagements to those that the novel generates if it is not to be found wanting.

Matthew Spangler, who is now Professor of Performance studies at San José State University and a playwright himself as well as an adaptor of prose fiction and nonfiction for the stage, undertook the theatrical adaptation of *Kite*. His first adaptation of a literary text, staged in 1995 when he was a student at the University of Sussex in the United Kingdom, was of Joseph Conrad's *Heart of Darkness*, a novel that, in its exploration of corruption and violence, has some thematic and tonal similarities to *Kite*. By Spangler's own account in the program for the 2018 UK tour of *Kite*, he first read Hosseini's novel in 2005, two years after its publication. His interest in adaptation, as a dramatist and a lecturer, meant that he imagined any book he read as a play, and *Kite*'s "complex characters, nonstop narrative, many heartbreaking moments, representation of the Afghan immigrant experience in the United States" and "broad historical canvas seemed naturally theatrical" (Spangler). In the program, he offers an interesting inventory of what he sees as the themes of *Kite*. It is primarily "a story of guilt and redemption," but also "a story about a father and son," about "two best friends," about "transnational immigration and refugees," about "the relative peace in Afghanistan in the 1970s," about "global politics," and about "class and ethnicity." Spangler's sense of the multiple themes of *Kite* means that his adaptation, insofar as it aimed to encompass all these, had to bear quite a load.

Spangler drafted the script in 2006, so he was not influenced by the movie, which was then in production and did not appear until the following year. He cooperated closely with Hosseini himself in shaping the script into a version ready for performance. A developmental production, which Spangler himself directed, was mounted at San José State University in March 2007, and its world premiere, also directed by Spangler, was on March 21, 2009, at the San José Repertory Theatre. Later US stagings included the Arizona Theatre Company's at Tucson (Sept. 10–Oct. 3, 2009) and Phoenix (Oct. 8–25, 2009); the Actors Theatre in Louisville, Kentucky (Aug. 31–Sept. 25, 2010); the Cleveland Playhouse in Ohio (Oct. 15—Nov.7, 2010); and the New Repertory Theatre at the Mosesian Center for the Arts in Watertown, Massachusetts (Sept. 9–30, 2012).

In all these productions, two actors played Amir in Act I: "a younger Amir and an older/storyteller Amir" (loc. 85).

The European premiere of the play was on April 26, 2013, at Nottingham Playhouse in the Midlands city of Nottingham in the United Kingdom. In this and subsequent productions, one actor played Amir, switching between his older and younger selves as required. The production transferred to Wyndham's Theatre in the West End of London, where it opened on December 21, 2016. It moved to Richmond Theatre in the London suburbs from March 11–14, 2017, and subsequently went on tour in England, Scotland, the Republic of Ireland and Northern Ireland, playing at theatres in Guildford, Southampton, Newcastle, York, Aberdeen, Blackpool, Buxton, Dublin, Cork, and Belfast. We shall sample reviews of the stage productions later, but we will now focus on the play as it exists in the published script (in which one actor plays both young and older Amir, rather than two actors as in pre-2013 productions). We shall look first at how that script follows and departs from the novel and then consider the representation of violence in the play, its use of physical action, and its deployment of music.

Any adaptation of a novel for the theater cannot follow the original slavishly. The media are different and an adaptor has to select, compress, and alter as appropriate to fit into what the Prologue to Shakespeare's *Romeo and Juliet* calls "the two hours' traffic of our stage" (Prologue, 5; line 12)—or whatever span of time is appropriate and available. While audiences, even those well aware of this necessary difference between novel and stage, are still likely to harbor, on some level, residual expectations that the play will deliver an equivalent experience to that of reading the novel, they would perhaps also be disappointed if, *per impossibile*, it did so. What would be the point of going to the theater if you could have the same experience sitting at home with a script? But although audiences want some sense of difference between an adaptation and its original, they may not want too much. Some of them may draw the line at what we now call "hyperadaptations," which depart from the original text to such a great extent that it feels like entering a familiar house that has been radically refurbished and refurnished and even acquired new occupants without its owner's approval. Hyperadaptations can be liberating and thought-provoking, but may seem, at least sometimes, to go too far. The idea that an adaptation should be, in important or essential ways, *faithful* to the original persists, even if it is not wholly clear what such fidelity might mean. Spangler's adaptation of *Kite* does satisfy the criterion of fidelity; but there are also significant and interesting differences, and we shall now consider key examples of these. It should be said that in exploring these differences, the general intention is not to rank the novel above the play, or vice versa, but to grasp what the differences are and consider the effects they have.

Differences

The play retains the narrative voice of the novel in the sense that Amir switches between immersion in roles in which he plays his past selves and his role as a narrator, looking back and summarizing and commenting on his past thoughts, feelings, motives, and actions with a degree of detachment. But he should not be too detached: the playscript recommends that he should relive "much of what he describes with the emotional energy of the present moment." (loc. 74).

Given that the play cannot be as long as the novel, at least not without making demands on its audiences that might reduce their number considerably, the adaptor must cut and compress. We can see an example of the result of this process if we compare and contrast the first paragraph of the novel with the first speech of the play. In both cases, Amir (though we are not immediately told his name) is the source of those words, and he is in narratorial mode. But while the first paragraph of the novel runs to 88 words, the first speech in the play runs to 67 words: this 21-word difference in length is not huge, but nonetheless demonstrates that the two texts will differ in terms of length, the play being shorter than the novel.

Two important statements in these first words are identical in novel and play. The first is "I became what I am today at the age of twelve," which indicates that Amir is identifying what he sees as the moment that shaped his adult identity. The second is "I remember the precise moment," which signals that he believes he can locate that moment exactly. But while Amir in the novel describes his twelve-year old self "peeking" into the alley, and repeats the verb at the end of the first paragraph (1), Amir in the play uses the verb "looking" in the same places, which suggests a more direct form of visual perception. It is interesting and relevant to explore further the different connotations of the two verbs. "Peeking" can connote a furtive, somewhat guilty voyeurism, but can also, in other contexts, seem mischievous, playful, as in the phrase: "I'll just take a peek." "Looking" can connote a franker appropriation that is both unflinching and more openly gratifying in a voyeuristic and even sadistic sense. Both verbs, however, could serve to implicate Amir in the rape of Hassan, as if, on some level, Assef might have been doing something Amir himself wanted to do but dared not acknowledge. But "peeking," the verb used in the novel itself, is arguably closer to what Amir actually does, or does not do, when the rape is taking place, as described in Chapter 7. In that scene as the novel presents it, Amir does not look all the time; he shuts his eyes at one point (64) and a little later, he stops watching and turns away (67). [For further comments on this scene, see the earlier essay in this volume, "You have been in Afghanistan, I perceive"?]

One of the most striking episodes in the novel occurs just over halfway through Chapter 8. Earlier in that chapter Amir, tortured by guilt and other disturbing emotions at his failure in the previous chapter to try to prevent Hassan's rape, has suggested to Baba that he dismiss Ali and Hassan and get new servants. Baba firmly rebuts the suggestion (78–79). When summer comes, Amir asks Hassan out for a walk and, by the cemetery wall, starts to pelt him with pomegranates from the nearby tree in which, back in Chapter 4, Amir once carved their names (24), in an attempt to provoke Hassan to hit back and thus assuage his guilt to some degree, but Hassan refuses to retaliate and ends the conflict by crushing a pomegranate against his own forehead (80–81). This scene is both visually rich and full of symbolic significance.

In Act I, Scene 5 of the play, Amir, in his role of retrospective narrator, mentions the pomegranate tree and his carving of their names, and in Scene 7, Hassan asks Amir if he wants to go up to the pomegranate tree (loc. 399). In Scene 11, the merchant whom Amir questions, just after the kite contest, as to whether he has seen Hassan, and who asks disparagingly why he is looking for a Hazara boy, is carrying "a basket of bright red pomegranates," (loc. 611), which anticipates the racist, sexual violence that Assef will soon unleash upon Amir's kite runner. But the pomegranates are absent from the episode in Scene 12 in which Amir tries to provoke Hassan into hitting back. Instead of throwing the bright red fruit, Amir hits Hassan, first in the face, then again and again until he falls, and once more when he is down. Hassan gets up, but the play offers no equivalent to the crushing of the pomegranate against his own forehead in the novel, though his exit line is almost the same, with the one addition of "Amir" in the play: "Do you feel better"? (81; loc. 739).

Hassan's refusal to assuage Amir's guilt by retaliating makes Amir decide he must get rid of the friend whom he has betrayed and who is a living daily reminder of his guilt. Both Act I of the play and Chapter 9 of the novel end with the departure from Baba's house of Ali and Hassan in the rain after Amir has framed Hassan for theft and the latter has, it seems, knowingly taken the rap. But there is a notable contrast in the way novel and play present this departure. In the novel, Amir stays indoors, watching Baba's car drive off as he takes Ali and Hassan to the bus station (94–95; for further analysis of this scene, see the earlier essay in this volume, "You have been in Afghanistan, I presume"?). At first it seems as if the play will follow the same scenario: it is raining and Amir, in his narratorial voice, tells us that he watched Ali and Hassan "haul their bags to Baba's black Mustang" (loc. 882), thus positioning himself as staying behind when they leave. But then Amir starts to speak as if he had immediately transferred, through the instantaneous media of memory and stage flight, to the bus station itself. The Ensemble that is a key part of Spangler's cast (see further discussion below) compounds this impression by assuming the role of bus passengers forming a line that Ali and Hassan have joined. In the novel, Amir sees, for the first time, his father crying and pleading with Ali and

Hassan in vain to stay *before* they leave his house (93). In the play, the first time he sees Baba cry is at the bus station (loc. 882). In the play, however, Baba does not openly plead as he does in the novel (93). Instead, Amir *tells* us that his father hoped Ali and Hassan would stay, as if he were engaging, at the time of the actual departure or retrospectively when he looks back on it, in mind-reading, not in the telepathic sense but in the sense of inferring what is going on in someone's mind and feelings from their outward appearance and behavior.

The play also inserts at this point an explicit moment of self-blame on Amir's part that, in the novel, occurs earlier in Chapter 9: "I wondered how and when I'd become capable of causing this kind of pain" (91). In the novel, Amir wonders this when Hassan and Ali have come into Baba's study, and Baba is about to ask Hassan if he stole Amir's money and watch. In the play he wonders it aloud in the last speech before Act I ends, thus highlighting his agonized self-interrogation and self-laceration, which will fuel his quest for redemption in Act II.

The penultimate sentence of Chapter 9 in the novel runs "I caught one final blurry glimpse of Hassan slumped in the backseat [of the bus] before Baba turned left at the street corner where we'd played marbles so many times" (95). In the play, Amir's last words before Act I ends are "I caught one final glimpse of Hassan as the bus pulled away, taking with it the boy whose first spoken word was my name." The opening clause of the sentence is almost the same in play and novel, except that the latter omits the adjective "blurry." This is part of a more general omission of the evocation, in that part of the novel, of the visual effects of the rain and its symbolization of the blurring, not only of the disappearing Hassan, but also of Amir's moral perception. Moreover, Amir's memory in the sentence from Chapter 9 returns to his boyhood games of marbles with Hassan (which the novel has not in fact mentioned previously), but in the play it goes back to that defining moment of identity and bonding previously mentioned in Act I, Scene 2 (loc. 163) of the play and at the end of Chapter 2 in the novel. This is when Amir tells us of their first words: Amir's was Baba, Hassan's was Amir (10). It makes an effective ending for the first act, recalling the close bonding between them in infancy that Amir imagines he has now broken.

As well as differences of this kind, there are also important differences in the play's representation of violence, and we shall now consider these. Violence is, in a sense, a subset of physical action on the stage, which we shall discuss later; but given the importance of violence in both novel and play, it seems important to give it separate attention here.

Violence on Stage

The central act of violence in both play and novel is the rape of Hassan. This takes place in Chapter 7 of the novel and Act I, Scene 11 in the play. We mentioned in the previous section that, in the novel, Amir twice looks away and thus also diverts the attention of readers from a particularly painful moment in the narrative. In the play, the rape takes place offstage: Assef exits and Wali and Kamal follow, dragging Hassan. The stage direction says that Amir "describes the [offstage] scene while facing the audience":

> Hassan's pants were pulled off. Assef unzipped his jeans, dropped his underwear and knelt down. He lifted Hassan by the hips. Hassan didn't struggle. Didn't even whimper. And I knew I had one last chance to decide who I was going to be. I could step into that alley, stand up for Hassan and accept whatever would happen to me. Or, I could run. Then I saw tiny drops of blood fall from between Hassan's legs, stain the snow black . . . And I ran.

Here, the play telescopes into one passage of 83 words three passages that are, in the novel, on separate pages (66, 68, 69). Moreover, it omits three sentences in the novel that follow "Didn't even whimper" and that are, arguably important to its thematic and symbolic significance: "[Hassan] moved his head slightly and I caught a glimpse of his face. Saw the resignation in it. It was a look I had seen before. It was the look of the lamb." (66). The "lamb" metaphor conveys the idea that Hassan is a sacrifice whose rape, meekly endured and never made public, serves to maintain social equilibrium.

In the novel, the passage moves straight from "Didn't ever whimper" to Amir's framing of the moment as a decisive one in the formation of his identity. "I had one last chance to make a decision. One final opportunity to decide who I was going to be" (68). The play compresses these two sentences into one: "And I knew I had one last chance to decide who I was going to be" (loc. 670). The first ten words of the following sentence are identical in novel and play: "I could step into that alley, stand up for Hassan." Then they diverge, with the novel including, after "stand up for Hassan," an interpolated clause punctuated by dashes at either end: "the way he'd stood up for me all those times in the past." The play makes no reference at this point to Hassan's past defenses of Amir. But after this variation, the last clause of the sentence is the same in both novel and play; it runs "accept whatever would happen to me." And in both cases Amir runs—and in the play, he can suit the action to the words. It is a very different kind of running from that of Hassan in pursuit of the kite, motivated by fear rather than devoted friendship.

A further notable scene of violence in the novel, in Chapter 21 (233–37), is the detailed and harrowing account of the public stoning to death in the Ghazi football stadium in Kabul of the couple accused of adultery. In the novel, this is where Amir sees once again, after many years, Hassan's rapist Assef, though without recognizing him immediately: he is the powerful Taliban official wearing John Lennon spectacles (an ironic link to a popstar apostle of love and peace), who casts the first stone that triggers the public execution. The play entirely omits any direct representation of this stoning, perhaps because it could prove so powerful that it would upset the balance and focus of the play, overshadowing the story of Amir. Instead, Amir first encounters Assef again in the house the latter is occupying.

The play does refer back at that point to the lethal judicial violence in which Assef has just been involved. When he enters, he wears "a white robe with drops of blood splattered on the sleeve and front" (loc. 1256). A little later in his conversation with Amir, he notices Amir noticing the blood on his robe and asks him to excuse his appearance: "I haven't had a chance to clean up since the show at the soccer stadium this afternoon. Bringing justice to another adulterer" (loc. 1545). Audiences who do not know the novel may not be wholly clear what Assef is referring to, given his casual, insouciant phrasing. Audiences who do know the novel will be able to appreciate the disjunction between that phrasing and the brutality of the event.

To labor that brutality in the play, however, could detract from the horror and dramatic force of the event that soon follows, when Sohrab puts out Assef's eye with a projectile from his slingshot. In both novel and play, the projectile is a brass ball. In Chapter 22 of the novel, in a rather complicated bit of business, the brass ball comes from a ring in the base of a coffee table that Amir notices just before Assef comes in (241). The table reminds him of a similar one he had seen in a Peshawar tea shop in Chapter 18 on which a brass ball had become unscrewed and he had tightened it, wishing he "could fix [his] own life as easily" (197). In Chapter 22, we infer that Sohrab is able to unscrew the brass ball from the ring at the base of the table after Assef has pushed him into the table and it overturns (250), though we never actually see him detaching it.

In Act II, Scene 14 of the play, the matter is simplified because Assef enters tossing a brass ball (loc. 1530) and puts it down on a table just after Sohrab has been brought in. As Amir and Assef fight violently and the latter is about to deliver the decisive blow, the stage direction tells us that Sohrab gets out his slingshot, puts the brass ball in the cup and aims it at Assef (loc. 1599). This is a much clearer chain of events than in the novel, though it loses the symbolic dimension arising from the link of the loose brass ball in the Peshawar café with Amir's idea of fixing up one's life in Chapter 18 (197).

The fight between Amir and Assef and Sohrab's firing of the brass ball from his slingshot involve physical action on stage, which is a major element of Spangler's adaptation. We will now explore this element more widely, in relation to other bodily activities besides violence.

Physical Action on Stage

Spangler wanted physical action to play a major part in the stage adaptation, and the Ensemble, which we have already mentioned, makes an important contribution to this. The script clearly defines the play as "an ensemble piece" (loc. 71) and stipulates that the Ensemble should appear as often as possible, "to fill the stage with movement in necessary scenes and to embody many of the descriptive passages" (loc. 72). Amir, who is on stage throughout the performance, "should be physically active during his monologues" (loc. 73).

At the start of the first act, the Ensemble stand on stage "facing the audience" (loc. 94), with Amir center stage. This establishes a close visual connection between the Ensemble and Amir at the outset. The Ensemble become especially important in the kite flying and kite tournament scenes in Act I. In Scene 9, set in the streets of Kabul, the Ensemble "enters and darts around the stage, as if chasing kites." Then "[o]ne of them gives Amir a kite attached to a spool of glass-coated string." At this point, "the music [another important element of the adaptation that we shall discuss in the next section] stops and the Ensemble freezes, gazing up at the sky, as if watching for falling kites" (loc. 454). Amir gives a short speech and then "hands the spool to a member of the Ensemble" and "gives the kite to another." These two Ensemble members "stretch the string across the stage" and Amir runs his "fingers along [it] to show" the audience its sharpness. Then, after another short speech, he "snaps the string," at which point "suddenly the Ensemble comes to life and darts around the stage, yelling, as if chasing falling kites" (loc. 466). In the further short speech that follows, Amir describes the scramble for the last fallen kite, sometimes resulting in fights. The Ensemble "exits chasing the falling kites and yelling at one another with the energy of intense competition" (loc. 470). The Ensemble and its physical activity and noise makes a strong contribution to conveying the collective excitement the build-up to the kite contest generates.

The activity and noise of the Ensemble are even more important to the kite tournament itself in the same scene. The

Ensemble joins in with Amir when he starts to fly his kite. The stage direction states that "[t]he kite flying could either be done through mime and choreographed movement or by using actual kites and/or string" (loc. 514). Using mime and movement works on what Shakespeare's *Henry V* calls the "imaginary forces" of the audience (1997, 727; Prologue, line 18), their powers of imagination. Using actual kites or something like them can give a vivid polychromatic impression, filling the stage with many colors. The stage direction says the Ensemble should also cheer, clap and possibly utter words and phrases such as "'*shahbash!*' [bravo], '*aafarin!*' [good job], '*waa waa!*' [wow], and '*namekhoda!*' [God bless]" (loc. 251, square brackets and translations in original). Any member of the Ensemble whose kite is cut should switch to the role of a kite-chasing runner. The aim is that the "kite tournament should build to an intense explosion of energy" (loc. 524). We can see how important the presence and activity of the Ensemble is to achieve this exciting, energetic, explosive effect.

The Ensemble returns at other significant points throughout the play. For example, as we have already seen, they form the queue of passengers that Ali and Hassan join at the bus station after Amir has engineered their departure from Baba's house. At the start of Act II, they are among the refugees, including Baba and Amir, traveling in the almost asphyxiating tank of the fuel truck from Afghanistan to Pakistan. In Act II, Scene 2, when Amir and Baba arrive in San Francisco in 1981, the Ensemble members become representatives of America and each of them offers, in turn, metonymies for American life in that decade: for instance:

> 1980s American #1 Spandex!
> 1980s American #2 The Space Shuttle!
> 1980s American #3 McDonald's!
> 1980s American #4 Burger King!
> 1980s American #5 Kool and the Gang!
> 1980s American #6 Blondie!
> 1980s American #7 Prince! (loc. 976)

In Scene 5, the Ensemble form the customers at the San José flea market where both Baba and General Taheri have stalls, and in Scene 8 they are the guests at the wedding of Amir and Soraya. The Ensemble is a vital element in bringing the play alive on stage. A further element is music, and we shall now consider this.

Music

Jonathan Girling was the play's composer and musical director for the 2018 UK production and, in the program, he himself says that the most important instrument was the tabla, a pair of small hand drums of slightly different sizes that feature especially in Indian music. Girling chose Hanif Khan as his tabla drummer. Khan taught Girling a range of taals—classical Indian musical beats—and Girling adapted these to give emphasis in many scenes. For example, in Act I, Scene 1:

> **Amir** [. . .] I thought about Baba, Rahim Khan, Ali and most of all, Hassan, the best kite-runner in Kabul and my best friend.
> *Beat.*
> I thought about how the winter of 1975 changed everything. (loc. 105)

Another example occurs in Act II, Scene 17, when Sohrab is rushed to hospital after his suicide attempt:

> **Amir** [. . .] At the hospital, they put a white sheet over him and wheel him away.
> *Beat.*
> And I know what I have to do.
> **Amir** *gets down on his knees and assumes the position for prayer.* (loc. 1769)

The rhythm of the taal may change according to the situation. Girling gives an example from Act I, Scene 9, which shows the kite contest. As the first contest takes place, "Hanif plays Jhapthal medium taal." When Amir says "the real fun began when a kite was cut," he plays "Jhapathal fast." The tabla pauses on "a crucial line"—Amir's

"But Hassan was by far the greatest kite runner I'd ever seen" (loc. 471)—and then "Hanif plays Jhapthal fast again" to imitate "the runners chasing the fallen kite across the stage" (Girling).

As well as the tabla, Tibetan Singing Bowls, Schwirrbogen (big wooden rattles), the tampura (an Indian string instrument) and an oil drum and mallet all feature at key moments. This creates a many-stranded sound texture that enlivens the aural atmosphere of the play and amplifies its meanings. It is further enriched by songs in Dari, and, in Act I, Scene 13, by a Happy Birthday song in Farsi for Amir—'*Tawalod, tawalod, tawalod et mubarak, mubarak, mubarak, tawalod et mubarak*' (loc. 756, italics in original). There are also, in Girling's words, "beautiful Afghan songs" such as "Ahesta Boro" ["Walk Slowly"] sung at the wedding of Amir and Soraya (loc. 1243) in Act II, Scene 8. Western pop songs also feature: Kool and the Gang's "Celebration" (1980) at the start of Act II, Scene 2 (loc. 960), marks Amir's arrival in California in 1981 (the group's name is also one of the metonymies for that American decade used by "1980s American #5" a little later in that scene [loc. 978]). "Abracadabra" (1982) by the Steve Miller Band plays at the start of Act II, Scene 5, as the San José flea market is set up (loc. 1064). During the scene we hear a number originally recorded in an earlier decade, Van Morrison's "Brown Eyed Girl" (1967) (loc. 1109) as Amir "gazes [. . .] transfixed" at Soraya at the Taheri stall (loc. 1110). This pop music further contributes to the cultural and geographical scope of the adaptation.

Narratorial commentary, dialogue, vividly dramatized scenes, physical action, ensemble acting, noise, music, all these contribute to the stage production. We will now consider key examples of its reception by theatre reviewers.

Review Reception

In his review of the 2009 production at the San José Repertory Theatre, directed by David Ira Goldstein, artistic director of the Arizona Theatre Company, Robert Hurwitt, in the *San Francisco Chronicle* (Mar. 30, 2009), implicitly addressed in his first paragraph the question this essay flagged earlier: would an adaptation please enthusiastic readers of the novel? Hurwitt's answer was largely affirmative: "it's hard to imagine that fans of [*The Kite Runner*] will be disappointed in the play." He was struck by how much the adaptation got into its two-and-a-half hours: "it depicts most of what happens in the book at almost fast-forward speed." For him, however, this had both advantages and disadvantages.

On the one hand, "David Ira Goldstein stages the action with cinematic grace" and employs "Vicki Smith's effortlessly sliding sets and lovely kite montages to create a seamless flow and some striking tableaux." Moreover, "the play preserves the book's conflicted, guilt-ridden narrative voice." On the other hand, Hurwitt felt the adaptation did not provide "the immersion in Afghan sights and customs that is one of the novel's most fascinating aspects" and failed "to transport us into a foreign culture." Furthermore, he discerned a lack of proportion and measured pacing in the play: it "spen[ds] the whole first act on the first quarter of the novel, giving us the rest in a kind of CliffsNotes rush." He concluded that "[t]oo often, [the play] tells the story rather than immerse us in it."

J. Kelly Nestruck reviewed the production at Theatre Calgary and at the Citadel Theatre in Edmonton in that Canadian city's *Globe and Mail* (Mar. 20, 2013). Nestruck acknowledged at the outset that, unlike most other reviewers of the adaptation, he had "little prior knowledge" of the novel, which he saw as an advantage because the "ripping good yarn" the play delivered "kept [him] on the edge of [his] seat by its potboiler twists and turns." It is interesting to note that this production adopted the alternative two-actors approach to playing Amir that, as we observed above, the published script mentions. One actor (Anousha Alamian) took the role of Amir as an adult, while another (Conor Wylie) played him as a boy. Nestruck seemed to feel this gave the first act an unduly retrospective and pictorial quality. "The fact that Alamian tells Amir's story, while Wylie depicts it makes the first act play out like a picture storybook. It's all very past tense."

In Act II, Nestruck thought that the sense that "we are watching a book on stage becomes more problematic," "as 20 years clunk by in quick succession." Nestruck also highlighted the absence of one of the "sign[s] of sophisticated storytelling": the representation of the "villains" as "well-rounded characters." When the "simplistic strokes" with which Assef is rendered "are applied to the Taliban in the second half, the result is a series of scenes that seem transplanted from a Hollywood thriller." The Taliban, Nestruck suggested, were far more formidable than such caricatures suggest. "This part of the play plops like propaganda—dated and deadly."

Edmund Chow, in an important analysis of the production of *Kite* staged at the Birmingham Repertory Theatre in the English Midlands (Sept. 22–Oct. 4, 2014), drew on "Walter Benjamin's concept of aura or 'getting closer to things' [. . .] to argue that Spangler's intention of adapting the original text intimately allows audiences to come closer to Afghan histories, cultures, and traditions" (162). Chow "critically investigate[d] the use of music, infusion of Dari language, and interjecting dialogues to create cultural 'effects' on stage," in order not only to "inculcate a sense of wonder towards an unknown culture," but also to "foster a strong connection toward the Afghan characters." (163). He contended that Spangler's careful and extensive research for the adaptation, and his close cooperation with Hosseini himself, could be seen as an attempt to make some kind of reparation in theatrical terms for the US invasion of Afghanistan, as "*a way to be good again*," to use that significant phrase of Rahim Khan's that reverberates in both novel and play (2, 168 [twice], 198, 270 [twice]; loc. 100, 1332, 1335, 1439). How successful the adaptation is in its "cultural effects," is open to question, however, as we see from Marissa Khaos's attack below.

In a review of the 2016–17 Wyndham's Theatre production in London, Emma Henderson, in the British *Independent* (Jan. 13, 2017), generally approved the adaptation, but found the "adults acting as their child selves [. . .] distracting" and making "a poor attempt at [. . .] trying to behave like 12-year-olds, when child actors could easily have taken on the role as in the film." This last observation, however, begs the ethical question of whether "child actors" should be used in a play that turns on the rape of a child and whether such actors might incur opprobrium and even, like the boy actors in the movie, death threats. Despite her reservation about adults playing children, however, Henderson, using the metaphor in Hosseini's title as an image of how the adaptation itself works, concluded that "the touching story of the novel is carried on stage by the turbulent ups and downs, echoing the ducking and diving of a fighting kite that will come up winning."

In the *Guardian* (Jan. 27, 2017), veteran theatre critic Michael Billington, also reviewing the Wyndham's Theatre production, called the play "a workmanlike summation of the book, but one that rarely captures its ability to glide seamlessly from the intimate to the epic." He argued that the adaptation's fidelity to certain aspects of the novel is the very thing that impairs its capacity to capture other important aspects. "By faithfully following the first-person narration and rhythmic structure of Hosseini's book, Spangler reduces it to a series of chronological events." Billington also observed that, "[a]s in any adaptation, crucial detail also gets lost," instancing the omissions of Assef's admiration for Hitler and Baba's "big-heartedness."

Aliya Al-Hassan, reviewing the production in *Broadway World* (Mar. 11, 2017) after its transfer from Wyndham's to Richmond Theatre in the London suburbs, judged that the play stays "fairly faithful to the story." Al-Hassan also argued, however, that the "effort to fit everything from the [novel] in" loses "some of the poetry" and makes the narration—here she echoes Billington—sometimes feel "like a retelling of the chronology of events, rather than an exploration of the events themselves." But she concluded that, "despite the heaviness of the narration at points," it was an "evocative," "touching," and deeply moving production.

Writer and arts journalist Victoria Sadler enthused about the adaptation in her review (Apr. 20, 2018) of the production at the Yvonne Arnaud Theatre in Guildford in the United Kingdom. She began by addressing the same question that Robert Hurwitz had raised in 2009, which we mentioned earlier in this essay: would this adaptation please enthusiastic readers of the novel? Sadler observed that adapting "a famous and much-loved book" for the theater guarantees an audience but runs "the risk that the show will not be able to capture the beauty and the fascination" that "made readers fall in love with the novel" and will leave them feeling "disappointed." But for her the production succeeded triumphantly and stayed "wonderfully faithful to the full story" of the novel. Sadler acknowledged that the play's coverage of that story "in just over 2h 30m" meant that, "particularly in the second half, it does lean more towards telling us what is happening, rather than showing us." Since she felt, however, that "the momentum and the plot must be kept moving on," this emphasis on "telling" did not bother her too much, and nor, she inferred, did it bother the audience around her who, on their way out after the final curtain, "were humming with admiration, marvelling at the show they'd just enjoyed." Sadler concluded that the play, "a heady mix of the personal and political," was a "powerful and quite brilliant production that investigates the complexity of power balances between people—and how these can fluctuate and change on the toss of a coin—with aplomb."

In a review in the *Irish Times* (Jun. 5, 2018) of the touring production at The Gaiety Theatre in Dublin in the Republic of Ireland, Peter Crawley hinted at a strong homoerotic subtext in both novel and play. He contended that "kite fighting was a metaphor that dare not speak its name," alluding to "the love that dare not speak its name," a phrase often taken to refer to homosexuality that comes from the last line of Lord Alfred Douglas's poem "Two Loves." Crawley compared *Kite* with the film *Brokeback Mountain* (2005), which is about a romantic and sexual relation between two men that develops when they are herding sheep in Wyoming. "S[t]eeped in shame, desire and eternal debt, *The Kite Runner* does for kite flying what *Brokeback Mountain* did for shepherding."

Crawley found "a becoming bright naïvety in the production's stagecraft." Like Emma Henderson in her *Guardian* review above, however, he was not keen on Amir's transitions between boyhood and adulthood. He described, somewhat satirically, how Raj Ghatak as Amir "slips into broad emulations of boyhood, or—under Giles Croft's less than subtle direction—sticks out his chest, throws back his arms and pronounces his dreadful shame to the audience in a fixed spotlight." Crawley observed ironically that "Afghanistan is conveyed with similar restraint, in exotic tones and imagery, with an onstage tabla player upon an Afghan rug, illustrations such as a pomegranate tree projected across huge fanned kite wings, or the drone of singing bowls sounding at significant intervals." Here Crawley, though approaching from a different angle, came close to Khaos's critique above of the production as an "Orientalist" mobilization of stereotypes. He also found the metonymies of America in Barney George's set stereotypical: "the curve of a skateboard ramp and a jagged backdrop rising into the shape of the San Francisco skyline."

Crawley contended that the naïvety he identifies "accentuates the more breathless peaks of the [second] act, a tortuous melodrama of revelations, cruel disasters and fated deliverance, at which, to borrow from Oscar Wilde, you would need a heart of stone not to laugh." The allusion here is to Wilde's reported remark on a famous tear-jerking scene in Charles Dickens's novel *The Old Curiosity Shop* (1840–41), that "[o]ne must have a heart of stone to read the death of Little Nell without laughing" (qtd. Eaton 269). Crawley went on to say, however, that whether or not you laugh "will depend on your submission to storytelling—the more overt and winding theme of the novel and the play—with its combination of surface pleasures and smuggled meanings. The kite is pretty enough, but the lacerating edge in its tail is much more fascinating." Crawley did not spell it out at this point, but the "smuggled meanings" and "lacerating edge" toward which he gestured were of a homoerotic kind.

A strongly critical review of the most recent production of the play, at Richmond Theatre came from author and activist Marissa Khaos, in *The Upcoming* (Mar. 12, 2020). She condemned it as "an Orientalist, culturally incorrect play with bad English about an othered people" and highlighted what she saw as its "confusion of languages and Indo-Iranian traditions." Citing Jonathan Steele's article on "Afghanistan: Battleground of Empires" in the program for the play, she argued that what Steele "calls 'Western mistakes' are, to this reviewer of Afghan heritage, colonial violence that is watered down to be made intelligible to the Western audience."

As these reviews show, the stage adaptation of *Kite* has aroused a range of responses, from an enthusiasm that overrides any possible flaws, through varieties of qualified praise, to a dismissal of it as stereotypical and Orientalizing. All these responses prove that the play is theatrically alive, able to engage its audiences emotionally, alert their critical faculties, raise their hackles, and generate controversy.

Conclusion

Matthew Spangler has continued to modify his adaptation of *Kite*, and each new production will interpret and present it differently. Spangler's adaptation, however, is now an established part of the intertexts and contexts of the original novel. The adaptation uses a great many of the novel's words and, because of this, it retains a good sense of its narrative voice. As we have seen, however, the play also, in the necessary work of adaptation, compresses, alters and omits elements of the novel and adds visual, aural, and kinetic dimensions that aim to bring the play theatrically alive. It seems likely, as history moves on, that the play will be further modified, that new adaptations by different scriptwriters, and new productions, will emerge, and that novels and adaptations by other authors, exploring similar territory, will alter the intertexts and contexts in which *Kite*, as play and novel, is read, interpreted, and received. Audiences watching an adaptation of *Kite* in the actual or virtual theatres of 2053, fifty years after the first publication of the novel, or in 2103, a hundred years after it appeared, are in for an interesting experience.

Note

The author of this essay would like to thank Matthew Spangler for supplying a copy of the unpublished script of his version of the adaptation in which the older and younger Amir are to be played by two actors and for his most helpful information about productions that used this approach.

Works Cited

Alfred, Lord Douglas. "Two Loves." *The Chameleon*. vol. 1, no. 1., R. L. Stevenson, Dec. 1894, law2.umkc.edu/faculty/projects/ftrials/wilde/poemsofdouglas.htm.

Al-Hassan, Aliya. "BWW Review: *THE KITE RUNNER.*" Richmond Theatre. Directed by Giles Croft. Adapted by Matthew Spangler. *Broadway World.* 11 Mar. 2017. www.broadwayworld.com/ westend/article/BWW-Review-THE-KITE-RUNNER-Richmond-Theatre-20200311.

Billington, Michael. "*The Kite Runner* Review—Loses Its Grip on Khaled Hosseini's Engaging Tale." Wyndham's, London. Directed by Giles Croft. Adapted by Matthew Spangler. *The Guardian,* 10 Jan. 2017, www.theguardian.com/stage/2017/jan/10/the-kite-runner-review-khaled-hosseini-wyndhams-matthew-spangler.

Chow, Edmund. "Adapting *The Kite Runner*: A Fidelity Project to Re-Imagine Afghan Aura." In *Contemporary Approaches to Adaptation in Theatre,* edited by Kara Reilly. Adaptation in Theatre and Performance series. Palgrave Macmillan, 2018, Chapter 8, pp. 161–74. www.academia.edu/37389231/Adapting_The_Kite_Runner_A_Fidelity_Project_to_Re-Imagine_Afghan_Aura.

Crawley, Peter. "*The Kite Runner* at Gaiety Review: Becomingly Naive Stage Version Lays Much of Subtext Bare." Gaiety Theatre, Dublin, Ireland. Directed by Giles Croft. Adapted by Matthew Spangler. *Irish Times,* 5 June 2018, www.irishtimes.com/culture/stage/theatre/the-kite-runner-at-gaiety-review-becomingly-naive-stage-version-lays-much-of-subtext-bare-1.3520095.

Eaton, Marcia Muelder. "Laughing at the Death of Little Nell: Sentimental Art and Sentimental People." *American Philosophical Quarterly,* vol. 26, no. 4, Oct. 1989, pp. 269–82. *JSTOR,* www.jstor.org/stable/20014296?seq=1#metadata_info_tab_contents.

Girling, Jonathan. "*The Kite Runner* Music." *The Kite Runner* program. Devonshire Park Theatre, Eastbourne. 13–17 Feb. 2018, n.p., www.whatsonstage.com/shows/eastbourne-theatre/the-kite-runner_213376.

Henderson, Emma. "*The Kite Runner*, Wyndham's Theatre, London, Review: A Performance That Lacked Children Still Comes Up Winning." Directed by Giles Croft. Adapted by Matthew Spangler. *The Independent,* 13 Jan. 2017, www.independent.co.uk/arts-entertainment/theatre-dance/the-kite-runner-wyndhams-theatre-london-review-a-performance-that-lacked-children-still-comes-up-a7524341.html

Hosseini, Khaled. *The Kite Runner.* 2003; Bloomsbury, 2011.

Hosseini, Khaled. *The Kite Runner*, adapted by Matthew Spangler. Modern Plays series. Bloomsbury Publishing. Kindle Edition. 3 Jan. 2017.

Hurwitt, Robert. "Play review: 'The Kite Runner' True to Source." San José Rep. Directed by David Ira Goldstein and Matthew Spangler. Adapted by Matthew Spangler. *San Francisco Chronicle*, 30 Mar. 2009, n.p., www.sfgate.com/performance/article/Play-review-The-Kite-Runner-true-to-source-3166477.php.

Khaos, Marissa. "*The Kite Runner* at Richmond Theatre." Directed by Giles Croft. Adapted by Matthew Spangler. *The Upcoming*, 12 Mar. 2020, www.theupcoming.co.uk/2020/03/12/the-kite-runner-at-richmond-theatre-theatre-review/.

Nestruck, J. Kelly. "From Book to Stage, *The Kite Runner* Is a Ripping Good Yarn." *The Globe and Mail*, Theatre Reviews. [Edmonton, Canada]. Directed by Giles Croft. Adapted by Matthew Spangler. 20 Mar. 2013. Updated 11 May 2018, www.theglobeandmail.com/arts/theatre-and-performance/theatre-reviews/from-book-to-stage-the-kite-runner-is-a-ripping-good-yarn/article10024003/.

Sadler, Victoria. "Theatre Review: The Kite Runner (Touring) 'Faithful to the Famous Book.'" Yvonne Arnaud Theatre, Guildford, UK. *Victoria Sadler*. 20 Apr. 2018, www.victoriasadler.com/theatre-review-the-kite-runner-touring-faithful-to-the-famous-book.

Shakespeare, William. *Henry V.* In *The Norton Shakespeare Based on The Oxford Edition; Histories*, edited by Stephen Greenblatt, Walter Cohen, Jean E. Howard, and Katharine Eisaman Maus. With an essay on the Shakespearean stage by Andrew Gurr. W. W. Norton, 1997, pp. 717–95.

_____. *Romeo and Juliet.*, edited with a Commentary by T. J. B. Spencer. Introduction by Adrian Poole. Penguin Shakespeare series. Penguin, 2005.

Spangler, Matthew. "A Note from The Adaptor." *The Kite Runner* program. Devonshire Park Theatre, Eastbourne. 13–17 Feb. 2018, n.p.

Steele, Jonathan. "Afghanistan: Battleground of Empires." In *The Kite Runner* program. Devonshire Park Theatre, Eastbourne. 13–17 Feb. 2018, n.p.

The Kite Runner: The Graphic Novel_____

Nicolas Tredell

The graphic novel version of *The Kite Runner* is a powerful work that, like Matthew Spangler's stage adaptation, creates a new context and intertext for the original novel and stands as an example of artistic creativity in its own right, with vigorous draftsmanship by Fabio Celoni, vivid color by Mirka Andolfo, and a compelling script by Tommaso Valsecchi. This essay will explore three key aspects of the graphic novel. First, we shall examine the interaction between its narrative voice and its visual images. Second, we shall consider the impact of those capitalized and often onomatopoeic words that are such a distinctive feature of graphic novels and of comic books more generally, such as "THUMP" (110), "CRASH" (116) and "BAM" (116). Third, we shall focus on those very significant moments in a graphic novel when panels appear in which there are strong visual images but no words at all.

Narrative Voice

There is no doubt that the graphic novel of *Kite* packs into its 127 pages a great deal of the original novel, which runs to 324 pages in the first US and UK editions. Of course, readers who come to it after having read Hosseini's novel will supplement it with the knowledge and experience of the original that they have gained from their reading, expanding hints, filling in gaps, and comparing and contrasting the perspectives each text offers. Even allowing for the contribution of such prior knowledge and experience, however, it is impressive that the graphic novel version succeeds in encompassing so much.

While the dialogue that is the key verbal element of the graphic novel appears in oval bubbles, the narrative voice is in rectangular boxes. At the start of the graphic novel, for example, after Amir has received the phone call from Rahim Khan that triggers the narrative and told his wife, Soraya, that he must go to Pakistan, a panel shows

Soraya saying, in an oval bubble "TO PAKISTAN? B-BUT. . . HOW? WHY? AND WHEN?!" (6; panel 3). [All words in bubbles and boxes in the graphic novel are in block capitals, and this essay quotes them in that format to emphasize that they come from a source other than prose fiction.] The image of Soraya in this panel is tilted thirty degrees from the vertical to the reader's left, as if to signify the upset in their life that Amir's sudden announcement has caused. At the bottom right of the panel, a rectangular box has the words of Amir as narrator: "MY WIFE, SORAYA, CONTINUED SPEAKING, BUT BY THEN I WAS NO LONGER LISTENING. THE LAST THING RAHIM KAHN HAD SAID WAS ECHOING IN MY HEAD. *THERE IS A WAY TO BE GOOD AGAIN*" (6, panel 3, italics in original). It is worth noting that this particular example of narrative prose contains a line of dialogue, typographically stressed by italics, which is one of the key lines in the original novel and in the stage adaptation, "*There is a way to be good again*," which offers Amir the prospect of a road to redemption, is, in a sense, the idea that drives the whole narrative.

Here, the narrator is recalling a very recent event, the phone call he has just received. At other points, the narrator goes back much further, establishing a time span that covers years as the original novel does. In an image on page 15 of Amir as a boy sitting behind a wall, the narrative voice, in a rectangular box at the top left of the panel, says: "SOMETIMES, IN THINKING BACK ON THE PAST IT SEEMS I'VE SPENT THE LAST TWENTY-SIX YEARS BEHIND A WALL. ONE OF THOSE TUMBLEDOWN MUD WALLS OF WHICH THERE ARE A THOUSAND IN KABUL" (15, panel 1). While three references to the "twenty-six years" that have elapsed since Hassan's rape occur in the original novel, in Chapters 1, 7 and 19 (1, 59, 223), the adjective "tumbledown" does not appear there—the novel applies the adjective "crumbling" to the wall from which Amir witnesses Hassan's rape (1)—and the scene-setting reference in the graphic novel to its being one of many walls, a distinctive feature of Kabul, is also absent from the original.

As well as scene-setting information, the narrative voice in the graphic novel also gives historical and political information, as the original does. One night, for instance, the then unusual sounds of explosions and gunfire are heard in Kabul. Ali tells Amir and Hassan, rather improbably, that "THEY'RE SHOOTING DUCKS" (22, panel 4). But three panels later the narrator says: "LATER I DISCOVERED THAT THEY WEREN'T SHOOTING DUCKS AFTER ALL. KABUL AWOKE THE NEXT MORNING TO FIND THAT THE MONARCHY WAS A THING OF THE PAST. DAOUD KHAN, IN THE ABSENCE OF HIS COUSIN, THE KING, ZAHIR SHAH, HAD TAKEN AFGHANISTAN IN A BLOODLESS COUP" (22). The wording here is close to that in Chapter 5 of Hosseini's novel (32), though the latter gives a precise date for the event: July 17, 1973.

In the graphic novel, however, there is a notable counterpoint between the retrospective voice-over, calmly giving information, and the visual image in the same panel, a night scene that shows Amir being comforted in Baba's arms with Ali and Hassan looking on from a similar viewpoint to that of the reader and seeming relatively composed. For Amir, this is one of those rare moments when Baba shows affection to him rather than Hassan. Their momentary bonding is stressed in the next panel, the last on the page, which closes up on Baba's face and on Amir seen from behind as his arms cling round his father's neck and Baba's large hand supports him. The narrative voice here, in the rectangular box in the bottom right of the panel, says: "WHATEVER IT WAS THAT HAPPENED, ALL I REMEMBER WAS SUDDENLY FEELING HAPPY" (22, panel 8). The visual image gives body to this feeling and makes it more immediate than a memory. It anticipates, visually and emotionally, a later scene of close contact between father and son when Baba and Amir, at Baba's request, hug each other after Amir's triumph in the kite-fighting contest (46, panels 5, 6); but the tears we see in Amir's eyes in that latter instance mingle joy at his bonding with his father with his guilt and distress at having witnessed Hassan's rape without intervening shortly before (42–43).

We can see a further example of the process whereby a visual image gives body to the narrative voice in a much later scene where the words in the rectangular box, in the bottom right of the panel, say: AFTER SOME TIME THERE WAS NO MORE THAT COULD BE DONE. BABA WOULD HAVE TO STAY IN THE HOSPITAL IF HE WANTED TO LIVE LONGER (82, panel 1). The image is a close-up of Baba's strong-featured face and his still powerful-looking chest, torso, and left arm, as he lies in a hospital bed with eyes closed and an oxygen mask over his face. This gains greater poignancy from the many earlier images in the graphic novel of a healthy Baba that show a man of great vigor, and from those occasional moments, of which we have seen two examples, in which Baba and Amir came into close and loving bodily contact. Once more an image gives body to the words, even if this time it is an ailing body bound for death.

There is an especially notable image in the graphic novel when one panel expands to fill the whole page, with the narrative voice in a box at the top (68). It occurs at one of the moments of particularly intense trauma in the novel, when Amir, Baba, and other refugees try to escape from Afghanistan into Pakistan inside the tank of a fuel truck. The penultimate panel on the page previous to this image shows Baba and Amir inside the tanker just after they have climbed into it, with Amir clutching his throat and saying, "I CAN'T BREATHE!" (67, panel 7). This near-suffocation and the panic it brings is a powerful and extended moment in Chapter 10 of the original novel (105–06), but it is given less attention in the graphic version. The next and last panel on the same page closes up on Amir's right eye, which is shut and from which a tear is escaping; Baba is not visible but we "hear" his voice in a speech bubble: "THINK OF SOMETHING GOOD, AMIR, SOMETHING HAPPY" (67, panel 8; Baba's words here are identical to those in direct speech in the original novel at this point [106]). Readers then turn over to find a spectacular full-page image that is likely to strike their eyes before they register the words in the rectangular box at the top left of the page. Those words, however, provide an interesting counterpoint to the image. They show Amir taking the advice Baba gave in the last panel on the previous page: "SOMETHING HAPPY, BABA HAD SAID" (68). So he thinks about "RUNNING A KITE," "HANDS BEING CUT BY THE GLASSED STRING [of the kite]," "STANDING ANKLE-DEEP IN UNTAMED GRASS," "BLACK TEA," "CHARLTON HESTON" (one of his and Hassan's film star heroes), "AN OLD FAMILIAR MELODY"—and, finally and perhaps above all, "HASSAN" (68). These are rather different from the things Amir thinks about in the novel (106–07). But the visual image in the graphic novel does not match the words; it shows none of the things Amir itemizes in the rectangular box. It takes us not only away from Amir's thoughts but from the constricting interior of the fuel tanker. It is as if a camera had drawn far back and up from the intimate close-ups of the last two panels on the previous page to give us a panoramic vista of sky and mountains at night, rendered in a nocturne of blue, white, and green with, near the bottom of the image, a sinuous white-lined brown, that of the road, winding through the vertiginous heights and depths, along which the small blue-white fuel tanker is moving. The smallness of the tanker compared to the mountains around it and to the night blue sky above increases our senses, awakened by Amir's difficulty in breathing, of the confinement of those who are traveling concealed within it. At the same time, the scale of the landscape and skyscape gives us an awareness of freedom and awe. It is the effect that eighteenth-century aestheticians called "the sublime," an impression of awe and terror as human beings are dwarfed by the huge magnificence of nature, as in a picture by J. M. W. Turner (see Burke). The image could stand alone, without words, as a landscape painting.

As well as the intermittent narrative voice that the images complement or counterpoint, the graphic novel of *Kite* also makes much use of onomatopoeia, of words that supposedly imitate the sounds they denote.

Onomatopoeia

Onomatopoeia figures significantly in the opening of the graphic novel of *Kite*. The action in both this and the original is triggered by a phone call, though the original does not mention this until its second paragraph (1). The graphic novel does not initially show the phone itself shown but we "hear" it ringing. Brief markers of place and date appear in the rectangular boxes at the top of the first and second panels—respectively, "SAN FRANCISCO" and "SUMMER 2001"—but the graphic verbal element that thrusts itself upon the eye is the "RRRIIIIINGG" of a telephone. We notice here a characteristic feature of such words in graphic novels: the repetition, in order to stress the sound, of letters that would only occur once in conventional orthography: "R" occurs three times, "I" five times, "G" twice.

Two further features of such words in graphic novels is that they are sometimes either truncated within, or extended beyond, the confines of one panel. In the first panel, showing what we later infer to be the San Francisco home of Amir and Soraya, the "RRRIIIIINGG" is contained within the panel. In the second panel, showing blue sky and white sun to mark the season indicated in the rectangular box, it is partly obscured by the bottom of the panel, as if it were rising from below into the sky. In the third panel, it emerges from the left-hand side of the page near the top, with the first two "R"s cut off by the frame, and then rises over a steaming cup of coffee and above the top of the panel, as if to indicate the increasing insistence of the sound, not in the sense that it is actually getting louder, but in the sense that the person hearing it feels more and more impelled to answer. In the fourth panel, which shows an open box with new copies of what we later learn is Amir's first published novel, *A Season for Ashes*, the ring sounds again, but this time the letters increase in size and spill over into the next panel, adding two more "G"'s at the end: "RRRIIIIINGGGG." The letters signal with increasing vehemence that this is a phone call that cannot be ignored, that must be answered.

In a key historical event in Afghanistan that we mentioned in the previous section, Daoud Khan's overthrow of King Zahir Shah, the coup was bloodless but still signalled by the gunfire and explosions that alarmed Baba's household. In the graphic novel, these are represented by the "BOOOOOM" and "BOOOOM" (the first with three extra "O"'s, the second with two) that wakes Amir at night and frightens him badly (21, panel 1). In contrast, on the next page, Hassan's approval of the story of Sohrab and Rostam that Amir has just read to him is signalled not only by his exclamations—"AH, AH, AH! BRAVO!"—but by the words that indicate the noise made by his hands (which we can just see, as Hassan's back is to us): "CLAP CLAP CLAP" (23, panel) The word "CLAP" will recur in the graphic novel on the five panels, filling a page, that show Amir's graduation from high school in America at the late age of 20 (69, panels 1–5). There it features eighteen times, three times each in panels one to four and six times in the fifth and final panel. This is indeed cause for celebration, a stage in Amir's assimilation to American life and to the English language that will help him to enter higher education and eventually become a writer. Moreover, it brings him close to his usually distant father, who is proud of his son's achievement. But it may be that it cannot compare with the heartfelt spontaneous applause, unprompted by any formal ceremony in contrast to the graduation applause, which Hassan gave him for his reading the story of Sohrab and Rostam. Moreover, it was arguably Hassan's favorable reception of his storytelling that was the most important first step on Amir's road to becoming a writer. It is Baba himself who, at the end of the evening celebrating Amir's graduation, reminds him of the friend (and half-brother, as Baba but not Amir knows at this stage) whom he betrayed: "HASSAN WOULD HAVE BEEN VERY PROUD OF YOU. I WISH HE COULD HAVE BEEN WITH US TODAY . . . ." Amir says "YES. . ." but we see from his expression in the graphic novel that the mention of Hassan distresses him (71, panel 7).

The graphic novel uses onomatopoeia to potent effect in one of the most harrowing scenes in the original: the stoning to death of the adulterous couple in the football stadium in Kabul. The last panel on the page prior to the execution itself shows stones cascading from the tipped-up back of a truck, and the word that accompanies this, tilted about twenty degrees from the horizontal to the reader's right, at a similar angle to that tilted truck back, is "RUMBLE"—a word often preceded by the adjective "ominous," which seems all too appropriate in this case (109, panel 7). On the next page, the fifth and sixth panels show the stones striking the hooded prisoners, with the word "CRACK" in the fifth panel and "THUMP" and "CRACK" (the latter in red letters this time) in the sixth (110). It may be objected that the use of this technique is inappropriate here, reducing the deep human trauma of the execution to an occasion for comic book sensation. On one level, however, public executions are and always have been a source of sensation, arousing a mixture of horror, fascination, self-righteousness, sadism, and sympathy. But in context the overall effect in the graphic novel of *Kite* is to intensify rather than diminish the sense of trauma, especially since Amir, with his own burden of guilt, is witnessing it even if, as with Hassan's rape, he tries not to see it all. The last panel shows him in profile, with one hand covering his left eye, and his right eye closed; but while he can shut out the sight, he cannot, as the onomatopoeic words in the previous two panels emphasize, shut out the sound (110, panel 7).

This scene is soon followed by Amir's confrontation with Assef and his first encounter with Hassan's son, Sohrab—Amir knows by now that Hassan is dead, executed by the Taliban. A smaller panel set within a larger panel shows a finger pressing a switch; a "CLICK" indicates the sound this makes, and visual symbols of musical notes flow out from the smaller inset panel into the larger one that surrounds it, which shows a black-and-white shadow-image of a dancer's ankles with rings around them that hold small bells. The next panel, a disturbing image because of its connotations of the exploitation of a young boy, shows Sohrab dancing. The sound the bells on the rings around his ankles makes is indicated by the words "DING," "DING," "DING," in red, one above the other near Sohrab's feet (114, panels 4, 5). The onomatopoeia here draws attention to the bells, one of which will soon assume a blinding significance.

On the next-but-one page, the fight between Assef and Amir starts, accompanied by the onomatopoeic words characteristically associated with physical combat in comic books: "SOCK," as Assef delivers a right hook to Amir's jaw; "CRASH" as Assef knocks him off his feet and onto a table that splits under the impact; "BAM BAM BAM," extending into the adjacent panel as he kicks Amir repeatedly in the back; "STOK" as he grasps him by the hair and bangs his head (116, panel 3, 4, 5–6, 7). But on the next page, three panels later, we hear a different sound that accompanies the image of Sohrab unleashing his slingshot: "FFFSSSSSTTT!" (117, panel 4). The original novel also uses onomatopoeia at this point but the sounds it indicates is different: "The slingshot made a *thwiiiiit* sound when Sohrab released the cup" (254). It is worth noting that in the graphic novel the projectile Sohrab fires from his slingshot is different from the brass ball employed in both the original novel and the play. The panel that includes the onomatopoeic "FFFSSSSSTTT!" we have just mentioned shows that he uses one of the bells that were on the rings round his ankles when he was dancing as the ammunition that puts Assef's eye out. It seems particularly appropriate to hit back at his oppressor with this symbol of his servitude; it has a strong element of poetic justice, hoisting Assef with his own petard. We should stress, however, that Sohrab's primary motivation here is not a desire for revenge for his own sufferings but a wish to protect Amir from a brutal and possibly lethal beating.

Onomatopoeia, one of the classic resources of graphic fiction, can add powerfully to a scene, as these examples show. They provide a further demonstration of how language can feature and function in such fiction. But there are moments in graphic novels when words stop (whether they are in dialogue bubbles, rectangular boxes, or onomatopoeic splashes across an image); moments when the visual image alone carries the meaning. It is to key moments of this kind in the graphic novel of *Kite* that we shall now turn.

Pictures Without Words

Standalone images in graphic novels are not, of course, wholly independent of the rest of the narratives in which they occur. They emerge out of and feed back into verbal-visual continuums and would have somewhat different effects if they were completely isolated from these. Consider, for example, the image early in the graphic novel that shows Amir as a young boy crouched behind a wall, hands over his knees, arms crossed and concealing the lower part of his face, eyeballs looking to his right (15, panel 4). If we saw this image in isolation, without knowing the context, we might wonder what it signifies; is he hiding, cowering, perhaps in fear? If we return it to the context of the narrative, we find that Amir is cowering playfully rather than fearfully at this point; he is playing a game of hide and seek with Hassan, who has already told him that it is "USELESS TO HIDE" (15, panel 3) and quickly finds him, provoking Amir to complain: "HOW COME I CAN NEVER FIND A GOOD HIDING PLACE?!" (15, panel 5).

The narrative voice, however, has already established, in the first and third panels on the same page, that hiding behind a wall has a greater significance for the adult Amir, looking back, than a mere recurrent episode in a children's game; that, in one notable instance, it has been crucial in fixing his identity. As it says in the rectangular box at the top left of panel 3: "IT WAS BEHIND JUST ONE OF THESE THAT I BECAME THE PERSON I AM TODAY" (15). It is from behind a mud wall of this kind that he will witness—and turn his eyes from—the rape of Hassan. In that sense, his boyhood lament in panel 5 that he can "NEVER FIND A GOOD HIDING PLACE" takes on far more importance in retrospect, seeming to anticipate his failure ever to find a good place to hide from the memory of what he did, or failed to do, in relation to Hassan. This enables us to look back on the wordless image in panel 4 and see it differently: Amir is cowering not only from Hassan but also from his future as Hassan's betrayer, when he runs but cannot hide from his own memories.

The close bond between Amir and Hassan becomes perhaps most intense in the kite-fighting contest when Hassan runs off to seize the blue kite, the last one to fall, the trophy of Amir's victory, The relevant image positions readers behind Amir's head, which fills most of the left-hand side of the picture space as we look at it; but we also see the large hand of Baba resting firmly on Amir's shoulder, an unusual moment of close physical contact between father and legitimate son and a sign of Baba's approval of that son's victory—in which Baba's illegitimate son, whom he does not publicly acknowledge, played a crucial role. We also see Hassan some distance away waving and saying, "FOR YOU A THOUSAND TIMES OVER!" (39, panel 6). The next and final panel on that page has no words: it is a close-up of Amir's face, tilted twenty degrees from the vertical to the reader's left, and it shows tears starting from his eyes (39, panel 7). It is the moment of Amir's greatest triumph and of the most intense bonding between him and Hassan.

Amir, however, is about to betray Hassan. This is the moment just before the rape. If we move to the scene of the rape itself, which drives the narrative of the novel and is the most disturbing of several traumatic episodes in the narrative, we find another example of a wordless image that proves eloquent. In the first panel on page 43, Amir turns away, eyes closed, biting his fist in anguish, as in Chapter

7 of the novel (64) and we "hear from offstage" Assef's menacing words in a speech bubble: "READY, HAZARA?" The next panel has no words; it shows two huge green, hairy legs, trousers pooled around the ankles, opened in an inverted "V" and converging as they rise to just above the knees at the top of the panel. In between them, just visible over the pooled trousers, we see the small face of Amir rising above the top of the wall, witnessing the rape that is about to take place (43, panel 2). Here the graphic novel comes closer to a depiction of the actual rape than either the original novel (which focuses more on Amir's aversion of his gaze) or the theatrical adaptation (where it takes place offstage). It makes Assef look like a monstrous, corrupt Colossus and strongly conveys how Amir is overwhelmed by him. The next panel shows Amir, from the back, running away and this does include a rectangular box with a narrative fragment that is almost identically worded to that in Chapter 7 of the novel: "I RAN AWAY. I RAN BECAUSE I WAS A COWARD" (43, Panel 3). [The novel has: "In the end, I ran," set as a separate paragraph, and then "I ran because I was a coward" (68).] The wordless visual image we have seen in the previous panel is so unpleasant that readers can empathize with his flight even if, on another level, they reprove it, as does Amir with another part of himself.

Amir's failure to intervene to try to save Hassan from the rape makes him plot to have Ali and Hassan dismissed from Baba's house and his service. This does not quite work—indeed, Baba begs them to stay—but Ali has decided they must go after Hassan has told him everything, including the fact of Amir's betrayal. It is interesting to compare and contrast the handling of the last moments of the departure of Ali and Hassan in the graphic novel, play, and original text. In Chapter 9 of the original, Baba takes Ali and Hassan in his car to the bus station and Amir watches their departure through a rain-soaked window (94–95). In the play, Amir is actually present at the bus station watching them go (loc. 882). In the graphic novel, however, they depart by means of a more traditional form of transport: a mule or donkey, and the episode concludes with four wordless images. First we see, looking from below, Amir at the window, turned grey and white by the glass, and with his fingers and thumbs pressed against the pane; this appears to be an image from Hassan's point of view (62, panel 3). We then draw back and have an image of part of the mule or donkey's nose and the side of Hassan's head as he looks up to the window, through which Amir, behind the pane, is hardly visible (62, panel 4). The following image switches to a point of view close to Amir's; we see the front of his profile and part of his right hand pressing against the pane and, through the whitish-grey glass, Hassan tightening a strap on the donkey but turning to look up (62, panel 5). The last panel on the page closes up on part of Baba's face as he stands watching with anguish the departure of Hassan and Ali; his face partly obscures the image of Amir up in the window, behind glass, emphasizing the pain Amir's machinations have caused his father as well as himself (62, panel 6). These four wordless images, in the context of the narrative, are eloquent of depths and complexities of emotion that it would take many words to evoke and explore adequately.

A particularly powerful wordless and large-scale image occurs immediately after Baba's death. The last panel of the previous page also has no words but offers a monochrome close-up of a section of Amir's face on the night his father dies, with a tear dropping down from a closed left eye almost to the level of his nostril (89, panel 6). When readers turn over, the next image fills the whole page—only the second image in the graphic novel of *Kite* to do so. The first full-page image, which we discussed earlier, was of the nighttime scene of the vast mountains and wide expanse of sky through which the fuel tanker in which Baba and Amir and other refugees are confined is making its way from Afghanistan to Pakistan (68). Like that image, this one is, to borrow cinematic terminology, shot from high above, looking down, but this time into an interior rather than an exterior space. It shows Amir kneeling on the floor beside his father's corpse, bent over him, his head buried in his neck, his arms around him, experiencing the kind of close physical contact that he rarely enjoyed when his father was alive. Soraya stands in the foreground, a little distance from the end of the bed and even further from her husband, with her head bent, presumably weeping. Her physical distance from her husband is perhaps appropriate to the implicit codes for female behavior on this occasion, but it does also show the extent to which, here as at other times in *Kite*, male bonding seems stronger than male-female bonding. A particularly poignant touch is the pair of slippers we can see on the opposite side of the bed to Amir—Baba's slippers, which he will never wear again. A cigarette stub in the ashtray on the table on that side of the bed also reminds us that Baba has only just departed from life. The palette of the image is of sombre greens and greys, with just a note of crimson on the bedside table (90). The five panels on the next page also have no words: they show the mourners at the funeral, the imam reading the burial service, and the coffin of rough-grained wood, symbolic of Baba's rough-hewn nature, being lowered with ropes into the grave (91).

A further example of panels without words—and in this case sometimes without figurative images—occurs when Amir is in the hospital in Peshawar after his almost fatal beating by Assef. The last panel on the previous page is wholly black, apart from three words from the narrative voice in a rectangular box near the top left of the page: "THEN I FAINTED" (118, panel 6). The first panel of the next page is also black but contains a longer narrative passage in a rectangular box about how Amir kept fainting from the pain (119, panel 1). The next panel is completely black (119, panel 2). Then there is an image of either Hassan or Sohrab standing and a voice, perhaps Amir's own, that says questioningly "HASSAN. . ."? (119, panel 3). The fourth panel is also completely black, and the next panel is an image of Baba wrestling with a bear (119, panel 4, 5). This fifth panel illustrates the passage in Chapter 23 of the original novel in which, in the Peshawar hospital, Amir finds himself, in a dream, "in the Sulaiman mountains of Baluchistan" where "Baba is wrestling the black bear" (258). In the original, this refers back to the first paragraph of Chapter 3, which starts "Lore has it my father once wrestled a black bear in Baluchistan with his bare hands" and, slightly later in the same paragraph, continues "I have imagined Baba's wrestling match countless times, even dreamed about it" (11). The graphic novel here provides an image of one of those dreams as Amir recovers fitfully from his own wrestling match with the monstrous Assef. Two more wholly black and wordless panels follow before, in the last two panels on that page, Amir begins to emerge into full consciousness and becomes aware of the doctor talking to him (119, 6, 7, 8, 9). The use of a solid black rectangle to represent unconsciousness or death has a good literary pedigree; it is famously used to represent the black blankness of death in Laurence Sterne's eighteenth-century classic *The Life and Opinions of Tristram Shandy, Gentleman* (1760–67; 1962, 33–34); and it is appropriate here, as Amir has been often unconscious and sometimes close to death. As the doctor tells him in the last panel: "YOU'RE VERY LUCKY TO BE ALIVE" (119, panel 9).

Panels without words also prove highly effective in the scenes of Sohrab's attempted suicide and subsequent hospitalization. The panel that shows what has happened positions readers behind Amir's head as he looks between curtains into a bathroom and sees a very pale Sohrab lying in a bath almost brimful of water red with blood. Sohrab's left hand and wrist, hanging over the edge of the bath, have dripped blood on to the side of the bath and the floor (128, panel 1). Sohrab has tried to kill himself to avoid being sent to an orphanage again, unaware that Amir has just found out that this will not have to happen. The following panels show, in succession, Amir at Sohrab's bedside in the ambulance; Amir pacing the hospital corridor; and Amir on a prayer mat in the corridor, head bent to the floor (128, panels 2, 3, 4). This last panel corresponds to the moment in Chapter 25 of the original novel where he prays to Allah that Sohrab may live and swears he will hereafter be a devout Muslim if Sohrab does so (301–02). In the dynamic of the plot, Sohrab's recovery is essential if Amir is ever to realize the prospect, which the graphic novel, play and original text of *Kite* all highlight, of finding "*a way to be good again.*"

Conclusion

The last image in the graphic novel is a complex one. It is a full-page image but, in contrast to the two earlier full-page images we have discussed, into which no other image is interpolated, this one has a smaller square image inset on the left of the page near the top (132).

The large image shows Sohrab, seen from behind in three-quarter view, with a left arm and hand, which we know from the last image on the previous page to be Soraya's, resting on his shoulder. In that image on the previous page, Sohrab has just won the kite contest in California and Amir has offered to run the kite for him (131, panel 8). In both the graphic novel and original text, Sohrab makes no verbal reply to this question, though in the original Amir thinks he sees Sohrab nod. On the last page of the graphic novel, Amir is starting to run to get the kite and turning back as he does so to wave at Sohrab and say: "FOR YOU, A THOUSAND TIMES OVER!" (132)—the same words, minus the exclamation mark, that he uses at this point in the original novel (323).

This moment in the graphic novel both parallels and reverses, in part, an image discussed earlier, when we see Amir, as a boy, from behind, with Baba's hand resting on his shoulder and Hassan, about to run the kite, waves to him and says "FOR YOU A THOUSAND TIMES OVER!" (39, panel 6). The panel that immediately follows that earlier one, as we have mentioned, offers a wordless close-up of Amir's face, tilted twenty degrees from the vertical to the reader's left (39, panel 7). The inset panel on the final page of the graphic novel is a close-up of Sohrab's face that is likewise titled slightly to his right (and, therefore, to our left as we look at it) and it is rather similar to Amir's face in that earlier close-up, though not identical: there are differences in skin tone, eye-color and eyebrow shapes. Nonetheless, the likeness suggests a kinship between Amir as a boy and the son of the best friend he betrayed that has, as the narrative has by now revealed, some biological as well as psychological basis. But, in contrast to the young Amir, no tears start from Sohrab's eyes; his expression is still serious and ambiguous; we do not quite know what he is thinking and feeling, how far he wants to cooperate in this strange game of self-redemption that Amir is playing.

Amir is trying, to an extent, to reverse the original positions of himself and Hassan; Amir is becoming the kite runner, the person who would do things for his friend "a thousand times over," and Sohrab is becoming the person he wants to please and to bond with more strongly and closely. But the final image, echoing those images earlier in the graphic novel from the moment just before Amir betrayed Hassan, could raise the issue of whether history might, in a way, repeat itself. If Amir has become an adult version of Hassan and wants Sohrab to become a boyhood version of Amir, might not Sohrab betray him at some point as Amir betrayed Sohrab's father, if not in the same way? Is it not a kind of abuse on Amir's part to try to mold Sohrab into the person responsible for his uncle's own redemption? These are among the many questions that the end of the graphic novel, like the end of the original novel, poses. It is to the credit of both that they leave these questions open.

Works Cited or Consulted

Burke, Edmund. *A Philosophical [E]nquiry into the Origin of Our Ideas of the Sublime and Beautiful with an Introductory Discourse Concerning Taste, and Several Other Additions*. 1757. Cassell's National Library series. Cassell, 1891.

Hosseini, Khaled. *The Kite Runner*. 2003; Bloomsbury, 2011.

_____. *The Kite Runner: The Graphic Novel*. Illustrated by Fabio Celoni (ink) and Mirka Andolfo (color). Script by Tommaso Valsecchi. Bloomsbury, 2011.

_____. *The Kite Runner*, adapted by Matthew Spangler. Modern Plays series. Bloomsbury Publishing. Kindle Edition.

Sterne, Laurence. *The Life and Opinions of Tristram Shandy, Gentleman*. With an Afterword by Gerald Weales. Signet Classics. The New American Library of World Literature, 1962.

Reconfiguring *The Kite Runner*_____

Nicolas Tredell

It is worth recalling, as we reach the last essay in this Critical Insights volume, that *The Kite Runner* was the debut novel of a hitherto wholly unknown writer—Hosseini had published no previous fiction. As we know, it unexpectedly became a hugely popular bestseller, often arousing intense emotional engagements in its readers, and Hosseini himself achieved global fame. This reconfigured the cultural field in which the novel was read and received; it was impossible to approach it without some awareness of the immense impact it had made on many people around the world. For example, later editions of the novel emphasized both its commercial success and the praise it had received from reviewers. The 2011 Bloomsbury paperback bore the legend, near the top of its front cover: "OVER 21 MILLION COPIES SOLD WORLDWIDE." Further down that cover, below the title, four capsule quotes summed up its strong effects: "'Devastating' *Daily Telegraph*"; "'Heartbreaking' *The Times*"; "'Unforgettable' Isabel Allende"; "'Deeply moving' *Sunday Express*." The back cover carried five longer laudatory quotes from national newspapers, and inside the book, the first two pages consisted, apart from a brief biography of Hosseini, of a section headed "Praise for *The Kite Runner*" containing twelve highly approving quotes.

The sales information and quotations form part of what the French literary theorist Gérard Genette called the "seuil," literally the "threshold" of a text—the usual English translation of Genette's term is "paratext." A paratext creates a threshold that readers have to cross (even if they try to ignore it) before accessing the main text, a kind of text around that text—and in the case of *Kite*, this part of the paratext strongly conveys the idea that the novel has enjoyed huge sales and made a large emotional impact, primes readers to expect to participate in a widespread collective experience involving deep and intense feelings. This kind of paratextual element will also provoke dissent in some readers, at least initially, a desire to resist what they see as hype, to demonstrate that they are not one of the herd by refusing the novel's emotional appeals and finding fault with it.

If reviewers and publishers have significantly reconfigured the field in which we receive *Kite*, a major contribution, however much literary theory may have challenged the concept of "the author," has come from Hosseini himself in his public statements about his first novel in writing, speeches, and interviews, and, above all from a literary viewpoint, by his two later novels, *A Thousand Splendid Suns* (2007) and *And the Mountains Echoed* (2013). The review responses to those two novels have also contributed to that reconfiguration. This essay first samples Hosseini's own retrospective takes on *Kite* and then considers key instances of the review responses to his next two novels, which often refer back to his first.

Kite in Retrospect

In his "Foreword" to the tenth anniversary edition of *Kite*, published in 2013, Hosseini recalled his surprise at the success of his first novel. He had thought he was writing it for himself and was astonished at its seemingly worldwide resonance, exemplified, for him, by the letters he received from a variety of places across the globe: "India, South Africa, Tel Aviv, Sydney, London, Arkansas" (Hosseini 2013, loc. 57). They came from readers "who express their passion to [him]" (loc. 58). We see once more exemplified here the *kind* of response *Kite* evokes in its enthusiastic readers: an impassioned, emotional one. For Hosseini, "these letters" (loc. 59) offered an insight into "the unique ability fiction has to connect people" and into "how universal some human experiences are: shame, guilt, regret, friendship, love, forgiveness, atonement." The claim of universality for human experiences has been much contested in literary criticism and theory since the later twentieth century; it is argued that "universality" is a mystifying category that obscures differences in terms of, for instance, power, wealth, gender, and social status. It could be charged that Hosseini, in such a statement, contributes to such mystification, making himself acceptable to readers, especially in the West, who are averse to addressing issues of material inequality that only political change

---

could mitigate. But it does seem reasonable to suggest that there are experiences of the kind Hosseini describes that are universal and that asserting this need not entail ideological mystification. In this respect, reconfiguration is not so much a matter of changing the contexts in which *Kite* is seen as of recognizing that *Kite* itself changes those contexts. Hosseini's first novel, its reception, and his own response to that reception, may, among many other things, alter the ways in which we understand "universality."

In that "Foreword," Hosseini went on to argue that, while life can feed into and fashion the form and content of fiction, the same can happen in reverse: fiction can feed into and fashion the form and content of a life, "in its readers, and even in its author" (loc. 62). Hosseini acknowledged that many of his own experiences had fed into his portrayal of Amir; *Kite* was not an autobiography, but it had autobiographical elements. But it also had an element of what we might call anticipatory autobiography. In *Kite*, Hosseini had evoked the adult Amir's return to Afghanistan, a major part of the novel that is crucial to its plot and action, but he had not, at that point, actually returned to Afghanistan as an adult himself. In March 2003, when *Kite* was in production, he did so. In that respect, art anticipated life.

Moreover, it shaped perceptions of life. Hosseini's fortnight in Kabul assumed "a decidedly surreal quality because every day, I saw places and things I had already seen with my mind's eye, with Amir's eyes" (loc. 67). Parts of a passage from Chapter 19 of *Kite* came to his mind, and "Amir's thoughts suddenly became my own." He quoted directly from *Kite* at this point in the "Foreword": "The kinship I felt suddenly for the old land . . . it surprised me [. . .] I thought I had forgotten about this land. But I hadn't. [. . .] Maybe Afghanistan hadn't forgotten me either" (Hosseini 211; first ellipsis in original text of *Kite*; two later ellipses, inserted, presumably by Hosseini himself, in quote in "Foreword"). Hosseini cited the familiar advice to aspiring authors to "write about what you've experienced," but pointed out that the reverse can happen: "I was going to experience what I had already written about" (loc. 70).

For Hosseini, the most striking collision between fiction and life was his rediscovery of his old childhood home in Kabul, which

---

echoed Amir's rediscovery of his in Chapter 21 of the novel (227–29). In the "Foreword," he swore that, on stepping through the front gates, he "saw a Rorscha[..]ch blot-shaped oil stain on the driveway, just as Amir had on his father's driveway" (loc. 79). He went on to make the interesting observation that the "emotional impact of finding my father's house would have been even more intense if I hadn't written" *Kite* (loc. 80; Hosseini 2011, 229). In a sense, he had already undergone this experience in imagination. "I had stood beside Amir at the gates of his father's house and felt his loss. I'd watched him set his hands on the rusty wrought-iron bars, and together we'd gazed at the sagging roof and crumbling front steps" (loc. 81). He even suggested that this imaginative anticipation "took some of the edge off my own experience" (loc. 83). He summed it up as an example of "Art stealing Life's thunder" (loc. 83).

This is a very evocative and nuanced passage that clearly also has more general implications with regard to the complex relationships between life and art, fictional and real experience. It is a rich and concise piece of paratext for *Kite* and helps to reconfigure the context in which we see the novel, while also endowing the novel itself with considerable reconfigurative power. Fiction can not only reshape life; it can also reshape the way in which fiction itself is perceived.

The "Foreword" concluded with an account of how Hosseini now felt about the book. He still loved it in "the way you would love your troublesome, awkward, unruly, ungainly, but ultimately decent and bighearted child" (loc. 84)—an implicit acknowledgment, perhaps, that he did not see it, from a decade's distance, as a fully "mature" novel, to invoke a critical criterion that was widely deployed in mid-twentieth century Anglo-American literary criticism. And the adjectives "awkward" and "ungainly" also suggest aesthetic reservations about the novel. Of course, this is very much what might traditionally have been expected of a first novel, though perhaps more so by an author rather younger than Hosseini was when he wrote it. But he did feel, from readers' responses, that it could claim a solid achievement: it had "helped make Afghanistan a real place" for those readers (loc. 88). "It's quite an honor when readers tell me that this novel helped put a personal face on Afghanistan for them, and that they now see my homeland as more than just another unhappy, chronically troubled, afflicted land" (loc. 89). This kind of testimony from readers has itself helped to reconfigure the contexts in which we read and receive the novel. As we have seen, some reviewers and critics have argued that *Kite* misrepresents Afghanistan; and this, too, is part of the reconfiguration of the contexts in which we see the novel.

In a 2013 interview with Hermione Hoby in the *Guardian* (June 1, 2013), when his third novel, *And the Mountains Echoed*, was about to be published, Hosseini also looked back on *Kite* with reservations: "I think if I were to write my first novel now it would be a different book, and it may not be the book that everybody wants to read. But if I were given a red pen now and I went back . . . I'd take that thing apart" (ellipsis in original). In this context, "a red pen" usually means an instrument for crossing things out or at least marking them for amendment, and it would have been interesting to have examples and more details of what Hosseini might have wanted, from the vantage point of 2013, to excise and/or emend. Even without these, however, his remarks do help to reconfigure the field in which we see *Kite*. His suggestion that a *Kite* amended in this way might have a smaller readership is also intriguing.

As well as Hosseini's retrospective remarks on *Kite*, his next two novels and their reception also help to reconfigure the ways in which we see his first novel and we shall now consider the two novels in turn.

Burden of Comparison

Any author who has a large success with their first novel will feel under pressure to produce a second that equals or surpasses that success. It may not happen. In the United States, Norman Mailer's first novel, *The Naked and the Dead* (1948), made a big impact; but while he continued to publish, and to attract publicity, he never wrote a *novel* that received the same degree of acclaim as his first, turning mainly to what he called "creative non-fiction" that used techniques drawn from fiction such as dialogue and dramatized scenes to depict actual events. Ralph Ellison's superb first novel *Invisible Man* came out in 1952 and seemed like a large first step in a distinguished literary career; but he never published another novel in his lifetime. In the United Kingdom, John Braine's *Room at the Top* (1957) and Alan Sillitoe's *Saturday Night and Sunday Morning* (1958) were widely praised and bestselling first novels; but although both writers continued to produce and publish fiction throughout their lives, none of their later works received the same level of attention as their debut books had done.

The pressure was greater for Hosseini because it came not primarily from a relatively small number of literary critics occupying influential positions in newspapers and magazines but from the large fan base that *Kite* had created. He acknowledged this in his "Postscript" to the 2008 paperback edition of his second novel, which is an extract from a speech he gave at Book Expo America on June 2, 2007. The letters of praise for *Kite* that he received from across the globe had made him see "how [he] had unwittingly placed [him]self in a daunting position—that of following up [*Kite*], and writing a book that, through no fault of its own, would bear the burden of comparison to [his first novel]" (408).

There were two key differences between *Kite* and *Suns*. The first was in terms of gender. As readers, reviewers, and critics had observed, *Kite* is very male-centered, focusing on bonding, or the failure to bond, between fathers and sons and boys of divergent ethnicities. *Suns* is very woman-centered, focusing on bonding between mother and daughter and between two women who share the same brutal husband. This change of focus, by Hosseini's own account, was a conscious decision he took when making the last editorial changes to *Kite*. As he put it in the *Suns'* postscript: "I wanted to write another love story set in Afghanistan but this time a mother/daughter tale and about the inner lives of two struggling Afghan women" (409). It seemed to him that there was no "more riveting or important or compelling story than the struggle of women in my country" (409). In dramatic terms, it was by far the most prominent topic. Such a topic would also, though Hosseini may not have consciously thought of it in this way, provide a riposte to the criticism that *Kite* was too male-centered, with women either subsidiary or absent.

The second key difference between *Kite* and *Suns* was in terms of structure and narrative stance. *Kite* was primarily one story told by a first-person narrator. For his second novel, Hosseini chose a third person narrative with two central characters, Mariam and Laila. (This prompts us to imagine how *Kite* would have read if Hassan had also been a first-person narrator sharing the storytelling with Amir, or if the story had been told in the third person alternating between Amir and Hassan [and later, perhaps, Sohrab] as viewpoint characters.)

Hosseini linked *Suns* with his return visit to Kabul in 2003 which, as mentioned above, *Kite* seemed to anticipate in some respects. But one of the things that the first novel did not seem to anticipate was his curiosity on that visit about the women he saw in the city, often trailing many children, whose faces were covered. He recalled his thoughts at the time as being in the interrogative mode, a series of questions: "who is that person inside? What has she seen? What has she endured? What makes her happy? What gives her sorrow? What are her hopes, her longings, her disappointments?" (411–12). *Suns*, he contended, "is in some way his attempt at imagining answers to those questions" (412) by exploring "the inner lives of [. . .] two fictional women," Mariam and Laila, and looking for "the very ordinary humanity beneath their veils" (412). We might see here a certain appropriative voyeurism, a degree of Orientalism, and a dubious universalizing, a desire that the male gaze should show how it can penetrate the veil, with its connotations of the mysterious East and hidden secrets and delights, and discover that these supposed aliens are really just like us. But Hosseini's conscious intention was to "leave you [the reader] with some sense of compassion and empathy for Afghan women," who have, he asserts, suffered more than most in recent global history (412). As in *Kite*, his primary aim was to extend the reach of human sympathy by means of imaginative fiction. We shall see how key reviewers responded to the result.

Better than *Kite*?

In the *Guardian* (May 19, 2007), the novelist, feminist writer and human rights activist Natasha Walter found that *Suns* did not disappoint the expectations of enthusiastic *Kite* readers. Her review reassured fans at the outset. "Anyone whose heart strings were pulled by Khaled Hosseini's first, hugely successful novel [. . .] should be more than satisfied with this follow-up." She appreciated the informational content of *Suns*, what it told readers about Afghanistan, though she found this competed with its fictional identity. "That sense that you are listening to a history lesson as much as experiencing a fiction becomes stronger as the narrative moves on." But Walter asserted that "Hosseini doesn't get bogged down" in the historical and political detail and that "[h]is energetic narrative speeds on."

Walter addressed a charge against Hosseini's fiction that was now becoming familiar. "You might think this novel is becoming too melodramatic, as one horror succeeds another, with rockets blowing families apart and attempted escapes and even murder, alongside the beatings and whippings and threats that make up the women's daily experiences." Against this charge, Walter invoked the authority of personal testimony, recalling "how many" of the "women [she herself] met in Kabul [. . .] had stories to tell almost as melodramatic as this." One person's melodrama is another's reality.

The "novel begins to sing," in Walter's view, in its depiction of "the slowly growing friendship of the two wives in the face of the horrific abuse from their shared husband." But if the verb "to sing" here suggests that *Suns* assumes a lyrical quality in evoking this friendship, Walter scotched this suggestion by calling its prose "stolidly direct" and discerned a tendency "to explain away not only the political but also the personal, presenting each experience in a wrapper on which the emotion is carefully labelled." "[E]ach distinct emotion," Walter went on, "is spelled out a touch too clearly." This continues and extends the kind of critical attack directed against *Kite* for its allegedly uninspired prose and over-explicit interpretative direction to the reader. Walter also charged that Hosseini's wish to believe that Afghanistan could one day be redeemed "means that the ending verges on the schmaltzy" and is "just a little flimsy."

Jonathan Yardley, a nonfiction author and an influential book critic and columnist at the *Washington Post* from 1981, when he won that year's Pulitzer Prize for Criticism, to 2014, might have allayed Hosseini's concern that *Suns* would not bear comparison with *Kite* when he declared, in his *Post* review of the novel (May 20, 2007): "just in case you're wondering whether in yours truly's judgment it's as good as *The Kite Runner*, here's the answer: No. It's better." This remark, in slightly modified form, understandably heads the review quotes on the back cover of the 2008 Bloomsbury paperback edition. But in its full context in Yardley's review, the praise is more qualified than it seems in isolation. In that review, Yardley almost immediately followed the claim by highlighting what he saw as "Hosseini's literary shortcomings" in three areas: style, structure, and genre. His style, while "competent" as a rule, "lacks grace and distinctiveness." In structural terms, *Suns* "moves swiftly," but is "unwieldy": Yardley gives as an example the sudden introduction of "an entirely new set of characters a quarter of the way through," which demands "another quarter of the [novel] to get them fully involved in the plot." In terms of genre, it lapses at moments into modes supposedly inferior to that of the serious realistic novel. Like *Kite*, *Suns* "is powerfully moving," but sometimes descends to "melodrama and heartstring-tugging." Natasha Walter, as we saw above, also used the "heartstring" metaphor, and it is a common one in accounts of the techniques and emotional effects of Hosseini's novels. *Suns* is, Yardley adjudged, "popular fiction of the first rank," and admirable as such; but we should not mistake it for literature.

This begs the question of what "literature" is, and Yardley's implied criteria seem open to challenge: Anthony Trollope arguably had an ungraceful and undistinguished style, and melodrama and the kind of emotional manipulation Yardley sums up in the term "heartstring-tugging" were part of Charles Dickens's stock-in-trade. Do we therefore exclude Trollope and Dickens from the category of "literature"?

Though *Suns* may not be "literature," Yardley found its informative content in regard to Afghanistan, even if that smacked more of history and journalism than of fiction, invaluable, especially for American readers, many of whom "learned much from" *Kite*. And there was, Yardley asserted, "much more to be learned from" *Suns*, which "is, for all its shortcomings, a brave, honorable, big-hearted book." Thus, Yardley's claim that *Suns* is "better" than *Kite* is hedged around with anxious assurances that this does not mean that Hosseini's second novel merits elevation to the literary canon—a recurrent issue with *Kite* itself.

Michiko Kakutani, chief book reviewer of the *New York Times* from 1979–2017 and winner of the 1998 Pulitzer Prize for Criticism, who has been called not only "America's most powerful literary critic" (Nevins 2017) but also "one of the world's most influential book reviewers" (Cochrane 2008), did not review *Kite* when it first appeared, perhaps an indication of its author's relative obscurity and relatively low literary status at that time. (Its *NYT* reviewer was Edward Hower, as discussed in "Catching *The Kite Runner*" earlier in this volume.) Kakutani did, however, begin her review of *Suns* in the *New York Times* (May 29, 2007) with some interesting observations on *Kite*. She saw it as "a kind of modern-day variation" on Joseph Conrad's novel *Lord Jim* (1900), in which the protagonist struggles over the years to atone for a youthful act of cowardice. Although Kakutani did not say so explicitly at this point, her reference later in the review to Hosseini's "straight-ahead, utilitarian prose" showed that she clearly meant the comparison in terms of theme rather than style. (Harold Bloom, who instances Conrad's *Nostromo* as one of the heights to which *Kite* could never aspire in his guide to the latter book, would have been outraged at any suggestion that Hosseini's style could be compared to Conrad's.) For Kakutani, *Kite* offered readers apparent insights into life in Afghanistan and showcased what she called "its author's accessible and very old-fashioned storytelling talents," which were threefold: "melodramatic plotlines; sharply drawn, black-and-white characters; and elemental boldfaced emotions."

Kakutani contrasted the narrative trajectory of *Kite* and *Suns* in a way that worked ultimately in favor of the latter. *Kite* "got off to a gripping start and stumbled into contrivance and sentimentality in its second half." *Suns*, by contrast, "starts off programmatically and gains speed and emotional power as it slowly unfurls." In some other respects the two novels were similar: both have a thoroughgoing villain and a saint-like, self-sacrificing "best friend." Both show the effects of Afghanistan's troubled politics on a small group of people. In both narratives, the Taliban kill one main character while life and hope remain for the other. Both also, in Kakutani's eyes, have the same flaw: "some embarrassingly hokey scenes" that might have come "from a B movie." But both also have "some genuinely heart-wrenching scenes that help redeem the overall story."

Kakutani declared that, in both *Kite* and *Suns*, Hosseini's "characters [. . .] have the simplicity and primary-colored emotions of people in a fairy tale or fable." It is not so much their "personalities" that arouse sympathy—she summed up Amir in *Kite* as "an unlikable coward who failed to come to the aid of his best friend"—as their "circumstances," which involve "unhappy families, abusive marriages, oppressive governments and repressive cultural mores." In *Suns* these are conveyed in what Kakutani calls "soap-opera-ish events": a mother's suicide, the illegitimate daughter's hastily arranged marriage to an older and brutal man.

In the early chapters of *Suns*, Kakutani claimed, "the characters are so one-dimensional that they feel like cartoons." But slowly, Kakutani acknowledged, the author's "instinctive storytelling skills take over, mowing down the reader's objections through sheer momentum and will." The "emotional reality of Mariam and Laila's lives" becomes "tangible" to us and the evocation of their quotidian activities conveys "a sense of what daily life was like in Kabul" before and during the time of the Taliban. For Kakutani, "these glimpses of daily life in Afghanistan" are what make *Suns*, like *Kite*, "so stirring, and that distract attention from its myriad flaws."

These thoughtful and well-argued reviews exemplify a growing critical consensus about Hosseini's strengths and weaknesses that applies to *Kite* as well as to *Suns*. But his third novel, *And the*

Mountains Echoed, perturbs and complicates that consensus and further reconfigures the contexts in which we view his first novel.

Ranging More Widely

In his 2013 interview with Hermione Hoby on the eve of the publication of *Mountains*, from which we have already quoted, Hosseini located the origin of his third novel in "a single image: a man towing a small wagon through the desert at night. In the wagon are two children, a brother and sister." He had heard stories that stressed how fearful for families, and fatal to children, winters in Afghanistan could be, and "suddenly this image came out of the blue, delivered with pristine, perfect clarity. And I was like: who are these people? Where are they going?" In *Mountains*, they are going to Kabul, where the father gives away his three-year-old daughter to a prosperous family so that she can have a better life, on condition that he will never see her again, and thus tears the close bond that linked her to her ten-year-old brother. Hosseini described the novel as "kind of like a fairytale turned on its head," with "a very painful rupture at the beginning and then this tearful reconciliation at the end, except the revelations and the reconciliations you're granted aren't the ones you're expecting." This, Hosseini suggested, is what life is really like.

Hoby drew a contrast between *Mountains* and *Kite* and *Suns*, calling the two later novels "fable-like," with characters whom the novelist E. M. Forster "might have classified as 'flat' rather than 'round'" (see Forster 73–81, 169–70). As we have seen, Kakutani made a similar point about both novels in her review of *Suns*. Hoby cited Hosseini's comment on *Kite*'s Hassan as an example of "flat" characterization, quoting Hosseini's comment that he is "a lovely guy and you root for him and you love him but he's not complicated."

Whether this is altogether true is open to question—*Kite* and *Suns* have "fable-like" elements but also some realistic ones, and while certain characters might be seen as "flat," not all of them are: Hassan may not be complicated, but Amir surely is. Hoby was concerned, however, to stress the features of the earlier novels that brought out the difference of his latest one, in which, she claimed, all the characters "find themselves morally compromised at some point." She highlighted Hosseini's desire to avoid, in this third novel, what might look like a contrived ending in which the brother and sister torn apart as children were eventually reunited: "I sort of dreaded this kind of Hollywood-ish thing and I could see it inching that way and was a little worried." But after rereading his first chapter, he saw "how the book needs to end, with this idea of memory as a way that we make sense of our life." Memory is an "amazing gift" that enables us "to treasure all those things that matter to us the most, that form our identity," but that is "also very cruel because we relive those parts of our lives that are so painful." He foresaw that if there were to be a brother/sister reunion at the end of the novel, "it would occur on these terms and it wouldn't be the reunion we'd expect and perhaps the one we want."

Mountains incorporates and develops many of Hosseini's earlier themes and techniques; but it is also a much more expansive, wider-ranging novel than *Kite* and *Suns*. We look at those earlier novels differently in light of this latest one. We shall now consider key review responses to it, which often referenced those earlier novels.

Narrative Chemistry

In her review of *Mountains* in the *Independent* (May 18, 2013), the English writer Rachel Hore, herself an author of eight novels, praised both *Kite* and *Suns* without the reservations other reviewers and critics had made. She called them "beautifully written epics of the oft bloody history of the land of his birth over the past 60 years" that "have justifiably earned him a reputation as a great storyteller." She found *Mountains* "a worthy successor," but did recognize that its narrative might seem to depart from the expectations it at first appears to arouse. When a devoted brother and sister are torn apart as children near the start of the novel, the reader whom Hore typified as "the average Hosseini fan" might, she believed, anticipate "a satisfying tug-of-love story in which" brother and sister suffer badly in their quest to be reunited but succeed, after a fashion, in the end. Instead, "the narrative thread is cut short," as Hore put it, and moves into a "whole network of new characters and narratives that weave back and forth in time and place." The "most fascinating" of these new characters, Hore contended, was "[h]alf-French Nila Wahdati," "a sensual but emotionally damaged woman who wears Western clothes and make-up as well as writing sexually charged poetry."

Hore denied that *Mountains* was "about Afghan politics," which are, for her, only "in the background." Instead, Hosseini's "interests this time are the human and the personal." But they did expand beyond the personal, not to the political, but to the mythical. Hore felt that "Hosseini's effectiveness as a storyteller" was due partly to "the way he draws on universal signifiers of myth and symbol." He "uses archetypes: the wicked stepmother, the master and the servant, the brothers (in this case cousins) who are friends yet rivals"; but he is able, Hore affirmed, "to put flesh on them, to make them real and individual."

In the *New York Times* (May 20, 2013), Michiko Kakutani also applauded *Mountains*, though with some reservations of the kind she had made in relation to *Suns*. She judged it to be "his most assured and emotionally gripping story yet, more fluent and ambitious" than *Kite*, "more narratively complex" than *Suns*. Many of its themes were like those "that crisscross his earl[ier] novels," such as "the relationship between parents and children, and the ways the past can haunt the present." But while *Kite* and *Suns* concentrated, respectively, on father/son and mother/daughter "dynamics," *Mountains* addressed "sibling relationships" and did so "through the lives of several pairs of brothers and sisters."

Like *Kite* and *Suns*, however, *Mountains* inhabited a generic interzone "midway between the boldly colored world of fable and the more shadowy, shaded world of realism." In the two earlier novels, this could, in Kakutani's view, result in "some soapy, melodramatic plot twists" and ultra-good or ultra-bad characters. *Mountains* also had an excess of "contrivance and sentimentality," but its author's "narrative gifts have deepened over the years," so that its narrative firmly grounded "the more maudlin aspects of his tale in genuine emotion and fine-grained details" to give readers "an intimate understanding" of his characters and their life-choices in fraught situations often bound up with Afghanistan's troubled history.

The primary story in *Mountains* is the enforced early separation of ten-year-old Abdullah and his three-year-old sister, Pari. But the novel constructs "a kind of echo chamber" containing a range of "other tales that mirror the stories of Abdullah and the older Pari." To Kakutani's ears, however, this echo chamber was full of banal and mechanical noises. The tales "shamelessly use [. . .] contrivance and cheesy melodrama to press every [possible] sentimental button." At this point in her review, Kakutani seemed, contrary to her earlier praise of the novel, to go on the attack once more, using familiar anti-Hosseini weapons. But she then turned her sword from a potentially lethal weapon into an instrument for singling out Hosseini and ceremoniously honoring him. With most writers, "such narrative manipulations would result in some truly cringe-making moments." Hosseini, however, largely avoids this and also "succeed(s) in spinning his characters' lives into a deeply affecting choral work [that] is a testament both to his intimate knowledge of their inner lives, and to his power as an old-fashioned storyteller."

At the start of his review in the *Observer* (May 26, 2013), Alexander Linklater also seemed to be preparing to attack. He contended that the title and blurb of *Mountains* conveyed the impression of a bland, almost formulaic product. In a somewhat satirical tone, he outlined, the ingredients that this product, the Hosseini brand, shared with *Kite*: "siblings separated by hardship and tragedy"; "nostalgia for old Afghanistan, ironized by its clashes with western freedoms and shattered by modern wars"; and "leaps in time, speaking of the cruel tricks of history through wildly emotive tales of loss, betrayal and redemption."

Like a skillful lawyer, however, Linklater began by outlining a case against Hosseini only to create a foil for a strong advocacy in his favor. He went on to affirm that "the threat of bland formula is instantly dissolved in Hosseini's elemental narrative chemistry." Its "opening myth" is a story about a father who makes a deal with a demon to secure a better life for his son on condition that he never sees the son again—and, as we have already seen, Saboor, the father who is relating this myth to his children, is about to give up his young daughter, Pari, for the same reason and thus tear her away from her brother Abdullah. This myth, Linklater argued, "is a substance that permeates a network of tales, its meaning developing and diversifying across 400 pages." In Linklater's view, the initial separation of Pari from Abdullah makes readers want to see brother and sister reunited one day. This desire for their reunion, in Linklater's perspective, "saturates the various layers and characters" of *Mountains*.

Linklater saw Hosseini as "a master" of a profound "narrative principle": "get your audience where they want to go, but not in the way they expect." Instead of a focus on one character (as in *Kite*) or two (as in *Suns*), the story moves slantwise and expands outward "across a web of family connections," and "delays gratification without frustrating desire." Thus the "multi-layered narrative," as Linklater described it, keeps postponing the anticipated brother-sister reunion in order to evoke and explore characters and situations that absorb the attention of readers in their own right rather than simply as staging posts on the road to an expected conclusion. As Linklater put it, Hosseini "compresse[s] a dozen life stories into his novel and unifie[s] them through" the reader's ongoing desire for the reunion of brother and sister. A reunion does eventually occur but, as Hosseini himself had pointed out in his interview with Hermione Hoby, it is not quite of the expected kind.

Linklater saw *Mountains* as more closely concerned with Afghan politics, history, and identity than Natasha Walter had done. Indeed, he argued that this concern linked *Mountains* more strongly with *Kite* and provided another unifying element in Hosseini's third novel. In Linklater's perspective, *Mountains* addressed "the relationship of Afghanistan to the wider world; what its traumas have done to those who remain and what happens to those who leave and then come back to rediscover their country." At the end of his review, Linklater circled back briefly to the negative take on Hosseini's fiction with which he had begun. In *Mountains*, he declared, Hosseini gives readers "what they want with a narrative facility as great as any blockbusting author alive" and suggested there might be "some hokey emotional chemistry at work here."

But Linklater nonetheless affirmed the value of Hosseini's latest novel not only as a compelling web of interwoven stories but also as a sophisticated educational text that "communicat[es] to millions of people a supple, conflicted and complex picture of his origin country, Afghanistan."

Conclusion

These reviews of *Mountains* exemplify a sense—not universal, but quite widespread—that Hosseini's third novel was a kind of advance on his earlier ones, especially *Kite*, his first novel. If that were true, he would have traced a familiar trajectory for a "serious" literary novelist, from a debut that showed talent and promise but also exhibited some flaws to more complex and searching work. There was still a reluctance, evident in Kakutani's review of *Mountains* for example, fully to acknowledge Hosseini as a significant contributor to "literature," still a tendency—sometimes almost a compulsion—to highlight his uses of popular genres, devices, and emotions, such as melodrama and sentimentality, as markers of literary deficiency. But with the publication of this third novel, the bid for literary status has been made and was unignorable, even if it could still meet with the kind of simplification and caricature of Hosseini's fiction that was one of the very charges typically laid against that fiction.

If *Mountains* is taken as an accomplished and intricate work—and it seems legitimate to do so, even by "traditional" literary standards—this has fruitful implications for reading, interpreting, and assessing the novel that is the topic of this Critical Insights volume. We can now approach *Kite* in two interrelated ways: as a more substantial work in its own right than it might previously have seemed, and as an anticipation of Hosseini's later fiction. Whatever interpretations and evaluations of Hosseini's first novel and of his whole oeuvre may emerge in the future, it looks as though *Kite* will run and run.

Works Cited

Cochrane, Kira. "Don't Mess with Michiko Kakutani.*" The Guardian,* 1 May 2008. www.theguardian.com/books/booksblog/2008/may/01/dontmesswithmichikokakutan.

Genette, Gérard. *Seuils.* Éditions du Seuil, 1987. English version: *Paratexts: Thresholds of Interpretation.* Translated by Jane E. Lewin. Foreword by Richard Macksey. Literature, Culture, Theory series no. 20. Cambridge UP, 1997.

Hore, Rachel. "Review: *And the Mountains Echoed,* By Khaled Hosseini. *The Independent,* 18 May 2013. www.independent.co.uk/arts-entertainment/books/reviews/review-and-the-mountains-echoed-by-khaled-hosseini-8622201.html.

Hosseini, Khaled. "Foreword to the Tenth Anniversary Edition." In *The Kite Runner.* Bloomsbury, 2013. Kindle Edition, loc. 52–87.

_____. "If I Could Go Back Now, I'd Take *The Kite Runner* Apart." Interview with Hermione Hoby. *The Guardian,* 1 June 2013. www.theguardian.com/books/2013/jun/01/khaled-hosseini-kite-runner-interview.

_____. "Postscript [. . .] This extract is taken from a speech given at Book Expo America [2 June] 2007." In *A Thousand Splendid Suns.* 2007. Bloomsbury, 2008, pp. 407–12.

Kakutani, Michiko. "A Woman's Lot in Kabul, Lower Than a House Cat's." Review of *A Thousand Splendid Suns* by Khaled Hosseini. *The New York Times,* 29 May 2007. www.nytimes.com/2007/05/29/books/29kaku.html.

_____. "Siblings Haunted by the Past, and by Afghanistan's Cycle of Misery." Review of *And the Mountains Echoed* by Khaled Hosseini. The *New York Times,* 20 May 2013. www.nytimes.com/2013/05/21/books/and-the-mountains-echoed-by-khaled-hosseini.html.

Linklater, Alexander. "*And the Mountains Echoed* by Khaled Hosseini— Review." *Observer,* 26 May 2013. www.theguardian.com/books/2013/may/26/mountains-echoed-khaled-hosseini-review.

Nevins, Jake. "The Literary Life of Michiko Kakutani: The Book Critic's Best Feuds and Reviews." *The Guardian,* 28 July 2017. www.theguardian.com/media/2017/jul/28/the-literary-life-of-michiko-kakutani-the-book-critics-best-feuds-and-reviews.

Walter, Natasha. "Behind the Veil." Review of *A Thousand Splendid Suns* by Khaled Hosseini. *The Guardian*, 19 May 2007. https://www.theguardian.com/books/2007/may/19/featuresreviews.guardianreview21.

Yardley, Jonathan. "*A Thousand Splendid Suns*." Review of *A Thousand Splendid Suns* by Khaled Hosseini. *The Washington Post*, 20 May 2007. https://www.washingtonpost.com/wp-dyn/content/article/2007/05/17/AR2007051701932.html.

RESOURCES

Chronology of Khaled Hosseini's Life

1965	Khaled Hossein born on March 4 in Kabul, Afghanistan. His family is upper-middle class. His father is a diplomat in the Ministry of Foreign Affairs in Kabul. His mother is a Persian language teacher at a high school for girls.
1970-73	The family lives in Tehran, Iran, while Hosseini's father works in the Embassy of Afghanistan there.
1973	The family returns to Kabul.
1973	In July, Hosseini's youngest brother is born.
1976	The family move to Paris because of Hosseini's father's job.
1978	Saur Revolution (April).
1980	Soviet Invasion of Afghanistan. Start of Soviet-Afghan War prevents family returning home. Family seeks political asylum in the United States, settling in San José, California. Father becomes driving instructor. Mother becomes waitress. Hosseini speaks no English on arrival in the United States at the age of 15.
1984	Hosseini graduates from Independence High School, San José.
1988	Hosseini graduates from Santa Clara University with a bachelor's degree (BS) in Biology.
1989	Hosseini enters University of California San Diego School of Medicine.

1989-96	Hosseini studies medicine at the University of California.
1993	Hosseini earns M.D.
1993	Hosseini marries Roya on October 3.
1996	Hosseini completes residency in internal medicine at Los Angeles Cedars-Sinai Medical Center.
1996	Hosseini becomes medical internist at Kaiser Hospital, Mountain View, California.
1999	Hosseini learns through news report that the Taliban have banned kite flying in Afghanistan. This prompts him to write a 25-page short story about two boys who fly kites in Kabul. Hosseini submits short story to *Esquire* and *The New Yorker*. Both reject it.
2000	Haris, Hosseini's son, born on December 22.
2001	In March, Hosseini rediscovers the manuscript of the short story in his garage and at the suggestion of a friend he decides to expand it into a novel, writing in the early morning before going to work as a doctor.
2002	In June, Hosseini sends the manuscript of *The Kite Runner* to literary agent Elaine Koster in New York City.
2003	Hosseini's daughter Farah is born on January 6.
2003	*The Kite Runner* is released in hardback on May 29 by Riverhead Books with an initial printing of 50,000 copies.

2003	Hosseini goes to Kabul where he sees the burqa-clad women begging in the streets. This experience is the inspiration for his second novel *A Thousand Splendid Suns*.
2004	Hosseini stops practicing medicine and begins writing *A Thousand Splendid Suns*. Paperback of *The Kite Runner* is released. This becomes popular with book groups.
2004	*The Kite Runner* starts appearing on bestseller lists in September.
2006	Hosseini becomes Goodwill Envoy for the UN.
2007	Matthew Spangler's stage adaptation of *The Kite Runner*, directed by Spangler himself, was performed at San José State University by a cast of student actors.
2007	*A Thousand Splendid Suns* is published in hardback on May 22 by Riverhead Books and by Simon Schuster as an audio CD. Original title was "Dreaming in Titanic City" referring to a neighborhood of Kabul that for a while was known as Titanic City. Revised title comes from a line in the poem "Kabul" by Saib Tabrizi, a seventeenth-century Iranian poet, in the translation by Josephine Davis.
2007	Columbia Pictures buys the film rights to *A Thousand Splendid Suns*.
2007	Hosseini goes on a UNHCR (United Nations High Commissioner for Refugees) trip to Afghanistan. Stories he is told about poor young children dying in winter by a number of village elders start him considering the plot for *And the Mountains Echoed*.

2007	The screening of the film of *The Kite Runner* takes place on September 16 at the White House for President George W. Bush and First Lady Mrs. Laura Bush. Also at the screening are Vice President Dick Cheney; Secretary of Defense Robert Gates; Chairman of the Joint Chiefs of Staff General Peter Pace; National Security Advisor Stephen Hadley; Ambassador Said T. Jawad of Afghanistan; former Ambassador to Afghanistan now U.S. Ambassador to the United Nations Zalmay Khalilzad; former U.S. Ambassador to Afghanistan Ronald E. Neumann; President of the American University in Afghanistan Tom Stauffer.
2007	Illustrated edition of *The Kite Runner* is published in hardback on October 4.
2007	On November 2, film of *The Kite Runner* scheduled to premiere. Release date pushed back six weeks to evacuate the Afghan child stars from the country after they had received death threats.
2007	Film of *The Kite Runner* released on December 14.
2008	Inspired by UNHCR trip Hosseini establishes The Khaled Hosseini Foundation in Afghanistan. This is a non-profit organization "providing funding for shelter, education, healthcare," etc. to women and children in Afghanistan.
2009	Steven Zaillian finishes writing the first draft of the screenplay of *A Thousand Splendid Suns*.
2009	Hosseini goes on a UNHCR trip to Afghanistan. His meeting with two young sisters in a remote village outside Kabul provides material for *And the Mountains Echoed* in the relationship between Abdullah and Pari.

2009	World premiere of Matthew Spangler's stage adaptation of *The Kite Runner* directed by David Ira Goldstein of the Arizona Theatre Company at San José Repertory Theatre, March 21—April 19.
2009	Spangler's *Kite Runner* stage adaptation performed by the Arizona Theatre Company at the Temple of Music and Art in Tucson, September 10–October 3.
2009	Spangler's *Kite Runner* stage adaptation performed by the Arizona Theatre Company at the Herberger Theater Center in Phoenix, October 8–October 25.
2009	Illustrated edition of *A Thousand Splendid Suns* is published on October 29.
2010	Spangler's *Kite Runner* stage adaptation performed at the Actors' Theatre of Louisville, August 31–September 25.
2010	Spangler's *Kite Runner* stage adaptation performed at the Cleveland Playhouse, October 15–November 11.
2011	Graphic Novel edition of *The Kite Runner* published, with illustrations by Fabio Celoni and Mirka Andolfo.
2012	Spangler's *Kite Runner* stage adaptation performed at The New Repertory Theatre of Watertown, Massachusetts, September 9–September 30.
2013	Spangler's *Kite Runner* stage adaptation performed at the Theatre Calgary, Alberta, Canada, January 29–February 24. Co-production with the Citadel Theatre (Edmonton).

2013	In January, *Publishers Weekly* announces May 21, 2013, as the publication date for *And the Mountains Echoed.*
2013	European premiere of Spangler's *Kite Runner* stage adaptation at Nottingham Playhouse April 26–May 18.
2013	Riverhead Books releases a tenth anniversary edition of *The Kite Runner* with a new gold-rimmed cover and a Foreword by Hosseini.
2013	In May, Columbia Pictures confirms the tentative release date of 2015 for the film of *A Thousand Splendid Suns*. This film does not yet seem to have appeared.
2013	*And the Mountains Echoed* is published on May 21 by Riverhead Books. The title was inspired by the line "And all the hills echoed" from William Blake's poem "Nurse's Song: Innocence."
2013	Hosseini makes a five-week promotional tour for *And the Mountains Echoed* to 41 cities across America.
2013	Plans are confirmed in October to translate *And the Mountains Echoed* into 40 languages including Icelandic and Malay.
2016	Spangler's *Kite Runner* stage adaptation performed at Wyndham's Theatre, London, December 21–March 11, 2017.
2017	The first theatrical adaptation of *A Thousand Splendid Suns* premieres on February 1 at the American Conservatory Theatre in San Francisco, California (co-produced by American Conservatory Theater and Theatre Calgary).

2017	The *Guardian* newspaper asks Hosseini to write the narrative for *Sea Prayer* "an illustrated story animated in a virtual reality film" to commemorate the death on September 2, 2015, of the three-year-old Syrian refugee, Alan Kurdi.
2017	April 3, UK tour of Spangler's *Kite Runner* adaptation starts at Hull New Theatre and goes on to play at 25 more venues before the final performance at the Grand Opera House in Belfast in Northern Ireland on June 18–23 2018.
2017	*Sea Prayer* released on September 1 "as a virtual reality experience in collaboration with UNHCR, the *Guardian* and Google" "to mark the second anniversary" of Alan Kurdi's death.
2018	To mark the third anniversary of Alan Kurdi's death, *Sea Prayer* published in September in print and e-book form by Riverhead Books, with watercolor illustrations by Dan Williams.
2019	Theatrical production of *A Thousand Splendid Suns*, adapted by Ursula Rani Sarma, has brief run at Birmingham Repertory Theatre, May 2–18.

Works by Khaled Hosseini

Novels

The Kite Runner. Riverhead Books, 2003.
A Thousand Splendid Suns. Riverhead Books, 2007.
And the Mountains Echoed. Riverhead Books, 2013.

Short Fiction

Sea Prayer, with illustrations by Dan Williams. Riverhead Books, 2018.

Bibliography

Ashdown, Kate. "Places of Safety or Threat: Afghanistan and America in *The Kite Runner*." EMC, *emagazine*, vol. 68, Apr. 2015. www. englishandmedia.co.uk/e-magazine/articles/17327. [Paywall].

Aubry, Timothy. "Afghanistan Meets the *Amazon*: Reading *The Kite Runner* in America." *PMLA*, vol. 124, no. 1, 2009, pp. 25–43. *JSTOR*, www.jstor.org/stable/25614246.

Banita, Georgiana. *"The Kite Runner's* Transnational Allegory: Anatomy of an Afghan-American Bestseller." *Must Read: Rediscovering American Bestsellers: From* Charlotte Temple *to* The Da Vinci Code, edited by Sarah Churchwell and Thomas Ruys Smith. Continuum, 2012, pp. 319–39.

Bickley, Pamela. "Living Inside History—Novels that Deal in Real Time." EMC, *emagazine* vol. 45, Sept. 2009. www.englishandmedia.co.uk/e-magazine/articles/15131. [Paywall].

Bleiman, Barbara. "In the Beginning—The Opening of *The Kite Runner*." EMC, *emagazine* vol. 41, Sept. 2008. www.englishandmedia.co.uk/e-magazine/articles/15025. [Paywall].

_____. "Stories, Novels, and Films in *The Kite Runner*." EMC, *emagazine* vol. 51, Dec. 2011. www.englishandmedia.co.uk/e-magazine. [Paywall].

Bloom, Harold. Introduction. Khaled Hosseini's *The Kite Runner*, edited by Harold Bloom. Bloom's Literary Criticism. Infobase Publishing, 2009, pp 7–8.

Blumenthal, Rachel. "Looking for Home in the Islamic Diaspora of Ayaan Hirsi Ali, Azar Nafisi, and Khaled Hosseini." *Arab Studies Quarterly*, vol. 34, no. 4, 2012, pp. 250–64. *JSTOR*, www.jstor.org/stable/41858711.

Davies, Dominic. "Exploiting Afghan Victimhood." *The Oxonian Review*, vol. 23, no. 1, 14 Oct. 2013. www.oxonianreview.org/wp/exploiting-afghan-victimhood/.

Desai, Chetan. *"The Kite Runner* and *Wuthering Heights*." EMC, *emagazine* vol. 50, Dec. 2010. www.englishandmedia.co.uk/e-magazine/articles/15242. [Paywall].

Fowler, Corinne. *Chasing Tales: Travel Writing, Journalism, and the History of British Ideas about Afghanistan*. Rodopi, 2007.

_____. "Khaled Hosseini: *The Kite Runner*." The Literary Encyclopedia. First published 18 Dec. 2009, www.litencyc.com/php/sworks.php?rec=true&UID=23019.

Hayes, Judi Slayden. *In Search of* The Kite Runner. Popular Insights Series. Chalice P, 2007.

Ivanchikova, Alla. *Imagining Afghanistan: Global Fiction and Film of the 9/11 Wars*. Purdue UP, 2019.

Jefferess, David. "To Be Good (Again): *The Kite Runner* as Allegory of Global Ethics." *Journal of Postcolonial Writing*, vol. 45, no. 4, Nov. 2009, pp. 389–400, needoc.net/to-be-good-again-the-kite-runner-as-allegory-of-global-ethics.

Kahf, Mohja. *The Girl in the Tangerine Scarf: A Novel*. Carroll & Graf, 2006.

Kerr, Calum. *The Kite Runner: York Notes Advanced*. Longman, 2009.

Keshavarz, Fatemeh. "Banishing the Ghosts of Iran." *The Chronicle of Higher Education*, vol. 53, no. 45, 13 July 2007, p. B6. www.chronicle.com/article/Banishing-the-Ghosts-of-Iran/14693. [Paywall]. Reprinted Bloom, 2009, pp. 70–73.

_____. "*Reading More Than* Lolita *in Tehran*: An Interview with Fatemeh Keshavarz." *MRonline*. 12 Mar. 2007. mronline.org/2007/03/12/reading-more-than-lolita-in-tehran-an-interview-with-fatemeh-keshavarz/.

_____. *Jasmine and Stars: Reading More Than* Lolita *in Tehran*. U of North Carolina P, 2007.

The Kite Runner (film). Directed by Marc Forster. Screenplay by David Beniof. Perf. Khalid Abdalla. Distributed by Dream Works Pictures, 2007.

The Kite Runner: The Graphic Novel. Illustrated by Fabio Celoni (ink) and Mirka Andolfo (color). Script by Tommaso Valsecchi. Bloomsbury, 2011.

Maskell, Anthony. "Fertility and Friendship in *The Kite Runner*." EMC, *emagazine, vol.* 86, Dec. 2019. www.englishandmedia.co.uk/e-magazine/articles/36876. [Paywall].

Morey, Peter. *Islamophobia and the Novel*. Literature Now. Columbia UP, 2018.

Nafisi, Azar. *Reading* Lolita *in Tehran: A Story of Love, Books, and* Revolution. IB Tauris, 2003. Republished as *Reading* Lolita *in Tehran: A Memoir in Books*. Random House, 2004.

O'Doherty, Garrett. *The Kite Runner*: Khaled Hosseini. Oxford Literature Companions (AS/A Level). Oxford UP, 2019.

O'Kieran, Kelly. "The Tragedy of *The Kite Runner*." EMC, *emagazine* 45, Sept. 2009. www.englishandmedia.co.uk/e-magazine/articles/15134. [Paywall].

Schofield, Alistair. "A Flattering Portrayal? Americans and Afghans in *The Kite Runner*." EMC, *emagazine* 58, Dec. 2012. www. englishandmedia.co.uk/e-magazine/articles/15490. [Paywall].

Simons, Judy. "*The Handmaid's Tale* and *The Kite Runner*." EMC, *emagazine* 77, Sept. 2017. www.englishandmedia.co.uk/e-magazine/ articles/25932. [Paywall].

Slaughter, Joseph R. *Human Rights, Inc.: The World Novel, Narrative Form, and International Law*. Fordham UP, 2007.

Spangler, Matthew. *The Kite Runner [Play Script]*. Based on the novel by Khaled Hosseini. Riverhead Books, 2018.

Stuhr, Rebecca. *Reading Khaled Hosseini*. The Pop Lit Book Club. Greenwood P, 2009. works.bepress.com/rebecca_stuhr/3/.

Additional Resources

Interviews

"Despair in Kabul." Interview by Lucie Young. *The Telegraph*, 19 May 2007, www.telegraph.co.uk/culture/3665261/Despair-in-Kabul.html.

"If I Could Go Back Now, I'd Take *The Kite Runner* Apart." Interview by Hermione Hoby. *The Guardian*, 1 June 2013, theguardian.com/books/2013/jun/01/khaled-hosseini-kite-runner-interview.

"Interview with Khaled Hosseini." Interview by GR. Goodreads. 4 June 2013, www.goodreads.com/interviews/show/869.Khaled_Hosseini.

"Khaled Hosseini in Conversation with Book Passage's Elaine Petrocelli. Interview by Elaine Petrocelli, Book Passages, 18 Apr. 2020, bookpassage.extendedsession.com/session/khaled-hosseini/.

"An Old, Familiar Face: Writer Khaled Hosseini, Lifting the Veil on Afghanistan". Interview by Tamara Jones. *The Washington Post*, 28 May 2007, washingtonpost.com. [Paywall]

Websites

khaledhosseini.com/

www.khaledhosseinifoundation.org/

Social Media
Facebook

www.facebook.com/KhaledHosseini/

www.facebook.com/khfoundation/

Twitter

twitter.com/khaledhosseini

About the Editor

Nicolas Tredell is an independent scholar who has published 21 books and over 400 essays, articles, and reviews on authors ranging from Shakespeare to Zadie Smith and on key issues in literary, film, and cultural theory. His recent books include *Anatomy of Amis* (Paupers' Press, 2017), the most comprehensive account so far of the work of Martin Amis; *Conversations with Critics* (Verbivoracious, 2015), an updated edition of his interviews with leading literary figures; *Shakespeare: The Tragedies* (Palgrave, 2012); and *C. P. Snow: The Dynamics of Hope* (Palgrave, 2012).

He edited the Salem Press Critical Insights volume on *A Midsummer Night's Dream* (2020) and has contributed essays to other Salem Press volumes on Psychological, Moral, and Feminist Approaches to Literature; Greed, Rebellion, Satire, and Survival; *The Crucible, Hamlet, Heart of Darkness, Invisible Man, Lord of the Flies, The Odyssey* and *Paradise Lost*; and Thomas Jefferson, Abraham Lincoln, Martin Luther King, Malcolm X, and Walt Whitman. Two recent essays, on American literature from 1776–2018, and on literary theory, have appeared in *The Literature Reader: Key Thinkers on Key Topics* (English and Media Centre, 2019). He is a regular contributor to the English and Media Centre's *emagazine* for English A Level students.

He is Consultant Editor of the Essential Criticism series, published by Red Globe Press (formerly Palgrave), which numbers 88 titles so far, eight of which he has himself produced, including the volumes on *Macbeth* and *A Midsummer Night's Dream*. He was a judge of the Geoffrey Faber Memorial Prize for poetry in 1994 and of the English and Media Centre Close Reading Competition in 2016. He is a co-organizer of the Literary London Society Annual Conferences that attract distinguished speakers from across the globe.

He formerly taught literature, drama, film, and cultural studies at Sussex University and now gives live and video lectures and presentations, and leads discussions, at a wide range of school, university, and public venues in England and abroad. His website is *nicolastredell.co.uk/*.

Contributors

Georgiana Banita is a Fellow and Advisory Board member of the Trimberg Research Academy (TRAc) at the University of Bamberg, Germany, where she leads several research projects. Banita is also an Honorary Research Fellow of the United States Studies Centre at the University of Sydney, Australia. She has carried out research and taught at several universities including Konstanz, Yale, and Sydney. She is the author of *Plotting Justice: Narrative Ethics and Literary Culture after 9/11* (2012) as well as co-editor of *Electoral Cultures: American Democracy and Choice* (2015) and the forthcoming *Artful Breakdowns: The Comics of Art Spiegelman*. She has published widely on contemporary American fiction, literature and terrorism, and transnational American Studies. Current research interests include low intensity conflict and American fiction, the global refugee crisis, and petroleum as a literary subject.

Robert C. Evans is I. B. Young Professor of English at Auburn University at Montgomery. He earned his PhD from Princeton University in 1984. In 1982 he began teaching at AUM, where he has been named distinguished Research Professor, Distinguished Teaching Professor, and University Alumni Professor. External awards include fellowships from the American Council of Learned Societies, the American Philosophical Society, the National Endowment for the Humanities, the UCLA Center for Medieval and Renaissance Studies, and the Folger, Huntington, and Newberry Libraries. He is the author or editor of over fifty books and of more than four hundred essays, including recent work on various American writers.

Lucky Issar has worked in the field of education in India and Denmark. Currently, he is doing research at the Department of English Philology at Freie Universität of Berlin, Germany. He has done extensive research on queer theory that focuses on India and Indian writings in English. He has written articles on the works of Indian author Arundhati Roy, focussing on the issues of caste, urban violence, and sexuality in contemporary India. At present, he is working on a book-length project titled *Urban Friendships in Urban India*. He loves reading literature, traveling, and living in Denmark.

Alla Ivanchikova is Associate Professor of English and Comparative Literature at Hobart and William Smith Colleges in Geneva, NY. She is the author of *Imagining Afghanistan: Global Fiction and Film of the 9/11 Wars* (Purdue UP, 2019) and of a range of essays, including "Geomediations in the Anthropocene: Fictions of the Geologic Turn," "Imagining Afghanistan in Deep Time: Nadeem Aslam and the Aesthetics of the Geologic Turn" (2018), "Imagining Afghanistan in the Aftermath of 9/11: Conflicting Literary Chronographies of the Invasion" (2016), and "Living in the Shadow of Radicalism: Fundamental Identities in Monica Ali's *Brick Lane* and in Elena Chudinova's *2048: The Mosque of Notre Dame de Paris*" (2012)

Calum Kerr PhD is Lecturer in Creative Writing at the University of Portsmouth, United Kingdom. He has researched and taught in English Literature and Creative Writing since 2001. He has written academic study guides on a wide range of texts from Shakespeare plays to *Waiting for Godot*, and from *Candide* to *Fight Club*. He is the author of the York Notes on *The Kite Runner* and has given a number of talks on the book. His main areas of current research include themes in the works of Terry Pratchett, and theories of creation and creativity in writing.

Angela Tredell is a retired Chartered Librarian with a master's degree (MA) in Information Science from the University of Brighton, England.

Afghan society xi, 74, 77, 84, 86,
    88, 91, 92, 93, 94, 96, 97,
    98, 99, 100, 101, 116, 139
Afghan suffering 104, 121
Afghan women 72, 74, 96, 105,
    109, 120, 122, 236, 237
Africa 53, 55, 58, 232
African Americans 29
agony 183
Akrami, Sofia 74, 75
Alamian, Anousha 207
À La Recherche du Temps Perdu
    (In Search of Lost Time)
    163
Alexander the Great 3
Al-Hassan, Aliya 209
Ali (Babalu) xii, xiv, xxv, 5, 28,
    31, 36, 37, 40, 71, 74, 84,
    86, 87, 88, 92, 95, 96, 97,
    98, 99, 100, 101, 127, 128,
    129, 130, 132, 136, 137,
    141, 153, 161, 163, 165,
    197, 198, 199, 204, 205,
    217, 225, 226
Alice in Wonderland 42
Allah 63, 80, 154, 228
allegories 168
Allende, Isabel 231
alliances 7, 13, 107
allusion 20, 211
al-Qaeda 8, 13
al-Tashkenti, Juma 61
altruism 99
Amazon 21, 25, 28, 30, 54, 63,
    65, 122, 193
ambiguous 229
America vii, viii, xii, xv, xxvii,
    xxviii, xxx, xxxii, xxxiii, 8,
    11, 12, 13, 14, 25, 30, 34,

40, 42, 47, 54, 55, 58, 60,
    65, 83, 108, 109, 116, 121,
    122, 124, 128, 145, 177,
    185, 204, 211, 220, 236,
    240, 248
American acculturation 49
American Afghan Pashtun
    community 57
American culture 11, 58
American identity 56, 109
American Muslims 29
American popular culture 187
Amir xi, xii, xiii, xiv, xvii, xviii,
    xxiv, xxv, xxxiii, 3, 5, 6, 7,
    11, 12, 14, 17, 18, 21, 22,
    23, 27, 28, 33, 34, 35, 36,
    37, 38, 39, 40, 41, 42, 43,
    44, 45, 46, 47, 49, 50, 51,
    52, 53, 54, 55, 57, 58, 59,
    60, 61, 62, 63, 64, 69, 70,
    71, 74, 75, 76, 77, 78, 79,
    80, 82, 86, 87, 88, 89, 90,
    91, 92, 93, 94, 95, 96, 97,
    98, 99, 100, 101, 109, 113,
    117, 119, 126, 127, 128,
    129, 130, 131, 132, 133,
    134, 135, 136, 137, 138,
    139, 140, 141, 142, 143,
    144, 145, 146, 147, 148,
    149, 150, 151, 152, 153,
    154, 155, 157, 158, 159,
    160, 161, 162, 163, 164,
    165, 166, 167, 168, 169,
    170, 173, 174, 175, 176,
    177, 178, 180, 181, 183,
    184, 186, 195, 196, 197,
    198, 199, 200, 201, 202,
    203, 204, 205, 206, 207,
    210, 212, 215, 216, 217,

hope 25, 29, 51, 70, 72, 107, 116, 119, 140, 143, 184, 241
Hore, Rachel 243
horror 59, 202, 221, 238
Hosseini, Farah xxviii
Hosseini, Haris xxviii
Hosseini, Khaled vii, xvii, xxvii, xxix, xxx, xxxi, xxxiii, xxxiv, 16, 22, 28, 31, 32, 49, 83, 84, 104, 105, 125, 141, 171, 173, 185, 213, 238, 248, 249
Hosseini, Maimoona xxvii
Hosseini, Nasser xxvii
Hosseini, Roya xxviii
hostility 54, 95, 112
Hower, Edward viii, 17, 240
Hubbard, Orvil 56, 59
Hubbell, Sue 50
Hugo, Victor 82
Huis clos (*In Camera*) 143, 146, 156
human dignity 78
human identity 60
humanitarianism 26, 106, 109
humanity 26, 74, 181, 186, 237
human rights x, 70, 72, 82, 112, 180, 238
humiliations 139
Hurwitt, Robert 206
Hurwitz, Robert 209
Hussein, Aamer 17, 31
Hussein, Saddam 13
hyperadaptation 195
hypermasculine environment 96, 98
hyper-masculinity 86, 87
hypocrisy 99

identity 8, 44, 49, 54, 55, 56, 59, 60, 61, 70, 106, 109, 143, 168, 196, 199, 201, 224, 238, 243, 246
ideology 53, 91, 120
illegal immigrants 56
illness 76, 132, 188
imagery xxii, 64, 117, 159, 210
imagination 151, 163, 204, 234
immersion 168, 196, 207
immigrants xxvii, 56, 177
immigration 23, 194
imposition 104, 117
independence viii, 5
Independent, The 17, 213, 248
India 3, 4, 85, 102, 232
Indiana 49, 55, 56, 58, 59
Indian culture xi, 86
Indian Muslims 85
indifference 77, 81, 97
Infidel 28, 31
injustice 29, 82
in medias res (in the middle of things) xxiv, 34, 35, 36
In Search of The Kite Runner 21, 31
inspiration xxix, 14, 110
international tensions 14
interpretations 47, 81, 247
intimacy 150, 160, 162
invasion xi, 3, 4, 6, 7, 10, 13, 25, 69, 71, 105, 108, 109, 113, 208
Invisible Man 236
Iran xxvii, 3, 4, 8, 19, 32, 114
Iranian culture 106
Iraq 13, 110
Iraq War 13
Irish Times 210, 213

Islam ix, x, 7, 8, 9, 21, 51, 55, 60,
61, 63, 64, 65, 85, 92, 102
Islamic Diaspora 28, 31
Islamic extremists 12
Islamic faith 64
Islamic law 9, 10
Islamic Republic of Afghanistan
13
Islamic tradition 10

Jalalabad, Afghanistan 151, 153
James, Henry 17
Jameson, Fredric 114
James, William 64
Jane Eyre 62
Japanese invasion 69
*Jasmine and Stars: Reading More
Than Lolita in Tehran* 19,
32
Jawad, Said T. xxx
jealousy 39, 44, 45, 128, 130, 131,
137
Jefferess, David viii, 25, 26
Joes, Anthony 116
Jolin, Dan 186
Jones, Tamara xxix, xxxiv
journalism 240
journey xii, xvii, xxv, 38, 41, 42,
45, 78, 126, 131, 132, 135,
137, 138, 140, 153
justice 29, 72, 102, 117, 202, 223

"Kabul" xxx
Kabul, Afghanistan xv, xxvii,
xxviii, xxix, xxx, xxxi,
xxxiv, 6, 9, 17, 18, 20, 27,
32, 36, 43, 49, 52, 55, 57,
58, 71, 72, 75, 78, 99, 107,
109, 110, 111, 118, 119,

120, 121, 122, 123, 125,
128, 139, 145, 146, 151,
152, 155, 169, 176, 177,
178, 179, 180, 182, 183,
193, 201, 203, 205, 216,
217, 221, 233, 237, 238,
241, 242, 248
Kahf, Mohja ix, 49
Kaka Homayoun 149, 162
Kakutani, Michiko 240, 244, 248
kaleidoscope 51
Kamal 53, 83, 151, 153, 154, 200
Karim 154
Karzai, Hamid 13, 18
Keshavarz, Fatemeh viii, 18, 19,
29, 32
Khaled Hosseini Foundation, The
xxx, xxxiii, xxxiv
Khalilzad, Zalmay xxx
Khaliq, Abdul 5
Khan, Genghis 3
Khan, Hanif 205
Khan, King Amanullah 5, 6
Khan, Mohammed Daoud 5, 6, 7,
71, 149, 220
Khan, Mohammed Zahir 5, 6
Khan, Muhammad Nadir 5
Khan, Rahim xii, xxv, 17, 42, 47,
71, 75, 86, 87, 90, 94, 95,
97, 98, 99, 100, 129, 130,
131, 132, 133, 134, 135,
137, 138, 141, 143, 161,
165, 168, 170, 205, 208, 215
Khanum 141
Khaos, Marissa 208, 211
Khyber, Mir Akbar 7
Kim viii, 4, 15, 110, 122, 125
King Lear 45, 51, 66
Kipen, David viii, 16

---

odor 150
Odyssey, The 41
Old Curiosity Shop, The 211
Old Testament 21
olfactory sensation 151
Oliver Twist 39
Omar, Qais Akbar 119
onomatopoeia 150, 219, 221, 222
"Operation Enduring Freedom"
109
oppressed sexuality 92
oppression 29, 104, 110, 117
Oregonian, The 184, 191
Orientalism 20, 29, 115, 124, 145,
237
O'Rourke, Meghan viii, 18, 63
orphanage 71, 79, 126, 139, 228
Othello 45
"Our God, Our Help in Ages Past"
166
Overcoming the Monster plot ix,
37, 38, 41
Ovid (Publius Ovidius Naso) 166,
171

Pace, Peter xxx
pain xiii, 21, 25, 89, 128, 141,
142, 152, 153, 160, 164,
199, 226, 227
Pakistan xiii, 3, 8, 9, 85, 110, 111,
113, 122, 123, 141, 145,
153, 154, 204, 215, 218, 226
paratext 231, 234
Pari xxxi, 245, 246
partial remedy 155
Pashtun xi, 10, 37, 53, 54, 57, 69,
75, 77, 82, 84, 86, 88, 91,
92, 93, 94, 95, 99, 100, 101,
102, 117, 130, 134, 136,
144, 145, 170
Pashtun violence 94
passion 27, 49, 61, 173, 232
pathetic fallacy 164
patience 94
patriarchal culture 70
patriotism 57
Pentagon, the 13
People's Democratic Party of
Afghanistan (PDPA) 7
people trafficker 154
perception 141, 142, 143, 145,
147, 149, 151, 153, 155
Pericles xiv, 170
Persian Gulf 4
persuasion 189
Peshawar Accords 9
Peshawar, Pakistan 9, 132, 141,
150, 153, 193, 202, 227
Philadelphia Inquirer 185, 192
Philadelphia Weekly 176, 192
Phillips, Michael 175
Phipps, Keith 177
physical action xv, 195, 200, 202,
203, 206
physical distance 226
physical trauma 148, 152, 160
Pillalamarri, Akhilesh 3
plots, types of ix, 47
poetic justice 223
Political Unconscious 114, 124
political violence 73
pomegranates 90, 153, 159, 197,
198
post-colonial theory xix
post-structuralist theories xix
posttraumatic stress disorder
(PTSD) 78

power/powerlessness viii, xx, 5,
    7, 10, 11, 12, 14, 30, 39, 46,
    74, 77, 79, 81, 93, 101, 108,
    113, 126, 129, 136, 139,
    141, 146, 147, 160, 165,
    181, 184, 193, 210, 232,
    234, 241, 245
prejudice 52, 53, 54, 56, 57, 58,
    159
pride 45, 49
Prigge, Matt 176
Prince Charming 47
procreation 52, 60
progeny 62
protection 12, 82, 130
Protectors, the 56, 59
Proust, Marcel 162
psychological trauma vii
psychology 29, 146, 163
Punjab, India 85
purity xi, 72, 86

queer people 91
Quest plot ix, 37, 41, 42

racial exclusion 59
racial hygiene 92
racism 52, 53, 54, 58, 159, 165
Rags to Riches plot ix, xxxiii, 37,
    39, 40, 41
Rainer, Peter 185
Ramayana, The 85
Rambo 3 104, 106, 125
rape vii, x, xi, xiii, xv, 41, 51, 52,
    53, 58, 62, 69, 70, 72, 73,
    74, 76, 77, 78, 81, 82, 88,
    89, 90, 91, 117, 136, 138,
    143, 144, 145, 148, 149,
    150, 153, 160, 163, 167,

168, 175, 179, 182, 183,
    185, 193, 197, 200, 208,
    216, 217, 222, 224, 225
rape victim xi, 88, 90, 144
Reading Khaled Hosseini 22, 32,
    83, 125
Reading Lolita *in Tehran* 20, 28,
    32
Reagan administration 116
Reagan, Ronald 12
realism 115, 122, 169, 244
reawakening 47
Rebirth plot ix, 38, 46
recontextualization 161
recovery 19, 228
redemption xix, 18, 19, 37, 39,
    47, 128, 129, 130, 132, 155,
    174, 194, 199, 216, 229,
    230, 245
rediscovery 233, 234
redundancy 62
rejection xi, xii, 99, 132, 170
religion xi, xix, xx, 26, 36, 39, 52,
    85, 86, 116
religious experience 63, 64
religious faith ix, 21, 63
repression x, 86, 92, 100, 181
reservations 75, 234, 235, 243,
    244
resolution 41, 44, 62, 170
resurrection 46
reunion 161, 243, 246
revelation 54, 128, 129, 130, 132
revenge 147, 223
Revolutionary Association of
    Women in Afghanistan 104
Richmond Theatre 195, 209, 211,
    213, 214
Rickey, Carrie 185